Mastering OpenCV 3

Second Edition

Get hands-on with practical Computer Vision using OpenCV 3

Daniel Lélis Baggio
Shervin Emami
David Millán Escrivá
Khvedchenia Ievgen
Jason Saragih
Roy Shilkrot

BIRMINGHAM - MUMBAI

Mastering OpenCV 3

Second Edition

First published: December 2012
Second edition: April 2017

Production reference: 1260417

Published by Packt Publishing Ltd.
Livery Place
35 Livery Street
Birmingham
B3 2PB, UK.

ISBN 978-1-78646-717-1

www.packtpub.com

Credits

Authors
Daniel Lélis Baggio
Shervin Emami
David Millán Escrivá
Khvedchenia Ievgen
Jason Saragih
Roy Shilkrot

Reviewer
Vinícius Godoy

Commissioning Editor
Edward Gordon

Acquisition Editor
Nitin Dasan

Content Development Editor
Rohit Kumar Singh

Technical Editor
Pavan Ramchandani

Copy Editor
Safis Editing

Project Coordinator
Vaidehi Sawant

Proofreader
Safis Editing

Indexer
Tejal Daruwale Soni

Graphics
Jason Monteiro

Production Coordinator
Shantanu N. Zagade

About the Authors

Daniel Lélis Baggio started his work in computer vision through medical image processing at InCor (Instituto do Coração – Heart Institute) in São Paulo, where he worked with intravascular ultrasound image segmentation. Since then, he has focused on GPGPU and ported the segmentation algorithm to work with NVIDIA's CUDA. He has also dived into 6degrees of freedom head tracking with a natural user interface group through a project called ehci (http://code.google.com/p/ehci/). He now works for the Brazilian Air Force.

Shervin Emami, born in Iran, taught himself electronics and hobby robotics during his early teens in Australia. While building his first robot at the age of 15, he learned how RAM and CPUs work. He was so amazed by the concept that he soon designed and built a whole Z80 motherboard to control his robot, and wrote all the software purely in binary machine code using two push buttons for 0s and 1s.

After learning that computers can be programmed in much easier ways such as assembly language and even high-level compilers, Shervin became hooked on computer programming and has been programming desktops, robots, and smartphones nearly every day since then. During his late teens, he created Draw3D (http://draw3d.shervinemami.info/), a 3D modeler with 30,000 lines of optimized C and assembly code that rendered 3D graphics faster than all the commercial alternatives of the time, but he lost interest in graphics programming when 3D hardware acceleration became available.

In University, Shervin took a class on Computer Vision and became greatly interested in it. So, for his first thesis in 2003, he created a real-time face detection program based on Eigenfaces, using OpenCV (beta 3) for the camera input. For his master's thesis in 2005, he created a visual navigation system for several mobile robots using OpenCV (v0.96).

From 2008, he worked as a freelance Computer Vision Developer in Abu Dhabi and Philippines, using OpenCV for a large number of short-term commercial projects that included:

- Detecting faces using Haar or Eigenfaces
- Recognizing faces using Neural Networks, EHMM, or Eigenfaces
- Detecting the 3D position and orientation of a face from a single photo using AAM and POSIT
- Rotating a face in 3D using only a single photo

- Face preprocessing and artificial lighting using any 3D direction from a single photo
- Gender recognition
- Facial expression recognition
- Skin detection
- Iris detection
- Pupil detection
- Eye-gaze tracking
- Visual-saliency tracking
- Histogram matching
- Body-size detection
- Shirt and bikini detection
- Money recognition
- Video stabilization
- Face recognition on iPhone
- Food recognition on iPhone
- Marker-based augmented reality on iPhone (the second-fastest iPhone augmented reality app at the time)

OpenCV was putting food on the table for Shervin's family, so he began giving back to OpenCV through regular advice on the forums and by posting free OpenCV tutorials on his website (`http://www.shervinemami.info/openCV.html`). In 2011, he contacted the owners of other free OpenCV websites to write this book. He also began working on computer vision optimization for mobile devices at NVIDIA, working closely with the official OpenCV developers to produce an optimized version of OpenCV for Android. In 2012, he also joined the Khronos OpenVL committee for standardizing the hardware acceleration of computer vision for mobile devices, on which OpenCV will be based in the future.

David Millán Escrivá was 8 years old when he wrote his first program on an 8086 PC with basic language, which enabled the 2D plotting of basic equations. In 2005, he finished his studies in IT through the Universitat Politécnica de Valencia with honors in human-computer interaction supported by computer vision with OpenCV (v0.96). He had a final project based on this subject and published it on HCI Spanish congress. He participated in Blender, an open source, 3D-software project, and worked on his first commercial movie Plumiferos—Aventuras voladorasas, as a computer graphics software developer.

David now has more than 10 years of experience in IT, with experience in computer vision, computer graphics, and pattern recognition, working on different projects and start-ups, applying his knowledge of computer vision, optical character recognition, and augmented reality. He is the author of the DamilesBlog (`http://blog.damiles.com`), where he publishes research articles and tutorials about OpenCV, Computer Vision in general, and Optical Character Recognition algorithms. David has reviewed the book *gnuPlot Cookbook, Packt Publishing*, written by Lee Phillips.

Khvedchenia Ievgen is a Computer Vision expert from Ukraine. He started his career with research and development of a camera-based driver assistance system for Harman International. He then began working as a computer vision consultant for ESG. Nowadays, he is a self-employed developer focusing on the development of augmented reality applications. Ievgen is the author of the Computer Vision Talks blog (http://computer-vision-talks.com),where he publishes research articles and tutorials pertaining to computer vision and augmented reality.

Jason Saragih received his BE in mechatronics (with honors) and PhD in computer science from the Australian National University, Canberra, Australia, in 2004 and 2008, respectively. From 2008 to 2010, he was a Postdoctoral fellow at the Robotics Institute of Carnegie Mellon University, Pittsburgh, PA. From 2010 to 2012, he worked at the Commonwealth Scientific and Industrial Research Organization (CSIRO) as a research scientist. He is currently a senior research scientist at Visual Features, an Australian tech start-up company.

Dr. Saragih has made a number of contributions to the field of computer vision, specifically on the topic of deformable model registration and modeling. He is the author of two nonprofit open source libraries that are widely used in the scientific community; DeMoLib and FaceTracker, both of which make use of generic computer vision libraries, including OpenCV.

Roy Shilkrot is a researcher and professional in the area of computer vision and computer graphics. He obtained a BSc in computer science from Tel-Aviv-Yaffo Academic College, and an MSc from Tel-Aviv University. He is currently a PhD candidate in Media Laboratory of the Massachusetts Institute of Technology (MIT) in Cambridge.

Roy has over seven years of experience as a software engineer in start-up companies and enterprises. Before joining the MIT Media Lab as a research assistant, he worked as a technology strategist in the Innovation Laboratory of Comverse, a telecom solutions provider. He also dabbled in consultancy, and worked as an intern for Microsoft research at Redmond.

About the Reviewer

Vinícius Godoy is a professor at PUCPR and the owner of the game development website called Ponto V!. He has a Master'degree in Computer Vision and Image Processing (PUCPR), a specialization degree in game development (Universidade Positivo) and graduation in Technology in Informatics - Networking (UFPR). He is also one of the authors of the book *OpenCV by Example, Packt Publishing* and is currently working on his Doctoral thesis on medical imaging in PUCPR.

He is in the software development field for more than 20 years. His former professional experience includes the design and programming of a multithreaded framework for PBX tests at Siemens, coordination of Aurelio Dictionary Software 100 years edition project—including its mobile versions for Android, IOS, and Windows Phone—coordination of an augmented reality educational activity for Positivo's educational table Mesa Alfabeto, presented at CEBIT and the IT Management of a BPMS company called Sinax.

www.PacktPub.com

For support files and downloads related to your book, please visit `www.PacktPub.com`.

Did you know that Packt offers eBook versions of every book published, with PDF and ePub files available? You can upgrade to the eBook version at `www.PacktPub.com`and as a print book customer, you are entitled to a discount on the eBook copy. Get in touch with us at `service@packtpub.com` for more details.

At `www.PacktPub.com`, you can also read a collection of free technical articles, sign up for a range of free newsletters and receive exclusive discounts and offers on Packt books and eBooks.

`https://www.packtpub.com/mapt`

Get the most in-demand software skills with Mapt. Mapt gives you full access to all Packt books and video courses, as well as industry-leading tools to help you plan your personal development and advance your career.

Why subscribe?

- Fully searchable across every book published by Packt
- Copy and paste, print, and bookmark content
- On demand and accessible via a web browser

Customer Feedback

Thanks for purchasing this Packt book. At Packt, quality is at the heart of our editorial process. To help us improve, please leave us an honest review on this book's Amazon page at https://www.amazon.com/dp/1786467178.

If you'd like to join our team of regular reviewers, you can e-mail us at customerreviews@packtpub.com. We award our regular reviewers with free eBooks and videos in exchange for their valuable feedback. Help us be relentless in improving our products!

Table of Contents

Preface

Mastering OpenCV3, Second Edition contains seven chapters, where each chapter is a tutorial for an entire project from start to finish, based on OpenCV's C++ interface, including the full source code. The author of each chapter was chosen for their well-regarded online contributions to the OpenCV community on that topic, and the book was reviewed by one of the main OpenCV developers. Rather than explaining the basics of OpenCV functions, this book shows how to apply OpenCV to solve whole problems, including several 3D camera projects (augmented reality, and 3D structure from Motion) and several facial analysis projects (such as skin detection, simple face and eye detection, complex facial feature tracking, 3D head orientation estimation, and face recognition), therefore it makes a great companion to the existing OpenCV books.

What this book covers

Chapter 1, *Cartoonifier and Skin Changer for Raspberry Pi*, contains a complete tutorial and source code for both a desktop application and a Raspberry Pi that automatically generates a cartoon or painting from a real camera image, with several possible types of cartoons, including a skin color changer.

Chapter 2, *Exploring Structure from Motion Using OpenCV*, contains an introduction to Structure from Motion (SfM) via an implementation of SfM concepts in OpenCV. The reader will learn how to reconstruct 3D geometry from multiple 2D images and estimate camera positions.

Chapter 3, *Number Plate Recognition Using SVM and Neural Networks*, includes a complete tutorial and source code to build an automatic number plate recognition application using pattern recognition algorithms and also using a support vector machine and Artificial Neural Networks. The reader will learn how to train and predict pattern-recognition algorithms to decide whether an image is a number plate or not. It will also help classify a set of features into a character.

Chapter 4, *Non-Rigid Face Tracking*, contains a complete tutorial and source code to build a dynamic face tracking system that can model and track the many complex parts of a person's face.

Chapter 5, *3D Head Pose Estimation Using AAM and POSIT*, includes all the background required to understand what Active Appearance Models (AAMs) are and how to create them with OpenCV using a set of face frames with different facial expressions. Besides, this chapter explains how to match a given frame through fitting capabilities offered by AAMs. Then, by applying the POSIT algorithm, one can find the 3D head pose.

Chapter 6, *Face Recognition Using Eigenfaces or Fisherfaces*, contains a complete tutorial and source code for a real-time face-recognition application that includes basic face and eye detection to handle the rotation of faces and varying lighting conditions in the images.

Chapter 7, *Natural Feature Tracking for Augmented Reality*, includes a complete tutorial on how to build a marker-based Augmented Reality (AR) application for iPad and iPhone devices with an explanation of each step and source code. It also contains a complete tutorial on how to develop a marker-less augmented reality desktop application with an explanation of what marker-less AR is and the source code.

You can download this chapter from: https://www.packtpub.com/sites/default/files /downloads/NaturalFeatureTrackingforAugmentedReality.pdf.

What you need for this book

You don't need to have special knowledge in computer vision to read this book, but you should have good C/C++ programming skills and basic experience with OpenCV before reading this book. Readers without experience in OpenCV may wish to read the book *Learning OpenCV* for an introduction to the OpenCV features, or read *OpenCV 2 Cookbook* for examples on how to use OpenCV with recommended C/C++ patterns, because this book will show you how to solve real problems, assuming you are already familiar with the basics of OpenCV and C/C++ development.

In addition to C/C++ and OpenCV experience, you will also need a computer, and IDE of your choice (such as Visual Studio, XCode, Eclipse, or QtCreator, running on Windows, Mac, or Linux). Some chapters have further requirements, in particular:

- To develop an OpenCV program for Raspberry Pi, you will need the Raspberry Pi device, its tools, and basic Raspberry Pi development experience.
- To develop an iOS app, you will need an iPhone, iPad, or iPod Touch device, iOS development tools (including an Apple computer, XCode IDE, and an Apple Developer Certificate), and basic iOS and Objective-C development experience.
- Several desktop projects require a webcam connected to your computer. Any common USB webcam should suffice, but a webcam of at least 1 megapixel may be desirable.

- CMake is used in some projects, including OpenCV itself, to build across operating systems and compilers. A basic understanding of build systems is required, and knowledge of cross-platform building is recommended.

An understanding of linear algebra is expected, such as basic vector and matrix operations, and eigen decomposition.

Who this book is for

Mastering OpenCV 3, Second Edition is the perfect book for developers with basic OpenCV knowledge to use to create practical computer vision projects, as well as for seasoned OpenCV experts who want to add more computer vision topics to their skill set. It is aimed at senior computer science university students, graduates, researchers, and computer vision experts who wish to solve real problems using the OpenCV C++ interface, through practical step-by-step tutorials.

Conventions

In this book, you will find a number of text styles that distinguish between different kinds of information. Here are some examples of these styles and an explanation of their meaning.

Code words in text, database table names, folder names, filenames, file extensions, pathnames, dummy URLs, user input, and Twitter handles are shown as follows: "You should put most of the code from this chapter into the `cartoonifyImage()` function"

A block of code is set as follows:

```
int cameraNumber = 0;
if (argc> 1)
  cameraNumber = atoi(argv[1]);
// Get access to the camera.
cv::VideoCapture capture
```

When we wish to draw your attention to a particular part of a code block, the relevant lines or items are set in bold:

```
// Get access to the camera.
cv::VideoCapture capture;
camera.open(cameraNumber);
if (!camera.isOpened()) {
  std::cerr<< "ERROR: Could not access the camera or video!" <<
```

Any command-line input or output is written as follows:

```
cmake -G "Visual Studio 10"
```

New terms and **important words** are shown in bold. Words that you see on the screen, for example, in menus or dialog boxes, appear in the text like this: "In order to download new modules, we will go to **Files** | **Settings** | **Project Name** | **Project Interpreter**."

Warnings or important notes appear in a box like this.

Tips and tricks appear like this.

Reader feedback

Feedback from our readers is always welcome. Let us know what you think about this book-what you liked or disliked. Reader feedback is important for us as it helps us develop titles that you will really get the most out of.

To send us general feedback, simply e-mail feedback@packtpub.com, and mention the book's title in the subject of your message.

If there is a topic that you have expertise in and you are interested in either writing or contributing to a book, see our author guide at www.packtpub.com/authors.

Customer support

Now that you are the proud owner of a Packt book, we have a number of things to help you to get the most from your purchase.

Downloading the example code

You can download the example code files for this book from your account at http://www.packtpub.com. If you purchased this book elsewhere, you can visit http://www.packtpub.com/support and register to have the files e-mailed directly to you.

You can download the code files by following these steps:

1. Log in or register to our website using your e-mail address and password.
2. Hover the mouse pointer on the **SUPPORT** tab at the top.
3. Click on **Code Downloads & Errata**.
4. Enter the name of the book in the **Search** box.
5. Select the book for which you're looking to download the code files.
6. Choose from the drop-down menu where you purchased this book from.
7. Click on **Code Download**.

Once the file is downloaded, please make sure that you unzip or extract the folder using the latest version of:

- WinRAR / 7-Zip for Windows
- Zipeg / iZip / UnRarX for Mac
- 7-Zip / PeaZip for Linux

The code bundle for the book is also hosted on GitHub at `https://github.com/PacktPubl ishing/Mastering-OpenCV3-Second-Edition`. We also have other code bundles from our rich catalog of books and videos available at `https://github.com/PacktPublishing/`. Check them out!

Downloading the color images of this book

We also provide you with a PDF file that has color images of the screenshots/diagrams used in this book. The color images will help you better understand the changes in the output. You can download this file from `https://www.packtpub.com/sites/default/files/down loads/MasteringOpenCV3SecondEdition_ColorImages.pdf`.

Errata

Although we have taken every care to ensure the accuracy of our content, mistakes do happen. If you find a mistake in one of our books-maybe a mistake in the text or the code-we would be grateful if you could report this to us. By doing so, you can save other readers from frustration and help us improve subsequent versions of this book. If you find any errata, please report them by visiting `http://www.packtpub.com/submit-errata`, selecting your book, clicking on the **Errata Submission Form** link, and entering the details of your errata. Once your errata are verified, your submission will be accepted and the errata will be uploaded to our website or added to any list of existing errata under the Errata section of that title.

To view the previously submitted errata, go to https://www.packtpub.com/books/content/support and enter the name of the book in the search field. The required information will appear under the **Errata** section.

Piracy

Piracy of copyrighted material on the Internet is an ongoing problem across all media. At Packt, we take the protection of our copyright and licenses very seriously. If you come across any illegal copies of our works in any form on the Internet, please provide us with the location address or website name immediately so that we can pursue a remedy.

Please contact us at copyright@packtpub.com with a link to the suspected pirated material.

We appreciate your help in protecting our authors and our ability to bring you valuable content.

Questions

If you have a problem with any aspect of this book, you can contact us at questions@packtpub.com, and we will do our best to address the problem.

1
Cartoonifier and Skin Changer for Raspberry Pi

This chapter will show how to write some image processing filters for desktop and for small embedded systems such as Raspberry Pi. First, we develop it for the desktop (in C/C++) and then port the project to Raspberry Pi, since this is the recommended scenario when developing for embedded devices. This chapter will cover the following topics:

- How to convert a real-life image to a sketch drawing
- How to convert to a painting and overlay the sketch to produce a cartoon
- A scary evil mode to create bad characters instead of good characters
- A basic skin detector and skin color changer, to give someone green alien skin
- Finally, how to create an embedded system based on our desktop application

Note that an **embedded system** is basically a computer motherboard placed inside a product or device, designed to perform specific tasks, and **Raspberry Pi** is a very low-cost and popular motherboard for building an embedded system:

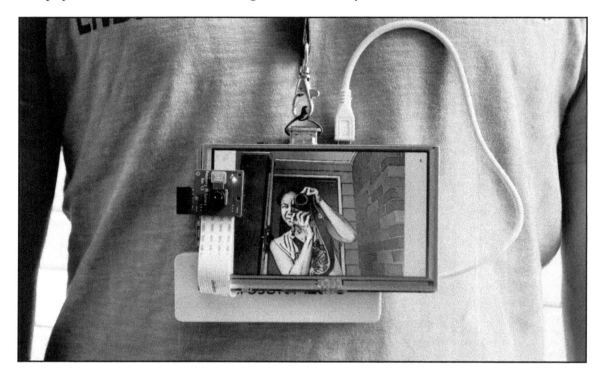

The preceding picture shows what you could make after this chapter: a battery-powered Raspberry Pi + screen you could wear to Comic Con, turning everyone into a cartoon!

We want to make the real-world camera frames automatically look like they are from a cartoon. The basic idea is to fill the flat parts with some color and then draw thick lines on the strong edges. In other words, the flat areas should become much more flat and the edges should become much more distinct. We will detect edges, smooth the flat areas, and draw enhanced edges back on top, to produce a cartoon or comic-book effect.

When developing an embedded computer vision system, it is a good idea to build a fully working desktop version first before porting it to an embedded system, since it is much easier to develop and debug a desktop program than an embedded system! So this chapter will begin with a complete Cartoonifier desktop program that you can create using your favorite IDE (for example, Visual Studio, XCode, Eclipse, QtCreator). After it is working properly on your desktop, the last section shows how to create an embedded system based on the desktop version. Many embedded projects require some custom code for the embedded system, such as to use different inputs and outputs or use some platform-specific code optimizations. However, for this chapter, we will actually be running identical code on the embedded system and the desktop, so we only need to create one project.

The application uses an **OpenCV** GUI window, initializes the camera, and with each camera frame it calls the function `cartoonifyImage()`, containing most of the code in this chapter. It then displays the processed image on the GUI window. This chapter will explain how to create the desktop application from scratch using a USB webcam, and the embedded system-based on the desktop application using a Raspberry Pi Camera Module. So first you would create a desktop project in your favorite IDE, with a `main.cpp` file to hold the GUI code given in the following sections such as the main loop, webcam functionality, and keyboard input, and you would create a `cartoon.cpp` file with the image processing operations with most of this chapter's code in a function called `cartoonifyImage()`.

The full source code of this book is available at
`http://github.com/MasteringOpenCV/code`.

Accessing the webcam

To access a computer's webcam or camera device, you can simply call the `open()` function on a `cv::VideoCapture` object (OpenCV's method of accessing your camera device), and pass 0 as the default camera ID number. Some computers have multiple cameras attached, or they do not work as default camera 0, so it is common practice to allow the user to pass the desired camera number as a command-line argument, in case they want to try camera 1, 2, or -1, for example. We will also try to set the camera resolution to 640x480 using `cv::VideoCapture::set()` to run faster on high-resolution cameras.

Depending on your camera model, driver, or system, OpenCV might not change the properties of your camera. It is not important for this project, so don't worry if it does not work with your webcam.

You can put this code in the main () function of your main.cpp file:

```
int cameraNumber = 0;
if (argc> 1)
cameraNumber = atoi(argv[1]);

// Get access to the camera.
cv::VideoCapture camera;
camera.open(cameraNumber);
if (!camera.isOpened()) {
  std::cerr<<"ERROR: Could not access the camera or video!"<<
  std::endl;
  exit(1);
}

// Try to set the camera resolution.
camera.set(cv::CV_CAP_PROP_FRAME_WIDTH, 640);
camera.set(cv::CV_CAP_PROP_FRAME_HEIGHT, 480);
```

After the webcam has been initialized, you can grab the current camera image as a cv::Mat object (OpenCV's image container). You can grab each camera frame by using the C++ streaming operator from your cv::VideoCapture object into a cv::Mat object, just like if you were getting input from a console.

OpenCV makes it very easy to capture frames from a video file (such as an AVI or MP4 file) or network stream instead of a webcam. Instead of passing an integer such as camera.open(0), pass a string such as camera.open("my_video.avi") and then grab frames just like it was a webcam. The source code provided with this book has an initCamera() function that opens a webcam, video file, or network stream.

Main camera processing loop for a desktop app

If you want to display a GUI window on the screen using OpenCV, you call the
`cv::namedWindow()` function and then `cv::imshow()` function for each image, but you
must also call `cv::waitKey()` once per frame, otherwise your windows will not update at
all! Calling `cv::waitKey(0)` waits forever until the user hits a key in the window, but a
positive number such as `waitKey(20)` or higher will wait for at least that many
milliseconds.

Put this main loop in the `main.cpp` file, as the base of your real-time camera app:

```cpp
while (true) {
  // Grab the next camera frame.
  cv::Mat cameraFrame;
  camera>>cameraFrame;
  if (cameraFrame.empty()) {
    std::cerr<<"ERROR: Couldn't grab a camera frame."<<
    std::endl;
    exit(1);
  }
  // Create a blank output image, that we will draw onto.
  cv::Mat displayedFrame(cameraFrame.size(), cv::CV_8UC3);

  // Run the cartoonifier filter on the camera frame.
  cartoonifyImage(cameraFrame, displayedFrame);

  // Display the processed image onto the screen.
  imshow("Cartoonifier", displayedFrame);

  // IMPORTANT: Wait for atleast 20 milliseconds,
  // so that the image can be displayed on the screen!
  // Also checks if a key was pressed in the GUI window.
  // Note that it should be a "char" to support Linux.
  char keypress = cv::waitKey(20);  // Needed to see anything!
  if (keypress == 27) {   // Escape Key
    // Quit the program!
    break;
  }
}//end while
```

Generating a black and white sketch

To obtain a sketch (black and white drawing) of the camera frame, we will use an edge detection filter, whereas to obtain a color painting, we will use an edge preserving filter (Bilateral filter) to further smoothen the flat regions while keeping edges intact. By overlaying the sketch drawing on top of the color painting, we obtain a cartoon effect, as shown earlier in the screenshot of the final app.

There are many different edge detection filters, such as Sobel, Scharr, Laplacian filters, or a Canny edge detector. We will use a Laplacian edge filter since it produces edges that look most similar to hand sketches compared to Sobel or Scharr, and are quite consistent compared to a Canny edge detector, which produces very clean line drawings but is affected more by random noise in the camera frames and therefore the line drawings would often change drastically between frames.

Nevertheless, we still need to reduce the noise in the image before we use a Laplacian edge filter. We will use a Median filter because it is good at removing noise while keeping edges sharp, but is not as slow as a Bilateral filter. Since Laplacian filters use grayscale images, we must convert from OpenCV's default BGR format to grayscale. In your empty `cartoon.cpp` file, put this code on the top so you can access OpenCV and STD C++ templates without typing `cv::` and `std::` everywhere:

```
// Include OpenCV's C++ Interface
#include "opencv2/opencv.hpp"

using namespace cv;
using namespace std;
```

Put this and all remaining code in a `cartoonifyImage()` function in your `cartoon.cpp` file:

```
Mat gray;
cvtColor(srcColor, gray, CV_BGR2GRAY);
const int MEDIAN_BLUR_FILTER_SIZE = 7;
medianBlur(gray, gray, MEDIAN_BLUR_FILTER_SIZE);
Mat edges;
const int LAPLACIAN_FILTER_SIZE = 5;
Laplacian(gray, edges, CV_8U, LAPLACIAN_FILTER_SIZE);
```

The Laplacian filter produces edges with varying brightness, so to make the edges look more like a sketch, we apply a binary threshold to make the edges either white or black:

```
Mat mask;
const int EDGES_THRESHOLD = 80;
threshold(edges, mask, EDGES_THRESHOLD, 255, THRESH_BINARY_INV);
```

In the following figure, you see the original image (to the left) and the generated edge mask (to the right) that looks similar to a sketch drawing. After we generate a color painting (explained later), we also put this edge mask on top to have black line drawings:

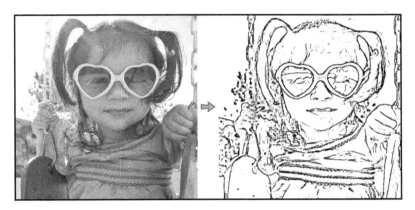

Generating a color painting and a cartoon

A strong Bilateral filter smoothens flat regions while keeping edges sharp; and therefore, is great as an automatic cartoonifier or painting filter, except that it is extremely slow (that is, measured in seconds or even minutes, rather than milliseconds!). Therefore, we will use some tricks to obtain a nice cartoonifier, while still running in acceptable speed. The most important trick we can use is that we can perform Bilateral filtering at a lower resolution and it will still have a similar effect as a full resolution, but run much faster. Lets reduce the total number of pixels by four (for example, half width and half height):

```
Size size = srcColor.size();
Size smallSize;
smallSize.width = size.width/2;
smallSize.height = size.height/2;
Mat smallImg = Mat(smallSize, CV_8UC3);
resize(srcColor, smallImg, smallSize, 0,0, INTER_LINEAR);
```

Rather than applying a large Bilateral filter, we will apply many small Bilateral filters, to produce a strong cartoon effect in less time. We will truncate the filter (see the following figure) so that instead of performing a whole filter (for example, a filter size of 21x21, when the bell curve is 21 pixels wide), it just uses the minimum filter size needed for a convincing result (for example, with a filter size of just 9x9 even if the bell curve is 21 pixels wide). This truncated filter will apply the major part of the filter (gray area) without wasting time on the minor part of the filter (white area under the curve), so it will run several times faster:

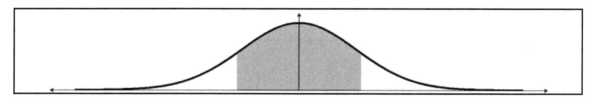

Therefore, we have four parameters that control the Bilateral filter: color strength, positional strength, size, and repetition count. We need a temp `Mat` since the `bilateralFilter()` function can't overwrite its input (referred to as *in-place processing*), but we can apply one filter storing a temp `Mat` and another filter storing back the input:

```
Mat tmp = Mat(smallSize, CV_8UC3);
int repetitions = 7;    // Repetitions for strong cartoon effect.
for (int i=0; i<repetitions; i++) {
   int ksize = 9;       // Filter size. Has large effect on speed.
   double sigmaColor = 9;     // Filter color strength.
   double sigmaSpace = 7;     // Spatial strength. Affects speed.
   bilateralFilter(smallImg, tmp, ksize, sigmaColor, sigmaSpace);
   bilateralFilter(tmp, smallImg, ksize, sigmaColor, sigmaSpace);
}
```

Remember that this was applied to the shrunken image, so we need to expand the image back to the original size. Then we can overlay the edge mask that we found earlier. To overlay the edge mask *sketch* onto the Bilateral filter *painting* (left side of the following figure), we can start with a black background and copy the *painting* pixels that aren't edges in the *sketch* mask:

```
Mat bigImg;
resize(smallImg, bigImg, size, 0,0, INTER_LINEAR);
dst.setTo(0);
bigImg.copyTo(dst, mask);
```

The result is a cartoon version of the original photo, as shown on the right side of the following figure, where the *sketch* mask is overlaid on the painting:

Generating an evil mode using edge filters

Cartoons and comics always have both good and bad characters. With the right combination of edge filters, a scary image can be generated from the most innocent looking people! The trick is to use a small-edge filter that will find many edges all over the image, then merge the edges using a small Median filter.

We will perform this on a grayscale image with some noise reduction, so the preceding code for converting the original image to grayscale and applying a 7x7 Median filter should still be used (the first image in the following figure shows the output of the grayscale Median blur). Instead of following it with a Laplacian filter and Binary threshold, we can get a more scary look if we apply a 3x3 Scharr gradient filter along *x* and *y* (second image in the figure), then a binary threshold with a very low cutoff (third image in the figure),and a 3x3 Median blur, producing the final *evil* mask (fourth image in the figure):

```
Mat gray;
cvtColor(srcColor, gray, CV_BGR2GRAY);
const int MEDIAN_BLUR_FILTER_SIZE = 7;
medianBlur(gray, gray, MEDIAN_BLUR_FILTER_SIZE);
Mat edges, edges2;
Scharr(srcGray, edges, CV_8U, 1, 0);
Scharr(srcGray, edges2, CV_8U, 1, 0, -1);
edges += edges2;
```

```
// Combine the x & y edges together.
const int EVIL_EDGE_THRESHOLD = 12
threshold(edges, mask, EVIL_EDGE_THRESHOLD, 255,
THRESH_BINARY_INV);
medianBlur(mask, mask, 3)
```

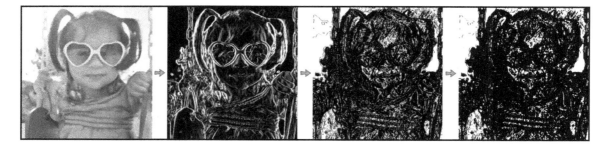

Now that we have an *evil* mask, we can overlay this mask onto the *cartoonified* painting image like we did with the regular *sketch* edge mask. The final result is shown on the right side of the following figure:

Generating an alien mode using skin detection

Now that we have a *sketch* mode, a *cartoon* mode (*painting + sketch* mask), and an *evil* mode (*painting + evil* mask), for fun, let's try something more complex: an *alien* mode, by detecting the skin regions of the face and then changing the skin color to green.

Skin detection algorithm

There are many different techniques used for detecting skin regions, from simple color thresholds using **RGB (Red-Green-Blue)**, **HSV (Hue-Saturation-Brightness)** values, or color histogram calculation and re-projection, to complex machine-learning algorithms of mixture models that need camera calibration in the **CIELab** color-space and offline training with many sample faces, and so on. But even the complex methods don't necessarily work robustly across various camera and lighting conditions and skin types. Since we want our skin detection to run on an embedded device, without any calibration or training, and we are just using skin detection for a fun image filter, it is sufficient for us to use a simple skin detection method. However, the color responses from the tiny camera sensor in the Raspberry Pi Camera Module tend to vary significantly, and we want to support skin detection for people of any skin color but without any calibration, so we need something more robust than simple color thresholds.

For example, a simple HSV skin detector can treat any pixel as skin if its hue color is fairly red, and saturation is fairly high but not extremely high, and its brightness is not too dark or extremely bright. But cameras in mobile phones or Raspberry Pi Camera Modules often have bad white balancing, therefore a person's skin might look slightly blue instead of red, and so on, and this would be a major problem for simple HSV thresholding.

A more robust solution is to perform face detection with a Haar or LBP cascade classifier (shown in `Chapter 6`, *Face Recognition using Eigenfaces or Fisherfaces*), then look at the range of colors for the pixels in the middle of the detected face, since you know that those pixels should be skin pixels of the actual person. You could then scan the whole image or nearby region for pixels of a similar color as the center of the face. This has the advantage that it is very likely to find at least some of the true skin region of any detected person, no matter what their skin color is or even if their skin appears somewhat blueish or redish in the camera image.

Unfortunately, face detection using cascade classifiers is quite slow on current embedded devices, so that method might be less ideal for some real-time embedded applications. On the other hand, we can take advantage of the fact that for mobile apps and some embedded systems, it can be expected that the user will be facing the camera directly from a very close distance, so it can be reasonable to ask the user to place their face at a specific location and distance, rather than try to detect the location and size of their face. This is the basis of many mobile phone apps, where the app asks the user to place their face at a certain position or perhaps to manually drag points on the screen to show where the corners of their face are in a photo. So let's simply draw the outline of a face in the center of the screen, and ask the user to move their face to the shown position and size.

Showing the user where to put their face

When the *alien* mode is first started, we will draw the face outline on top of the camera frame so the user knows where to put their face. We will draw a big ellipse covering 70% of the image height, with a fixed aspect ratio of 0.72, so that the face will not become too skinny or fat depending on the aspect ratio of the camera:

```
// Draw the color face onto a black background.
Mat faceOutline = Mat::zeros(size, CV_8UC3);
Scalar color = CV_RGB(255,255,0);    // Yellow.
int thickness = 4;

// Use 70% of the screen height as the face height.
int sw = size.width;
int sh = size.height;
int faceH = sh/2 * 70/100;  // "faceH" is radius of the ellipse.

// Scale the width to be the same nice shape for any screen width.
int faceW = faceH * 72/100;
// Draw the face outline.
ellipse(faceOutline, Point(sw/2, sh/2), Size(faceW, faceH),
        0, 0, 360, color, thickness, CV_AA);
```

To make it more obvious that it is a face, let's also draw two eye outlines. Rather than drawing an eye as an ellipse, we can give it a bit more realism (see the following figure) by drawing a truncated ellipse for the top of the eye and a truncated ellipse for the bottom of the eye, because we can specify the start and end angles when drawing with the `ellipse()` function:

```
// Draw the eye outlines, as 2 arcs per eye.
int eyeW = faceW * 23/100;
int eyeH = faceH * 11/100;
int eyeX = faceW * 48/100;
int eyeY = faceH * 13/100;
Size eyeSize = Size(eyeW, eyeH);

// Set the angle and shift for the eye half ellipses.
int eyeA = 15; // angle in degrees.
int eyeYshift = 11;

// Draw the top of the right eye.
ellipse(faceOutline, Point(sw/2 - eyeX, sh/2 -eyeY),
    eyeSize, 0, 180+eyeA, 360-eyeA, color, thickness, CV_AA);

// Draw the bottom of the right eye.
ellipse(faceOutline, Point(sw/2 - eyeX, sh/2 - eyeY-eyeYshift),
    eyeSize, 0, 0+eyeA, 180-eyeA, color, thickness, CV_AA);
```

```
// Draw the top of the left eye.
ellipse(faceOutline, Point(sw/2 + eyeX, sh/2 - eyeY),
eyeSize, 0, 180+eyeA, 360-eyeA, color, thickness, CV_AA);

// Draw the bottom of the left eye.
ellipse(faceOutline, Point(sw/2 + eyeX, sh/2 - eyeY-eyeYshift),
    eyeSize, 0, 0+eyeA, 180-eyeA, color, thickness, CV_AA);
```

We can do the same to draw the bottom lip of the mouth:

```
// Draw the bottom lip of the mouth.
int mouthY = faceH * 48/100;
int mouthW = faceW * 45/100;
int mouthH = faceH * 6/100;
ellipse(faceOutline, Point(sw/2, sh/2 + mouthY), Size(mouthW,
    mouthH), 0, 0, 180, color, thickness, CV_AA);
```

To make it even more obvious that the user should put their face where shown, let's write a message on the screen!

```
// Draw anti-aliased text.
int fontFace = FONT_HERSHEY_COMPLEX;
float fontScale = 1.0f;
int fontThickness = 2;
char *szMsg = "Put your face here";
putText(faceOutline, szMsg, Point(sw * 23/100, sh * 10/100),
fontFace, fontScale, color, fontThickness, CV_AA);
```

Now that we have the face outline drawn, we can overlay it onto the displayed image by using alpha blending, to combine the cartoonified image with this drawn outline:

```
addWeighted(dst, 1.0, faceOutline, 0.7, 0, dst, CV_8UC3);
```

This results in the outline in the following figure, showing the user where to put their face, so we don't have to detect the face location:

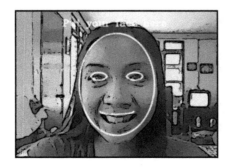

Implementation of the skin color changer

Rather than detecting the skin color and then the region with that skin color, we can use OpenCV's `floodFill()` function, which is similar to the bucket fill tool in many image editing software. We know that the regions in the middle of the screen should be skin pixels (since we asked the user to put their face in the middle), so to change the whole face to have green skin, we can just apply a green flood fill on the center pixel, which will always color some parts of the face green. In reality, the color, saturation, and brightness is likely to be different in different parts of the face, so a floodfill will rarely cover all the skin pixels of a face unless the threshold is so low that it also covers unwanted pixels outside of the face. So instead of applying a single flood fill in the center of the image, let's apply a flood fill on six different points around the face that should be skin pixels.

A nice feature of OpenCV's `floodFill()` is that it can draw the floodfill into an external image rather than modify the input image. So this feature can give us a mask image for adjusting the color of the skin pixels without necessarily changing the brightness or saturation, producing a more realistic image than if all the skin pixels became an identical green pixel(losing significant face detail).

Skin color changing does not work so well in the RGB color-space, because you want to allow brightness to vary in the face but not allow skin color to vary much, and RGB does not separate brightness from color. One solution is to use the HSV color-space, since it separates brightness from the color (Hue) as well as the corlorful-ness (Saturation). Unfortunately, HSV wraps the Hue value around red, and since skin is mostly red, it means that you need to work both with *Hue < 10%* and *Hue > 90%*, since these are both red. So, instead we will use the **Y'CrCb** color-space (the variant of YUV that is in OpenCV), since it separates brightness from color, and only has a single range of values for typical skin color rather than two. Note that most cameras, images, and videos actually use some type of YUV as their color-space before conversion to RGB, so in many cases you can get a YUV image free without converting it yourself.

Since we want our alien mode to look like a cartoon, we will apply the *alien* filter after the image has already been cartoonified. In other words, we have access to the shrunken color image produced by the Bilateral filter, and access to the full-sized edge mask. Skin detection often works better at low resolutions, since it is the equivalent of analyzing the average value of each high-resolution pixel's neighbors (or the low-frequency signal instead of the high-frequency noisy signal). So let's work at the same shrunk scale as the Bilateral filter (half-width and half-height). Let's convert the painting image to YUV:

```
Mat yuv = Mat(smallSize, CV_8UC3);
cvtColor(smallImg, yuv, CV_BGR2YCrCb);
```

We also need to shrink the edge mask so it is at the same scale as the painting image. There is a complication with OpenCV's `floodFill()` function, when storing to a separate mask image, in that the mask should have a 1 pixel border around the whole image, so if the input image is *WxH* pixels in size then the separate mask image should be *(W+2) x (H+2)* pixels in size. But the `floodFill()` function also allows us to initialize the mask with edges, that the flood fill algorithm will ensure it does not cross. Let's use this feature, in the hope that it helps prevent the flood fill from extending outside of the face. So we need to provide two mask images: one is the edge mask of *WxH* in size, and the other image is the exact same edge mask but *(W+2)x(H+2)* in size because it should include a border around the image. It is possible to have multiple `cv::Mat` objects (or headers) referencing the same data, or even to have a `cv::Mat` object that references a sub-region of another `cv::Mat` image. So, instead of allocating two separate images and copying the edge mask pixels across, let's allocate a single mask image including the border, and create an extra `cv::Mat` header of *WxH* (that just references the region-of-interest in the flood fill mask without the border). In other words, there is just one array of pixels of size *(W+2)x(H+2)* but two `cv::Mat` objects, where one is referencing the whole *(W+2)x(H+2)* image and the other is referencing the *WxH* region in the middle of that image:

```
int sw = smallSize.width;
int sh = smallSize.height;
Mat mask, maskPlusBorder;
maskPlusBorder = Mat::zeros(sh+2, sw+2, CV_8UC1);
mask = maskPlusBorder(Rect(1,1,sw,sh));
// mask is now in maskPlusBorder.
resize(edges, mask, smallSize);    // Put edges in both of them.
```

The edge mask (shown on the left of the following figure) is full of both strong and weak edges, but we only want strong edges, so we will apply a binary threshold (resulting in the middle image in the following figure). To join some gaps between edges, we will then combine the morphological operators `dilate()` and `erode()` to remove some gaps (also referred to as the close operator), resulting in the right of the figure:

```
const int EDGES_THRESHOLD = 80;
threshold(mask, mask, EDGES_THRESHOLD, 255, THRESH_BINARY);
dilate(mask, mask, Mat());
erode(mask, mask, Mat());
```

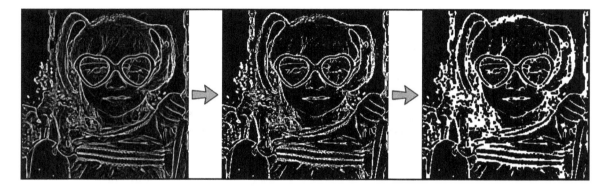

As mentioned earlier, we want to apply flood fills in numerous points around the face, to make sure we include the various colors and shades of the whole face. Let's choose six points around the nose, cheeks, and forehead, as shown on the left-hand side of the following figure. Note that these values are dependent on the face outline drawn earlier:

```
int const NUM_SKIN_POINTS = 6;
Point skinPts[NUM_SKIN_POINTS];
skinPts[0] = Point(sw/2,        sh/2 - sh/6);
skinPts[1] = Point(sw/2 - sw/11, sh/2 - sh/6);
skinPts[2] = Point(sw/2 + sw/11, sh/2 - sh/6);
skinPts[3] = Point(sw/2,        sh/2 + sh/16);
skinPts[4] = Point(sw/2 - sw/9,  sh/2 + sh/16);
skinPts[5] = Point(sw/2 + sw/9,  sh/2 + sh/16);
```

Now we just need to find some good lower and upper bounds for the flood fill. Remember that this is being performed in $Y'CrCb$ color-space, so we basically decide how much the brightness can vary, how much the red component can vary, and how much the blue component can vary. We want to allow the brightness to vary a lot, to include shadows as well as highlights and reflections, but we don't want the colors to vary much at all:

```
const int LOWER_Y = 60;
const int UPPER_Y = 80;
const int LOWER_Cr = 25;
const int UPPER_Cr = 15;
const int LOWER_Cb = 20;
const int UPPER_Cb = 15;
Scalar lowerDiff = Scalar(LOWER_Y, LOWER_Cr, LOWER_Cb);
Scalar upperDiff = Scalar(UPPER_Y, UPPER_Cr, UPPER_Cb);
```

We will use the `floodFill()` function with its default flags, except that we want to store to an external mask, so we must specify `FLOODFILL_MASK_ONLY`:

```
const int CONNECTED_COMPONENTS = 4;  // To fill diagonally, use 8.
const int flags = CONNECTED_COMPONENTS | FLOODFILL_FIXED_RANGE
  | FLOODFILL_MASK_ONLY;
Mat edgeMask = mask.clone();    // Keep a copy of the edge mask.
// "maskPlusBorder" is initialized with edges to block floodFill().
for (int i = 0; i < NUM_SKIN_POINTS; i++) {
    floodFill(yuv, maskPlusBorder, skinPts[i], Scalar(), NULL,
      lowerDiff, upperDiff, flags);
}
```

The following figure on the left-side shows the six flood fill locations (shown as circles), and the right-side of the figure shows the external mask that is generated, where skin is shown as gray and edges are shown as white. Note that the right-side image was modified for this book so that skin pixels (of value 1) are clearly visible:

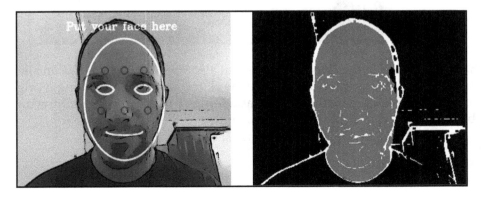

The `mask` image (shown on the right side of the previous figure) now contains the following:

- Pixels of value 255 for the edge pixels
- Pixels of value 1 for the skin regions
- Pixels of value 0 for the rest

Meanwhile, `edgeMask` just contains edge pixels (as value 255). So to get just the skin pixels, we can remove the edges from it:

```
mask -= edgeMask;
```

The `mask` variable now just contains 1's for skin pixels and 0's for non-skin pixels. To change the skin color and brightness of the original image, we can use the `cv::add()` function with the skin mask, to increase the green component in the original BGR image:

```
int Red = 0;
int Green = 70;
int Blue = 0;
add(smallImgBGR, CV_RGB(Red, Green, Blue), smallImgBGR, mask);
```

The following figure shows the original image on the left, and the final alien cartoon image on the right, where at least six parts of the face will now be green!

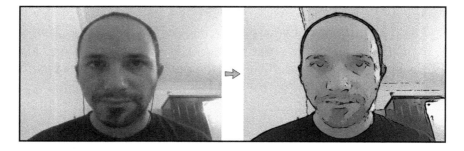

Notice that we have made the skin look green but also brighter (to look like an alien that glows in the dark). If you want to just change the skin color without making it brighter, you can use other color changing methods, such as adding 70 to green while subtracting 70 from red and blue, or convert to HSV color space using `cvtColor(src, dst, "CV_BGR2HSV_FULL")`, and adjust the hue and saturation.

Reducing the random pepper noise from the sketch image

Most of the tiny cameras in smartphones, RPi Camera Modules, and some webcams have significant image noise. This is normally acceptable, but it has a large effect on our 5x5 Laplacian edge filter. The edge mask (shown as the sketch mode) will often have thousands of small blobs of black pixels called **pepper noise**, made of several black pixels next to each other in a white background. We are already using a Median filter, which is usually strong enough to remove pepper noise, but in our case it may not be strong enough. Our edge mask is mostly a pure white background (value of 255) with some black edges (value of 0) and the dots of noise (also values of 0). We could use a standard closing morphological operator but it will remove a lot of edges. So instead, we will apply a custom filter that removes small black regions that are surrounded completely by white pixels. This will remove a lot of noise while having little effect on actual edges.

We will scan the image for black pixels, and at each black pixel, we'll check the border of the 5x5 square around it to see if all the 5x5 border pixels are white. If they are all white then we know we have a small island of black noise, so then we fill the whole block with white pixels to remove the black island. For simplicity in our 5x5 filter, we will ignore the two border pixels around the image and leave them as they are.

The following figure shows the original image from an Android tablet on the left-side, with a sketch mode in the center, showing small black dots of pepper noise, and the result of our pepper-noise removal shown on the right-side, where the skin looks cleaner:

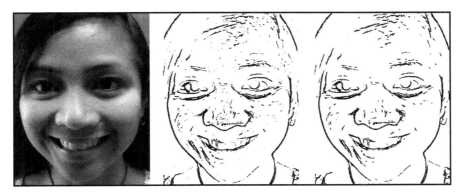

The following code can be named the `removePepperNoise()` function to edit the image in-place for simplicity:

```
void removePepperNoise(Mat &mask)
{
  for (int y=2; y<mask.rows-2; y++) {
    // Get access to each of the 5 rows near this pixel.
    uchar *pUp2 = mask.ptr(y-2);
    uchar *pUp1 = mask.ptr(y-1);
    uchar *pThis = mask.ptr(y);
    uchar *pDown1 = mask.ptr(y+1);
    uchar *pDown2 = mask.ptr(y+2);

    // Skip the first (and last) 2 pixels on each row.
    pThis += 2;
    pUp1 += 2;
    pUp2 += 2;
    pDown1 += 2;
    pDown2 += 2;
    for (int x=2; x<mask.cols-2; x++) {
      uchar value = *pThis;  // Get pixel value (0 or 255).
      // Check if it's a black pixel surrounded bywhite
      // pixels (ie: whether it is an "island" of black).
      if (value == 0) {
        bool above, left, below, right, surroundings;
        above = *(pUp2 - 2) && *(pUp2 - 1) && *(pUp2) &&
        *(pUp2 + 1) && *(pUp2 + 2);
        left = *(pUp1 - 2) && *(pThis - 2) && *(pDown1 - 2);
        below = *(pDown2 - 2) && *(pDown2 - 1) && *(pDown2)
          && *(pDown2 + 1) && *(pDown2 + 2);
        right = *(pUp1 + 2) && *(pThis + 2) && *(pDown1 + 2);
        surroundings = above && left && below && right;
        if (surroundings == true) {
          // Fill the whole 5x5 block as white. Since we
          // knowthe 5x5 borders are already white, we just
          // need tofill the 3x3 inner region.
          *(pUp1 - 1) = 255;
          *(pUp1 + 0) = 255;
          *(pUp1 + 1) = 255;
          *(pThis - 1) = 255;
          *(pThis + 0) = 255;
          *(pThis + 1) = 255;
          *(pDown1 - 1) = 255;
          *(pDown1 + 0) = 255;
          *(pDown1 + 1) = 255;
          // Since we just covered the whole 5x5 block with
          // white, we know the next 2 pixels won't be
          // black,so skip the next 2 pixels on the right.
```

```
            pThis += 2;
            pUp1 += 2;
            pUp2 += 2;
            pDown1 += 2;
            pDown2 += 2;
          }
        }
        // Move to the next pixel on the right.
        pThis++;
        pUp1++;
        pUp2++;
        pDown1++;
        pDown2++;
      }
    }
  }
```

That's all! Run the app in the different modes until you are ready to port it to embedded!

Porting from desktop to embedded

Now that the program works on desktop, we can make an embedded system from it. The details given here are specific to Raspberry Pi, but similar steps apply when developing for other embedded Linux systems such as BeagleBone, ODROID, Olimex, Jetson, and so on.

There are several different options for running our code on an embedded system, each with some advantages and disadvantages in different scenarios.

There are two common methods for compiling the code for an embedded device:

1. Copy the source code from the desktop onto the device and compile it directly onboard the device. This is often referred to as **native compilation**, since we are compiling our code natively on the same system that it will eventually run on.
2. Compile all the code on the desktop but using special methods to generate code for the device, and then you copy the final executable program onto the device. This is often referred to as **cross-compilation** since you need a special compiler that knows how to generate code for other types of CPUs.

Cross-compilation is often significantly harder to configure than native compilation, especially if you are using many shared libraries, but since your desktop is usually a lot faster than your embedded device, cross-compilation is often much faster at compiling large projects. If you expect to be compiling your project hundreds of times so as to work on it for months, and your device is quite slow compared to your desktop, such as the Raspberry Pi 1 or Raspberry Pi Zero that are very slow compared to a desktop, then cross-compilation is a good idea. But in most cases, especially for small simple projects, you should just stick with native compilation since it is easier.

Note that all the libraries used by your project will also need to be compiled for the device, so you will need to compile OpenCV for your device. Natively compiling OpenCV on a Raspberry Pi 1 can take hours, whereas, cross-compiling OpenCV on a desktop might take just 15 minutes. But you usually only need to compile OpenCV once and then you'll have it for all your projects, so it is still worth sticking with native compilation of your project (including native compilation of OpenCV) in most cases.

There are also several options for how to run the code on an embedded system:

- Use the same input and output methods you used on desktop, such as the same video files or USB webcam or keyboard as input, and display text or graphics to an HDMI monitor in the same way you were doing on desktop.
- Use special devices for input and output. For example, instead of sitting at a desk using a USB webcam and keyboard as input and displaying the output to a desktop monitor, you could use the special Raspberry Pi Camera Module for video input, use custom GPIO push-buttons or sensors for input, and use a 7-inch MIPI DSI screen or GPIO LED lights as the output, and then by powering it all with a common **portable USB charger**, you can be wearing the whole computer platform in your backpack or attach it on your bicycle!
- Another option is to stream data in or out of the embedded device to other computers, or even use one device to stream out the camera data and one device to use that data. For example, you can use the Gstreamer framework to configure the Raspberry Pi to stream H.264 compressed video from its Camera Module onto the Ethernet network or through Wi-Fi, so that a powerful PC or server rack on the local network or Amazon AWS cloud-computing services can process the video stream somewhere else. This method allows a small and cheap camera device to be used in a complex project requiring large processing resources located somewhere else.

If you do wish to perform computer vision onboard the device, beware that some low-cost embedded devices such as Raspberry Pi 1, Raspberry Pi Zero, and BeagleBone Black have significantly slower computing power than desktops or even cheap netbooks or smartphones, perhaps 10-50 times slower than your desktop, so depending on your application you might need a powerful embedded device or to stream video to a separate computer as mentioned previously. If you don't need much computing power (for example, you only need to process one frame every 2 seconds, or you only need to use 160x120 image resolution), then a Raspberry Pi Zero running some Computer Vision onboard might be fast enough for your requirements. But many Computer Vision systems need far more computing power, and so if you want to perform Computer Vision onboard the device, you will often want to use a much faster device with a CPU in the range of 2 GHz, such as a Raspberry Pi 3, ODROID-XU4, or Jetson TK1.

Equipment setup to develop code for an embedded device

Let's begin by keeping it as simple as possible, by using a USB keyboard and mouse and a HDMI monitor just like our desktop system, compiling the code natively on the device, and running our code on the device. Our first step will be to copy the code onto the device, install the build tools, and compile OpenCV and our source code on the embedded system.

Many embedded devices such as Raspberry Pi have an HDMI port and at least one USB port. Therefore, the easiest way to start using an embedded device is to plug in a HDMI monitor and USB keyboard and mouse for the device, to configure settings and see output, while doing the code development and testing using your desktop machine. If you have a spare HDMI monitor, plug that into the device, but if you don't have a spare HDMI monitor, you might consider buying a small HDMI screen just for your embedded device.

Also, if you don't have a spare USB keyboard and mouse, you might consider buying a wireless keyboard and mouse that has a single USB wireless dongle, so you only use up a single USB port for both the keyboard and mouse. Many embedded devices use a 5V power supply, but they usually need more power (electrical current) than a desktop or laptop will provide in its USB port. So you should obtain either a separate 5V USB charger (atleast 1.5 Amps, *ideally 2.5 Amps*), or a portable USB battery charger that can provide atleast 1.5 Amps of output current. Your device might only use 0.5 Amps most of the time, but there will be occasional times when it needs over 1 Amps, so it's important to use a power supply that is rated for at least 1.5 Amps or more, otherwise your device will occasionally reboot or some hardware could behave strangely at important times or the filesystem could become corrupt and you lose your files! A 1 Amp supply might be good enough if you don't use cameras or accessories, but 2.0-2.5 Amps is safer.

For example, the following photographs show a convenient setup containing a Raspberry Pi 3, a good quality 8 GB micro-SD card for $10 (http://ebay.to/2ayp6Bo), a 5-inch HDMI resistive-touchscreen for $30-$45 (http://bit.ly/2aHQO2G), a wireless USB keyboard and mouse for $30 (http://ebay.to/2aN2oXi), a **5V 2.5A** power supply for $5 (http://ebay.to/2aCBLVK), a USB webcam such as the very fast **PS3 Eye** for just $5 (http://ebay.to/2aVWCUS), a Raspberry Pi Camera Module v1 or v2 for $15-$30 (http://bit.ly/2aF9PxD), and an Ethernet cable for $2 (http://ebay.to/2aznnjd),connecting the Raspberry Pi into the same LAN network as your development PC or laptop. Notice that this HDMI screen is designed specifically for the Raspberry Pi, since the screen plugs directly into the Raspberry Pi below it, and has a HDMI male-to-male adapter (shown in the right-hand side photo) for the Raspberry Pi so you don't need an HDMI cable, whereas other screens may require an HDMI cable (http://ebay.to/2aW4Fko) or MIPI DSI or SPI cable. Also note that some screens and touch panels need configuration before they will work, whereas most HDMI screens should work without any configuration:

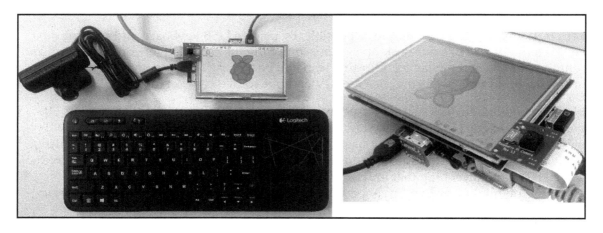

Notice the black USB webcam (on the far left of the LCD), the Raspberry Pi Camera Module (green and black board sitting on the top-left corner of the LCD), Raspberry Pi board (underneath the LCD), HDMI adapter (connecting the LCD to the Raspberry Pi below it), a blue Ethernet cable (plugged into a router), a small USB wireless keyboard and mouse dongle, and a micro-USB power cable (plugged into a **5V 2.5A** power supply).

Configuring a new Raspberry Pi

The following steps are specific to Raspberry Pi (also referred to as an **RPi**), so if you are using a different embedded device or you want a different type of setup, search the Web about how to setup your board. To setup an RPi 1, 2, or 3 (including their variants such as RPi Zero, RPi2B, 3B, and so on, and RPi 1A+ if you plug in a USB Ethernet dongle):

1. Get a fairly new, *good-quality micro-SD card* of at least 8 GB. If you use a cheap micro-SD card or an old micro-SD card that you already used many times before and it has degraded in quality, it might not be reliable enough to boot the RPi, so if you have trouble booting the RPi, you should try a good quality Class 10 micro-SD card (such as SanDisk Ultra or better) that says it handles at least 45 MB/s or can handle 4K video.

2. Download and burn the latest **Raspbian IMG** (not NOOBS) to the micro-SD card. Note that *burning an IMG is different to simply copying the file to SD*. Visit `https://www.raspberrypi.org/documentation/installation/installing-images/` and follow the instructions for your desktop's OS, to burn Raspbian to a micro-SD card. Be aware that you will lose any files that were previously on the card.

3. Plug a USB keyboard and mouse and HDMI display into the RPi, so you can easily run some commands and see the output.

4. Plug the RPi into a 5V USB power supply with atleast 1.5A, ideally 2.5A or higher. Computer USB ports aren't powerful enough.

5. You should see many pages of text scrolling while it is booting up Raspbian Linux, then it should be ready after 1 or 2 minutes.

6. If, after booting, it's just showing a black console screen with some text (such as if you downloaded **Raspbian Lite**), you are at the text-only login prompt. Log in by typing `pi` as the username and then hit *Enter*. Then type `raspberry` as the password and hit *Enter* again.

7. Or if it booted to the graphical display, click on the black **Terminal** icon at the top to open a shell (Command Prompt).

8. Initialize some settings in your RPi:

   - Type `sudo raspi-config` and hit *Enter* (see the following screenshot).
   - First, run **Expand Filesystem** and then finish and reboot your device, so the Raspberry Pi can use the whole micro-SD card.

- If you use a normal (US) keyboard, not a British keyboard, in Internationalization Options, change to Generic 104-key keyboard, Other, English (US), and then for the `AltGr` and similar questions just hit *Enter* unless you are use a special keyboard.
- In Enable Camera, enable the RPi Camera Module.
- In Overclock Options, set to RPi2 or similar so the device runs faster (but generates more heat).
- In Advanced Options, enable SSH server.
- In Advanced Options, if you are using Raspberry Pi 2 or 3, **change Memory Split to 256MB** so the GPU has plenty of RAM for video processing. For Raspberry Pi 1 or Zero, use 64 MB or the default.
- Finish then Reboot the device.

9. (Optional) Delete Wolfram, to save 600 MB of space on your SD card:

```
sudo apt-get purge -y wolfram-engine
```

It can be installed back using `sudo apt-get install wolfram-engine`

To see the remaining space on your SD card, run `df -h | head -2`

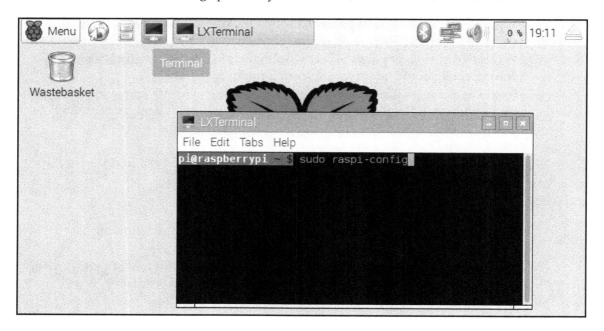

10. Assuming you plugged the RPi into your Internet router, it should already have Internet access. So update your RPi to the latest RPi firmware, software locations, OS, and software. **Warning**: Many Raspberry Pi tutorials say you should run `sudo rpi-update`; however, in recent years it's no longer a good idea to run `rpi-update` since it can give you an unstable system or firmware. The following instructions will update your Raspberry Pi to have stable software and firmware (note that these commands might take up to 1 hour):

```
sudo apt-get -y update
sudo apt-get -y upgrade
sudo apt-get -y dist-upgrade
sudo reboot
```

11. Find the IP address of the device:

```
hostname -I
```

12. Try accessing the device from your desktop.

    For example, assuming the device's IP address is `192.168.2.101`.

    On a Linux desktop:

    ```
    ssh-X pi@192.168.2.101
    ```

    Or on a Windows desktop:

    - Download, install, and run PuTTY
    - Then in PuTTY, connect to the IP address (192.168.2.101),
    - As user `pi` with password `raspberry`

13. (Optional) If you want your Command Prompt to be a different color than the commands and show the error value after each command:

    ```
    nano ~/.bashrc
    ```

    Add this line to the bottom:

    ```
    PS1="[e[0;44m]u@h: w ($?) $[e[0m] "
    ```

    Save the file (hit *Ctrl* + *X*, then hit *Y*, and then hit *Enter*).

Start using the new settings:

```
source ~/.bashrc
```

14. To disable the screensaver/screen blank power saving feature in Raspbian from turning off your screen on idle:

```
sudo nano /etc/lightdm/lightdm.conf
```

- Look for the line that says `#xserver-command=X` (jump to line 87 by pressing *Alt* + *G* and then typing `87` and hitting *Enter*).
- Change it to: **xserver-command=X -s 0 dpms**

- Save the file (hit *Ctrl* + *X* then hit *Y* then hit *Enter*).

```
sudo reboot
```

You should be ready to start developing on the device now!

Installing OpenCV on an embedded device

There is a very easy way to install OpenCV and all its dependencies on a Debian-based embedded device such as Raspberry Pi:

```
sudo apt-get install libopencv-dev
```

However, that might install an old version of OpenCV from 1 or 2 years ago.

To install the latest version of OpenCV on an embedded device such as Raspberry Pi, we need to build OpenCV from the source code. First we install a compiler and build system, then libraries for OpenCV to use, and finally OpenCV itself. Note that the steps for compiling OpenCV from source on Linux is the same whether you are compiling for desktop or for embedded. A Linux script `install_opencv_from_source.sh` is provided with this book; it is recommended you copy the file onto your Raspberry Pi (for example, with a USB flash stick) and run the script to download, build, and install OpenCV including potential multi-core CPU and **ARM NEON SIMD** optimizations (depending on hardware support):

```
chmod +x install_opencv_from_source.sh
./install_opencv_from_source.sh
```

The script will stop if there is any error; for example, if you don't have Internet access, or a dependency package conflicts with something else you already installed. If the script stops with an error, try using info on the Web to solve that error, then run the script again. The script will quickly check all the previous steps and then continue from where it finished last time. Note that it will take between 20 minutes to 12 hours depending on your hardware and software!

It's highly recommended to build and run a few OpenCV samples every time you've installed OpenCV, so when you have problems building your own code, at least you will know whether the problem is the OpenCV installation or a problem with your code.

Let's try to build the simple *edge* sample program. If we try the same Linux command to build it from OpenCV 2, we get a build error:

```
cd ~/opencv-3.*/samples/cpp
g++ edge.cpp -lopencv_core -lopencv_imgproc -lopencv_highgui
-o edge
/usr/bin/ld: /tmp/ccDqLWSz.o: undefined reference to symbol
'_ZN2cv6imreadERKNS_6StringEi'
/usr/local/lib/libopencv_imgcodecs.so.3.1: error adding symbols: DSO
missing from command line
collect2: error: ld returned 1 exit status
```

The second to last line of that error message tells us that a library was missing from the command line, so we simply need to add `-lopencv_imgcodecs` in our command next to the other OpenCV libraries we linked to. Now you know how to fix the problem anytime you are compiling an OpenCV 3 program and you see that error message. So let's do it correctly:

```
cd ~/opencv-3.*/samples/cpp
g++ edge.cpp -lopencv_core -lopencv_imgproc -lopencv_highgui
-lopencv_imgcodecs -o edge
```

It worked! So now you can run the program:

```
./edge
```

Hit *Ctrl + C* on your keyboard to quit the program. Note that the *edge* program might crash if you try running the command in an SSH terminal and you don't redirect the window to display on the device's LCD screen. So if you are using SSH to remotely run the program, add *DISPLAY=:0* before your command:

```
DISPLAY=:0 ./edge
```

You should also plug a USB webcam into the device and test that it works:

```
g++ starter_video.cpp -lopencv_core -lopencv_imgproc
-lopencv_highgui -lopencv_imgcodecs -lopencv_videoio \
-o starter_video
DISPLAY=:0 ./starter_video 0
```

Note: If you don't have a USB webcam, you can test using a video file:

```
DISPLAY=:0 ./starter_video ../data/768x576.avi
```

Now that OpenCV is successfully installed on your device, you can run the Cartoonifier applications we developed earlier. Copy the Cartoonifier folder onto the device (for example, by using a USB flash stick, or using scp to copy files over the network). Then build the code just like you did for desktop:

```
cd ~/Cartoonifier
export OpenCV_DIR="~/opencv-3.1.0/build"
mkdir build
cd build
cmake -D OpenCV_DIR=$OpenCV_DIR ..
make
```

And run it:

```
DISPLAY=:0 ./Cartoonifier
```

Using the Raspberry Pi Camera Module

While using a USB webcam on Raspberry Pi has the convenience of supporting identical behavior and code on desktop as on embedded device, you might consider using one of the official Raspberry Pi Camera Modules (referred to as the **RPi Cams**). They have some advantages and disadvantages over USB webcams.

The RPi Cams use the special MIPI CSI camera format, designed for smartphone cameras to use less power. They have smaller physical size, faster bandwidth, higher resolutions, higher frame rates, and reduced latency, compared to USB. Most USB 2.0 webcams can only deliver 640x480 or 1280x720 30 FPS video, since USB 2.0 is too slow for anything higher (except for some expensive USB webcams that perform onboard video compression) and USB 3.0 is still too expensive. Whereas, smartphone cameras (including the RPi Cams) can often deliver 1920x1080 30 FPS or even Ultra HD/4K resolutions. The RPi Cam v1 can in fact deliver upto 2592x1944 15 FPS or 1920x1080 30 FPS video even on a $5 Raspberry Pi Zero, thanks to the use of MIPI CSI for the camera and a compatible video processing ISP and GPU hardware inside the Raspberry Pi. The RPi Cams also support 640x480 in 90 FPS mode (such as for slow-motion capture), and this is quite useful for real-time computer vision so you can see very small movements in each frame, rather than large movements that are harder to analyze.

However, the RPi Cam is a plain circuit board that is *highly sensitive* to electrical interference, static electricity, or physical damage (simply touching the small orange flat cable with your finger can cause video interference or even permanently damage your camera!). The big flat white cable is far less sensitive but it is still very sensitive to electrical noise or physical damage. The RPi Cam comes with a very short 15 cm cable. It's possible to buy third-party cables on eBay with lengths between 5 cm to 1 m, but cables 50cm or longer are less reliable, whereas USB webcams can use 2 m to 5 m cables and can be plugged into USB hubs or active extension cables for longer distances.

There are currently several different RPi Cam models, notably the NoIR version that doesn't have an internal infrared filter; therefore, a NoIR camera can easily see in the dark (if you have an invisible infrared light source), or see infrared lasers or signals far clearer than regular cameras that includes an infrared filter inside them. There are also two different versions of RPi Cam: RPi Cam v1.3 and RPi Cam v2.1, where the v2.1 uses a wider angle lens with a Sony 8 Mega-Pixel sensor instead of a 5 Mega-Pixel **OmniVision** sensor, and has better support for motion in low lighting conditions, and adds support for 3240x2464 video at 15 FPS and potentially upto 120 FPS video at 720p. However, USB webcams come in thousands of different shapes and versions, making it easy to find specialized webcams such as waterproof or industrial-grade webcams, rather than requiring you to create your own custom housing for an RPi Cam.

IP cameras are also another option for a camera interface that can allow 1080p or higher resolution videos with Raspberry Pi, and IP cameras support not just very long cables, but potentially even work anywhere in the world using the Internet. But IP cameras aren't quite as easy to interface with OpenCV as USB webcams or the RPi Cam.

In the past, RPi Cams and the official drivers weren't directly compatible with OpenCV; you often used custom drivers and modified your code in order to grab frames from RPi Cams, but it's now possible to access an RPi Cam in OpenCV in the exact same way as a USB webcam! Thanks to recent improvements in the v4l2 drivers, once you load the v4l2 driver the RPi Cam will appear as a `/dev/video0` or `/dev/video1` file like a regular USB webcam. So traditional OpenCV webcam code such as `cv::VideoCapture(0)` will be able to use it just like a webcam.

Installing the Raspberry Pi Camera Module driver

First let's temporarily load the v4l2 driver for the RPi Cam to make sure our camera is plugged in correctly:

```
sudo modprobe bcm2835-v4l2
```

If the command failed (if it printed an error message to the console, or it froze, or the command returned a number besides 0), then perhaps your camera is not plugged in correctly. Shutdown and then unplug power from your RPi and try attaching the flat white cable again, looking at photos on the Web to make sure it's plugged in the correct way around. If it is the correct way around, it's possible the cable wasn't fully inserted before you closed the locking tab on the RPi. Also check whether you forgot to click **Enable Camera** when configuring your Raspberry Pi earlier, using the `sudoraspi-config` command.

If the command worked (if the command returned 0 and no error was printed to the console), then we can make sure the v4l2 driver for the RPi Cam is always loaded on bootup, by adding it to the bottom of the `/etc/modules` file:

```
sudo nano /etc/modules
# Load the Raspberry Pi Camera Module v4l2 driver on bootup:
bcm2835-v4l2
```

After you save the file and reboot your RPi, you should be able to run `ls /dev/video*` to see a list of cameras available on your RPi. If the RPi Cam is the only camera plugged into your board, you should see it as the default camera (`/dev/video0`), or if you also have a USB webcam plugged in then it will be either `/dev/video0` or `/dev/video1`.

Let's test the RPi Cam using the `starter_video` sample program we compiled earlier:

```
cd ~/opencv-3.*/samples/cpp
DISPLAY=:0 ./starter_video 0
```

If it's showing the wrong camera, try `DISPLAY=:0 ./starter_video 1`.

Now that we know the RPi Cam is working in OpenCV, let's try Cartoonifier:

```
cd ~/Cartoonifier
DISPLAY=:0 ./Cartoonifier 0
```

Or `DISPLAY=:0 ./Cartoonifier 1` for the other camera.

Making Cartoonifier to run full screen

In embedded systems, you often want your application to be full screen and hide the Linux GUI and menu. OpenCV offers an easy method to set the full screen window property, but make sure you created the window using the NORMAL flag:

```
// Create a fullscreen GUI window for display on the screen.
namedWindow(windowName, WINDOW_NORMAL);
setWindowProperty(windowName, WND_PROP_FULLSCREEN,
CV_WINDOW_FULLSCREEN);
```

Hiding the mouse cursor

You might notice the mouse cursor is shown on top of your window even though you don't want to use a mouse in your embedded system. To hide the mouse cursor, you can use the `xdotool` command to move it to the bottom-right corner pixel, so it's not noticeable, but is still available if you want to occasionally plug in your mouse to debug the device. Install `xdotool` and create a short Linux script to run it with Cartoonifier:

```
sudo apt-get install -y xdotool
cd ~/Cartoonifier/build
nano runCartoonifier.sh
#!/bin/sh
# Move the mouse cursor to the screen's bottom-right pixel.
xdotoolmousemove 3000 3000
# Run Cartoonifier with any arguments given.
/home/pi/Cartoonifier/build/Cartoonifier "$@"
```

Finally, make your script executable:

```
chmod +x runCartoonifier.sh
```

Try running your script, to make sure it works:

```
DISPLAY=:0 ./runCartoonifier.sh
```

Running Cartoonifier automatically after bootup

Often when you build an embedded device, you want your application to be executed automatically after the device has booted up, rather than requiring the user to manually run your application. To automatically run our application after the device has fully booted up and logged into the graphical desktop, create an autostart folder with a file in it with certain contents including the full path to your script or application:

```
mkdir ~/.config/autostart
nano ~/.config/autostart/Cartoonifier.desktop
       [Desktop Entry]
       Type=Application
       Exec=/home/pi/Cartoonifier/build/runCartoonifier.sh
       X-GNOME-Autostart-enabled=true
```

Now, whenever you turn the device on or reboot it, Cartoonifier will begin running!

Speed comparison of Cartoonifier on Desktop versus Embedded

You will notice that the code runs much slower on Raspberry Pi than on your desktop! By far the two easiest ways to run it faster are to use a faster device or use a smaller camera resolution. The following table shows some frame rates, **Frames per Seconds** (**FPS**) for both the *Sketch* and *Paint* modes of Cartoonifier on a desktop, RPi 1, RPi 2, RPi 3, and Jetson TK1. Note that the speeds don't have any custom optimizations and only run on a single CPU core, and the timings include the time for rendering images to the screen. The USB webcam used is the fast PS3 Eye webcam running at 640x480 since it is the fastest low-cost webcam on the market.

It's worth mentioning that Cartoonifier is only using a single CPU core, but all the devices listed have four CPU cores except for RPi 1 which has a single core, and many x86 computers have hyperthreading to give roughly eight CPU cores. So if you wrote your code to efficiently make use of multiple CPU cores (or GPU), the speeds might be 1.5 to 3 times faster than the single-threaded figures shown:

Computer	Sketch mode	Paint mode
Intel Core i7 PC	20 FPS	2.7 FPS
Jetson TK1ARM CPU	16 FPS	2.3 FPS
Raspberry Pi 3	4.3 FPS	0.32 FPS (3 seconds/frame)
Raspberry Pi 2	3.2 FPS	0.28 FPS (4 seconds/frame)
Raspberry Pi Zero	2.5 FPS	0.21 FPS (5 seconds/frame)
Raspberry Pi 1	1.9 FPS	0.12 FPS (8 seconds/frame)

Notice that Raspberry Pi is extremely slow at running the code, especially the *Paint* mode, so we will try simply changing the camera and the resolution of the camera.

Changing the camera and camera resolution

The following table shows how the speed of the *Sketch* mode compares on Raspberry Pi 2 using different types of cameras and different camera resolutions:

Hardware	640x480 resolution	320x240 resolution
RPi 2 with RPi Cam	3.8 FPS	12.9 FPS
RPi 2 with PS3 Eye webcam	3.2 FPS	11.7 FPS
RPi 2 with unbranded webcam	1.8 FPS	7.4 FPS

As you can see, when using the RPi Cam in 320x240, it seems we have a good enough solution to have some fun, even if it's not in the 20-30 FPS range that we would prefer.

Power draw of Cartoonifier running on desktop versus embedded system

We've seen that various embedded devices are slower than desktop, from the RPi 1 being roughly 20 times slower than a desktop, up to Jetson TK1 being roughly 1.5 times slower than a desktop. But for some tasks, low speed is acceptable if it means there will also be significantly lower battery draw, allowing for small batteries or low year-round electricity costs for a server or low heat generated.

Raspberry Pi has different models even for the same processor, such as Raspberry Pi 1B, Zero, and 1A+ that all run at similar speeds but have significantly different power draw. MIPI CSI cameras such as the RPi Cam also use less electricity than webcams. The following table shows how much electrical power is used by different hardware running the same Cartoonifier code. Power measurements of Raspberry Pi were performed as shown in the following photo using a simple USB current monitor (for example, J7-T Safety Tester--`http://bit.ly/2aSZa6H`--for $5), and a DMM multimeter for the other devices:

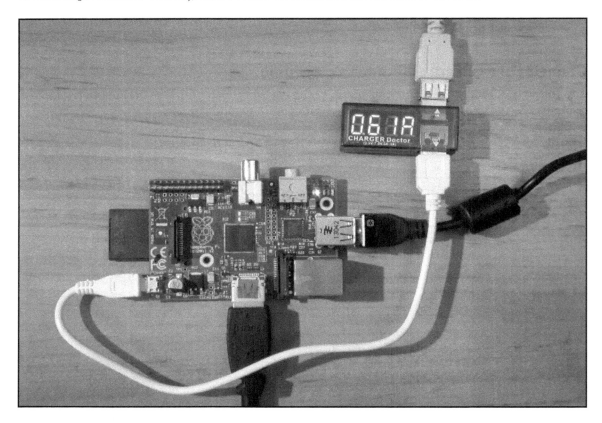

Idle Power measures power when the computer is running but no major applications are being used, whereas **Cartoonifier Power** measures power when Cartoonifier is running. **Efficiency** is Cartoonifier Power / Cartoonifier Speed in a 640x480 *Sketch* mode.

Hardware	Idle Power	Cartoonifier Power	Efficiency
RPi Zero with PS3 Eye	1.2 Watts	1.8 Watts	1.4 Frames per Watt
RPi 1A+ with PS3 Eye	**1.1 Watts**	**1.5 Watts**	1.1 Frames per Watt
RPi 1B with PS3 Eye	2.4 Watts	3.2 Watts	0.5 Frames per Watt
RPi 2B with PS3 Eye	1.8 Watts	2.2 Watts	1.4 Frames per Watt
RPi 3B with PS3 Eye	2.0 Watts	2.5 Watts	1.7 Frames per Watt
Jetson TK1 with PS3 Eye	2.8 Watts	4.3 Watts	**3.7 Frames per Watt**
Core i7 laptop with PS3 Eye	14.0 Watts	39.0 Watts	0.5 Frames per Watt

We can see that RPi 1A+ uses the least power, but the most power-efficient options are Jetson TK1 and Raspberry Pi 3B. Interestingly, the original Raspberry Pi (RPi1B) has roughly the same efficiency as an x86 laptop. All later Raspberry Pis are significantly more power-efficient than the original (RPi 1B).

Disclaimer: The author is a former employee of NVIDIA that produced the Jetson TK1, but the results and conclusions are believed to be authentic.

Lets also look at the power draw of different cameras that work with Raspberry Pi:

Hardware	Idle Power	Cartoonifier Power	Efficiency
RPi Zero with PS3 Eye	1.2 Watts	1.8 Watts	1.4 Frames per Watt
RPi Zero with RPi Cam v1.3	0.6 Watts	1.5 Watts	2.1 Frames per Watt
RPi Zero with RPi Cam v2.1	**0.55 Watts**	**1.3 Watts**	**2.4 Frames per Watt**

We see that RPi Cam v2.1 is slightly more power-efficient than RPi Cam v1.3, and significantly more power-efficient than a USB webcam.

Streaming video from Raspberry Pi to a powerful computer

Thanks to the hardware-accelerated video encoders in all modern ARM devices including Raspberry Pi, a valid alternative to performing Computer Vision onboard an embedded device is to use the device to just capture video and stream it across a network in realtime to a PC or server rack. All Raspberry Pi models contain the same video encoder hardware, so an RPi 1A+ or RPi Zero with a Pi Cam is quite a good option for a low-cost, low-power portable video streaming server. Raspberry Pi 3 adds Wi-Fi for additional portable functionality.

There are numerous ways live camera video can be streamed from a Raspberry Pi, such as using the official RPi V4L2 camera driver to allow the RPi Cam to appear like a webcam, then use Gstreamer, liveMedia, netcat, or VLC to stream the video across a network. However, these methods often introduce 1 or 2 seconds of latency and often require customizing the OpenCV client code or learning how to use Gstreamer efficiently. So instead, the following section will show how to perform both the camera capture and network streaming using an alternative camera driver named **UV4L**:

1. Install UV4L on the Raspberry Pi by following `http://www.linux-projects.org/uv4l/installation/`:

   ```
   curl http://www.linux-projects.org/listing/uv4l_repo/lrkey.asc
   sudo apt-key add -
   sudo su
   echo "# UV4L camera streaming repo:">> /etc/apt/sources.list
   echo "deb http://www.linux-
     projects.org/listing/uv4l_repo/raspbian/jessie main">>
     /etc/apt/sources.list
   exit
   sudo apt-get update
   sudo apt-get install uv4l uv4l-raspicam uv4l-server
   ```

2. Run the UV4L streaming server manually (on the RPi) to check that it works:

   ```
   sudo killall uv4l
   sudo LD_PRELOAD=/usr/lib/uv4l/uv4lext/armv6l/libuv4lext.so
   uv4l -v7 -f --sched-rr --mem-lock --auto-video_nr
   --driverraspicam --encoding mjpeg
   --width 640 --height 480 --framerate15
   ```

3. Test the camera's network stream from your desktop:

- Install VLC Media Player.
- **File** | **Open Network Stream** | visit `http://192.168.2.111:8080/str eam/video.mjpeg`.
- Adjust the URL to the IP address of your Raspberry Pi. Run `hostname -I` on RPi to find its IP address.

4. Now get the UV4L server to run automatically on bootup:

```
sudo apt-get install uv4l-raspicam-extras
```

5. Edit any UV4L server settings you want in `uv4l-raspicam.conf` such as resolution and frame rate:

```
sudo nano /etc/uv4l/uv4l-raspicam.conf
drop-bad-frames = yes
nopreview = yes
width = 640
height = 480
framerate = 24
sudo reboot
```

6. Now we can tell OpenCV to use our network stream as if it was a webcam. As long as your installation of OpenCV can use FFMPEG internally, OpenCV will be able to grab frames from an MJPEG network stream just like a webcam:

```
./Cartoonifier http://192.168.2.101:8080/stream/video.mjpeg
```

Your Raspberry Pi is now using UV4L to stream the live 640x480 24 FPS video to a PC that is running Cartoonifier in *Sketch* mode, achieving roughly 19 FPS (with 0.4 seconds of latency). Notice this is almost the same speed as using the PS3 Eye webcam directly on the PC (20 FPS)!

Note that when you are streaming the video to OpenCV, it won't be able to set the camera resolution; you need to adjust the UV4L server settings to change the camera resolution. Also note that instead of streaming MJPEG, we could have streamed H.264 video that uses lower bandwidth, but some computer vision algorithms don't handle video compression such as H.264 very well, so MJPEG will cause less algorithm problems than H.264.

If you have both the official RPi V4L2 driver and the UV4L driver installed, they will both be available as cameras 0 and 1 (devices `/dev/video0` and `/dev/video1`), but you can only use one camera driver at a time.

Customizing your embedded system!

Now that you have created a whole embedded Cartoonifier system, and you know the basics of how it works and which parts do what, you should customize it! Make the video full screen, change the GUI, or change the application behavior and workflow, or change the Cartoonifier filter constants, or the skin detector algorithm, or replace the Cartoonifier code with your own project ideas. Or stream the video to the cloud and process it there!

You can improve the skin detection algorithm in many ways, such as a more complex skin detection algorithm (for example, using trained Gaussian models from many recent CVPR or ICCV conference papers at `http://www.cvpapers.com`), or add face detection (see the *Face detection* section of `Chapter 6`, *Face Recognition using Eigenfaces and Fisherfaces*) to the skin detector, so it detects where the user's face is, rather than asking the user to put their face in the center of the screen. Beware that face detection may take many seconds on some devices or high-resolution cameras, so they may be limited in their current real-time uses. But embedded system platforms are getting faster every year, so this may be less of a problem over time.

The most significant way to speed up embedded computer vision applications is to reduce the camera resolution absolutely as much as possible (for example, 0.5 mega pixel instead of 5 megapixels), allocate and free images as rarely as possible, and do image format conversions as rarely as possible. In some cases, there might be some optimized image processing or math libraries, or optimized version of OpenCV from the CPU vendor of your device (for example, Broadcom, NVIDIA Tegra, Texas Instruments OMAP, Samsung Exynos), or for your CPU family (for example, ARM Cortex-A9).

To make customizing embedded and desktop image processing code easier, this book comes with the files, `ImageUtils.cpp` and `ImageUtils.h`, to help you experiment. They include functions such as `printMatInfo()` that prints a lot of info about a `cv::Mat` object, making debugging OpenCV much easier. There are also timing macros to easily add detailed timing statistics to your C/C++ code. For example:

```
DECLARE_TIMING(myFilter);

void myImageFunction(Mat img) {
  printMatInfo(img, "input");
```

```
    START_TIMING(myFilter);
    bilateralFilter(img, ...);
    STOP_TIMING(myFilter);
    SHOW_TIMING(myFilter, "My Filter");
}
```

You would then see something like the following printed to your console:

```
input: 800w600h 3ch 8bpp, range[19,255][17,243][47,251]
My Filter: time: 213ms (ave=215ms min=197ms max=312ms, across 57 runs).
```

This is useful when your OpenCV code is not working as expected, particularly for embedded development where it is often difficult to use an IDE debugger.

Summary

This chapter has shown several different types of image processing filters that can be used to generate various cartoon effects, from a plain sketch mode that looks like a pencil drawing, a paint mode that looks like a color painting, to a cartoon mode that overlays the *Sketch* mode on top of the paint mode to appear like a cartoon. It also shown that other fun effects can be obtained, such as the evil mode that greatly enhanced noisy edges, and the alien mode that changed the skin of a face to appear bright green.

There are many commercial smartphone apps that perform similar fun effects on the user's face, such as cartoon filters and skin color changers. There are also professional tools using similar concepts, such as skin-smoothing video post-processing tools that attempt to beautify women's faces by smoothing their skin while keeping the edges and non-skin regions sharp, in order to make their faces appear younger.

This chapter shows how to port the application from a desktop to an embedded system, by following the recommended guidelines of developing a working desktop version first, and then porting it to embedded, and creating a user interface that is suitable for the embedded application. The image processing code is shared between the two projects, so that the reader can modify the cartoon filters for the desktop application, and easily see those modifications in the embedded system as well.

Remember that this book includes an OpenCV installation script for Linux and full source code for all projects discussed.

2
Exploring Structure from Motion Using OpenCV

In this chapter, we will discuss the notion of **Structure from Motion (SfM)**, or better put, extracting geometric structures from images taken with a camera under motion, using OpenCV's API to help us. First, let's constrain the otherwise very b road approach to SfM using a single camera, usually called a **monocular** approach, and a discrete and sparse set of frames rather than a continuous video stream. These two constrains will greatly simplify the system we will sketch out in the coming pages, and help us understand the fundamentals of any SfM method. To implement our method, we will follow in the footsteps of Hartley and Zisserman (hereafter referred to as H&Z, for brevity), as documented in Chapters 9 through 12 of their seminal book *Multiple View Geometry in Computer Vision*.

In this chapter, we will cover the following:

- Structure from Motion concepts
- Estimating the camera motion from a pair of images
- Reconstructing the scene
- Reconstructing from many views
- Refining the reconstruction

Throughout the chapter, we assume the use of a calibrated camera, one that was calibrated beforehand. *Calibration* is a ubiquitous operation in Computer Vision, fully supported in OpenCV using command-line tools, and was discussed in previous chapters. We, therefore, assume the existence of the camera's **intrinsic parameters** embodied in the K matrix and distortionn coefficients vector - the outputs from the calibration process.

To make things clear in terms of language, from this point on, we will refer to a camera as a single view of the scene rather than to the optics and hardware taking the image. A camera has a 3D position in space (translation) and a 3D direction of view (orientation). In general, we describe this as the 6 **Degree of Freedom** (**DOF**) camera pose, sometimes referred to as **extrinsic parameters**. Between two cameras, therefore, there is a 3D translation element (movement through space) and a 3D rotation of the direction of view.

We will also unify the terms for the point in the scene, world, real, or 3D to be the same thing, a point that exists in our real world. The same goes for points in an image or 2D, which are points in the image coordinates of some real 3D point that was projected on the camera sensor at that location and time.

In the chapter's code sections, you will notice references to *Multiple View Geometry in Computer Vision*, for example // HZ 9.12. This refers to equation number 12 of Chapter 9 of the book. Also, the text will include excerpts of code only; while the complete runnable code is included in the material accompanied with the book.

The following flow diagram describes the process in the SfM pipeline we will implement. We begin by triangulating an initial reconstructed point cloud of the scene, using 2D features matched across the image set and a calculation of two camera poses. We then add more views to the reconstruction by matching more points into the forming point cloud, calculating camera poses and triangulating their matching points. In between, we will also perform bundle adjustment to minimize the error in the reconstruction. All the steps are detailed in the next sections of this chapter, with relevant code excerpts, pointers to useful OpenCV functions, and mathematical reasoning:

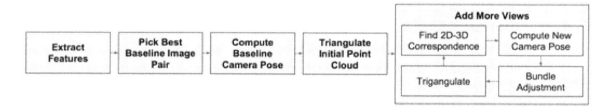

Structure from Motion concepts

The first discrimination we should make is the difference between stereo (or indeed any multiview) and 3D reconstruction using calibrated rigs and SfM. A rig of two or more cameras assumes that we already know the *motion* between the cameras, while in SfM, we don't know what this motion is and we wish to find it. Calibrated rigs, from a simplistic point of view, allow a much more accurate reconstruction of 3D geometry because there is no error in estimating the distance and rotation between the cameras, it is already known. The first step in implementing an SfM system is finding the motion between the cameras. OpenCV may help us in a number of ways to obtain this motion, specifically using the findFundamentalMat and findEssentialMat functions.

Let's think for one moment of the goal behind choosing an SfM algorithm. In most cases, we wish to obtain the geometry of the scene, for example, where objects are in relation to the camera and what their form is. Having found the motion between the cameras picturing the same scene, from a reasonably similar point of view, we would now like to reconstruct the geometry. In Computer Vision jargon, this is known as **triangulation**, and there are plenty of ways to go about it. It may be done by way of ray intersection, where we construct two rays-one from each camera's center of projection and a point on each of the image planes. The intersection of these rays in space will, ideally, intersect at one 3D point in the real world that is imaged in each camera, as shown in the following diagram:

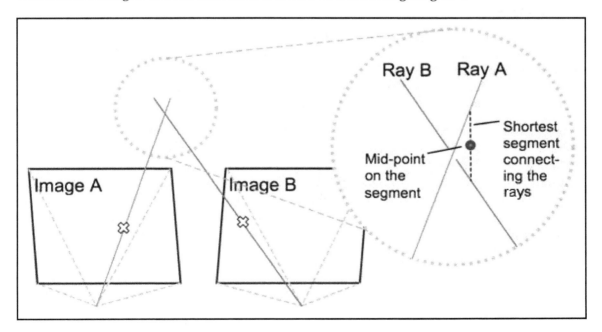

In reality, ray intersection is highly unreliable; H&Z recommend against it. This is because the rays usually do not intersect, making us fall back to using the middle point on the shortest segment connecting the two rays. OpenCV contains a simple API for a more accurate form of triangulation--the `triangulatePoints` function--so we do not need to code this part on our own.

After you learn how to recover 3D geometry from two views, we will see how we can incorporate more views of the same scene to get an even richer reconstruction. At that point, most SfM methods try to optimize the bundle of estimated positions of our cameras and 3D points by means of **Bundle Adjustment**, in the *Refinement of the reconstruction* section. OpenCV contains the means for Bundle Adjustment in its new Image Stitching Toolbox. However, the beauty of working with OpenCV and C++ is the abundance of external tools that can be easily integrated into the pipeline. We will, therefore, see how to integrate an external bundle adjuster, the Ceres nonlinear optimization package.

Now that we have sketched an outline of our approach to SfM using OpenCV, we will see how each element can be implemented.

Estimating the camera motion from a pair of images

Before we set out to actually find the motion between two cameras, let's examine the inputs and the tools we have at hand to perform this operation. First, we have two images of the same scene from (hopefully not extremely) different positions in space. This is a powerful asset, and we will make sure that we use it. As for tools, we should take a look at mathematical objects that impose constraints over our images, cameras, and the scene.

Two very useful mathematical objects are the fundamental matrix (denoted by F) and the essential matrix (denoted by E), which impose a constraint over corresponding 2D points in two images of the scene. They are mostly similar, except that the essential matrix is assuming usage of calibrated cameras; this is the case for us, so we will choose it. OpenCV allows us to find the fundamental matrix via the `findFundamentalMat` function and the essential matrix via the `findEssentialMatrix` function. Finding the essential matrix can be done as follows:

```
Mat E = findEssentialMat(leftPoints, rightPoints, focal, pp);
```

This function makes use of matching points in the left-hand side image, `leftPoints`, and right-hand side image, `rightPoints`, which we will discuss shortly, as well as two additional pieces of information from the camera's calibration: the focal length, `focal`, and principal point, `pp`.

The essential matrix E is a 3x3 sized matrix, which imposes the following constraint on a point x in one image and a point and a point x' corresponding image:

$$x'K^{T}EKx = 0$$

Here, K is the calibration matrix.

This is extremely useful, as we are about to see. Another important fact we use is that the essential matrix is all we need in order to recover the two cameras' positions from our images, although only up to an arbitrary unit of scale. So, if we obtain the essential matrix, we know where each camera is positioned in space, and where it is looking. We can easily calculate the matrix if we have enough of those constraint equations, simply because each equation can be used to solve for a small part of the matrix. In fact, OpenCV internally calculates it using just five point-pairs, but through the **Random Sample Consensus algorithm (RANSAC)**, many more pairs can be used and they make for a more robust solution.

Point matching using rich feature descriptors

Now, we will make use of our constraint equations to calculate the essential matrix. To get our constraints, remember that for each point in image A, we must find a corresponding point in image B. We can achieve such a matching using OpenCV's extensive 2D feature-matching framework, which has greatly matured in the past few years.

Feature extraction and descriptor matching is an essential process in Computer Vision, and is used in many methods to perform all sorts of operations, for example, detecting the position and orientation of an object in an image or searching a big database of images for similar images through a given query. In essence, *feature extraction* means selecting points in the image that would make for good features and computing a descriptor for them. A *descriptor* is a vector of numbers that describes the surrounding environment around a feature point in an image. Different methods have different length and data types for their descriptor vectors. **Descriptor Matching** is the process of finding a corresponding feature of one set in another using its descriptor. OpenCV provides very easy and powerful methods to support feature extraction and matching.

Let's examine a very simple feature extraction and matching scheme:

```
vector<KeyPoint> keypts1, keypts2;
Mat desc1, desc2;

// detect keypoints and extractORBdescriptors
Ptr<Feature2D>orb = ORB::create(2000);
orb->detectAndCompute(img1, noArray(), keypts1, desc1);
orb->detectAndCompute(img2, noArray(), keypts2, desc2);

// matching descriptors
Ptr<DescriptorMatcher>matcher
=DescriptorMatcher::create("BruteForce-Hamming");
vector<DMatch> matches;
matcher->match(desc1, desc2, matches);
```

You may have already seen similar OpenCV code, but let's review it quickly. Our goal is to obtain three elements: feature points for two images, descriptors for them, and a matching between the two sets of features. OpenCV provides a range of feature detectors, descriptor extractors, and matchers. In this simple example, we use the ORB class to get both the 2D location of **Oriented BRIEF (ORB)**(where, **BRIEF** stands for **Binary Robust Independent Elementary Features**) feature points and their respective descriptors. ORB may be preferred over traditional 2D features such as the **Speeded-Up Robust Features (SURF)** or **Scale Invariant Feature Transform (SIFT)** because it is unencumbered with intellectual property and shown to be faster to detect, compute, and match.

We use a *bruteforce* binary matcher to get the matching, which simply matches two feature sets by comparing each feature in the first set to each feature in the second set (hence the phrasing *bruteforce*).

In the following image, we will see a matching of feature points on two images from the Fountain P11 sequence can be found at `http://cvlab.epfl.ch/~strecha/multiview/dens eMVS.html`:

Practically, raw matching like we just performed is good only up to a certain level, and many matches are probably erroneous. For that reason, most SfM methods perform some form of filtering on the matches to ensure correctness and reduce errors. One form of filtering, which is built into OpenCV's brute-force matcher, is **cross-check filtering**. That is, a match is considered true if a feature of the first image matches a feature of the second image, and the reverse check also matches the feature of the second image with the feature of the first image. Another common filtering mechanism, used in the provided code, is to filter based on the fact that the two images are of the same scene and have a certain stereo-view relationship between them. In practice, the filter tries to robustly calculate the fundamental or essential matrix which we will learn about in the *Finding camera matrices* section and retain those feature pairs that correspond with this calculation with small errors.

An alternative to using rich features, such as ORB, is to use **optical flow**. The following information box provides a short overview of optical flow. It is possible to use optical flow instead of descriptor matching to find the required point matching between two images, while the rest of the SfM pipeline remains the same. OpenCV recently extended its API to get the flow field from two images and now it is faster and more powerful.

Optical flow is the process of matching selected points from one image to another, assuming both images are part of a sequence and relatively close to one another. Most optical flow methods compare a small region, known as the **search window** or patch, around each point from *image A* to the same area in *image B*. Following a very common rule in Computer Vision, called the **brightness constancy constraint** (and other names), the small patches of the image will not change drastically from one image to the other, and therefore the magnitude of their subtraction should be close to zero. In addition to matching patches, newer methods of optical flow use a number of additional methods to get better results. One is using image pyramids, which are smaller and smaller resized versions of the image, which allow for working *from-coarse-to-fine*, a very well-used trick in Computer Vision. Another method is to define global constraints on the flow field, assuming that the points close to each other move together in the same direction. A more in-depth review of optical flow methods in OpenCV can be found in a chapter named *Developing Fluid Wall Using the Microsoft Kinect* which is available on the Packt website.

Finding camera matrices

Now that we have obtained matches between keypoints, we can calculate the essential matrix. However, we must first align our matching points into two arrays, where an index in one array corresponds to the same index in the other. This is required by the findEssentialMat function as we've seen in the *Estimating Camera Motion* section. We would also need to convert the KeyPoint structure to a Point2f structure. We must pay special attention to the queryIdx and trainIdx member variables of DMatch, the OpenCV struct that holds a match between two keypoints, as they must align with the way we used the DescriptorMatcher::match() function. The following code section shows how to align a matching into two corresponding sets of 2D points, and how these can be used to find the essential matrix:

```cpp
vector<KeyPoint> leftKpts, rightKpts;
// ... obtain keypoints using a feature extractor

vector<DMatch> matches;
// ... obtain matches using a descriptor matcher

//align left and right point sets
vector<Point2f>leftPts, rightPts;
for(size_ti = 0; i < matches.size(); i++){
  // queryIdx is the "left" image
  leftPts.push_back(leftKpts[matches[i].queryIdx].pt);

  // trainIdx is the "right" image
  rightPts.push_back(rightKpts[matches[i].trainIdx].pt);
}

//robustly find the Essential Matrix
Mat status;
Mat E = findEssentialMat(
  leftPts,        // points from left image
  rightPts,       // points from right image
  focal,          // camera focal length factor
  pp,             // camera principal point
  cv::RANSAC,     // use RANSAC for a robust solution
  0.999,          // desired solution confidence level
  1.0,            // point-to-epipolar-line threshold
  status);        // binary vector for inliers
```

We may, later, use the `status` binary vector to prune those points that align with the recovered essential matrix. Look at the following image for an illustration of point matching after pruning. The red arrows mark feature matches that were removed in the process of finding the matrix, and the green arrows are feature matches that were retained:

Now we are ready to find the camera matrices. This process is described at length in a chapter of H&Z's book; however, the new OpenCV 3 API makes things very easy for us by introducing the `recoverPose` function. First, we will briefly examine the structure of the camera matrix we are going to use:

$$P = [R|t] = \begin{bmatrix} r_1 & r_2 & r_3 & t_1 \\ r_4 & r_5 & r_6 & t_2 \\ r_7 & r_8 & r_9 & t_3 \end{bmatrix}$$

This is the model for our camera pose, which consists of two elements: rotation (denoted by **R**) and translation (denoted by **t**). The interesting thing is that it holds a very essential equation: $x = PX$, where x is a 2D point on the image and X is a 3D point in space. There is more to it, but this matrix gives us a very important relationship between the image points and the scene points. So, now that we have a motivation for finding the camera matrices, we will see how it can be done. The following code section shows how to decompose the essential matrix into the rotation and translation elements:

```
Mat E;
// ... find the essential matrix

Mat R, t; //placeholders for rotation and translation

//Find Pright camera matrix from the essential matrix
//Cheirality check is performed internally.
recoverPose(E, leftPts, rightPts, R, t, focal, pp, mask);
```

Very simple. Without going too deeply into the mathematical interpretation, this conversion of the essential matrix to rotation and translation is possible because the essential matrix was originally composed by these two elements. Strictly for satisfying our curiosity, we can look at the following equation for the essential matrix, which appears in the literature: $E=[t]_x R$. We see it is composed of (some form of) a translation element t and a rotational element R.

Note that a *cheirality check* is internally performed in the `recoverPose` function. The cheirality check makes sure that all triangulated 3D points are *in front* of the reconstructed camera. H&Z show that camera matrix recovery from the essential matrix has in fact four possible solutions, but the only correct solution is the one that will produce triangulated points in front of the camera, hence the need for a cheirality check. We will learn about triangulation and 3D reconstruction in the next section.

Note what we just did only gives us one camera matrix, and for triangulation, we require two camera matrices. This operation assumes that one camera matrix is fixed and canonical (no rotation and no translation, placed at the *world origin*):

$$P_0 = \begin{bmatrix} 1 & 0 & 0 & 0 \\ 0 & 1 & 0 & 0 \\ 0 & 0 & 1 & 0 \end{bmatrix}$$

The other camera that we recovered from the essential matrix has moved and rotated in relation to the fixed one. This also means that any of the 3D points that we recover from these two camera matrices will have the first camera at the world origin point (0, 0, 0). The assumption of a canonical camera is just how `cv::recoverPose` works; however in other situations, the *origin* camera pose matrix may be different than the canonical and still be valid for 3D points' triangulation, as we will see later when we will not use `cv::recoverPose` to get a new camera pose matrix.

One more thing we can think of adding to our method is error checking. Many times, the calculation of an essential matrix from point matching is erroneous, and this affects the resulting camera matrices. Continuing to triangulate with faulty camera matrices is pointless. We can install a check to see if the rotation element is a valid rotation matrix. Keeping in mind that rotation matrices must have a determinant of 1 (or -1), we can simply do the following:

```
bool CheckCoherentRotation(const cv::Mat_<double>& R) {
  if(fabsf(determinant(R))-1.0 >EPS) {
    cerr <<"rotation matrix is invalid" <<endl;
    return false;
  }
  return true;
}
```

Think of `EPS` (from Epsilon) as a very small number that helps us cope with numerical calculation limits of our CPU. In reality, we may define the following in code:

```
#define EPS 1E-07
```

We can now see how all these elements combine into a function that recovers the P matrices. First, we will introduce some convenience data structures and type shorthand:

```
typedef std::vector<cv::KeyPoint> Keypoints;
typedef std::vector<cv::Point2f>  Points2f;
typedef std::vector<cv::Point3f>  Points3f;
typedef std::vector<cv::DMatch>   Matching;

struct Features { //2D features
  Keypoints keyPoints;
  Points2f  points;
  cv::Mat   descriptors;
};

struct Intrinsics { //camera intrinsic parameters
  cv::Mat K;
  cv::Mat Kinv;
  cv::Mat distortion;
```

```
};
```

Now we can write the camera matrix finding function:

```
void findCameraMatricesFromMatch(
  const Intrinsics&    intrin,
  const Matching&      matches,
  const Features&      featuresLeft,
  const Features&      featuresRight,
  cv::Matx34f&         Pleft,
  cv::Matx34f&         Pright) {
  {
    //Note: assuming fx = fy
    const double focal = intrin.K.at<float>(0, 0);
    const cv::Point2d pp(intrin.K.at<float>(0, 2),
                         intrin.K.at<float>(1, 2));

    //align left and right point sets using the matching
    Features left;
    Features right;
    GetAlignedPointsFromMatch(
      featuresLeft,
      featuresRight,
      matches,
      left,
      right);

    //find essential matrix
    Mat E, mask;
    E = findEssentialMat(
      left.points,
      right.points,
      focal,
      pp,
      RANSAC,
      0.999,
      1.0,
      mask);

    Mat_<double> R, t;

    //Find Pright camera matrix from the essential matrix
    recoverPose(E, left.points, right.points, R, t, focal, pp, mask);

    Pleft = Matx34f::eye();
    Pright = Matx34f(R(0,0), R(0,1), R(0,2), t(0),
                     R(1,0), R(1,1), R(1,2), t(1),
                     R(2,0), R(2,1), R(2,2), t(2));
```

```
}
```

At this point, we have the two cameras that we need in order to reconstruct the scene. The canonical first camera in the `Pleft` variable, and the second camera we calculated form the essential matrix in the `Pright` variable.

Choosing the image pair to use first

Given we have more than just two image views of the scene, we must choose which two views we will start the reconstruction from. In their paper, *Snavely et al.* suggest to picking the two views that have the least number of **homography** inliers. A homography is a relationship between two images or sets of points that lie on a plane; the **homography matrix** defines the transformation from one plane to another. In case of an image or a set of 2D points, the homography matrix is of size 3x3.

When *Snavely et al.* look for the lowest inlier ratio, they essentially suggest that you calculate the homography matrix between all pairs of images and pick the pair whose points mostly do not correspond with the homography matrix. This means that the geometry of the scene in these two views is not planar, or at least, not the same plane in both views, which helps when doing 3D reconstruction. For reconstruction, it is best to look at a complex scene with non-planar geometry, with things closer and farther away from the camera.

The following code snippet shows how to use OpenCV's `findHomography` function to count the number of inliers between two views whose features were already extracted and matched:

```
int findHomographyInliers(
const Features& left,
const Features& right,
const Matching& matches) {
  //Get aligned feature vectors
  Features alignedLeft;
  Features alignedRight;
  GetAlignedPointsFromMatch(left, right, matches, alignedLeft,
  alignedRight);

  //Calculate homography with at least 4 points
  Mat inlierMask;
  Mat homography;
  if(matches.size() >= 4) {
    homography = findHomography(alignedLeft.points,
                                alignedRight.points,
                                cv::RANSAC, RANSAC_THRESHOLD,
                                inlierMask);
```

```
      }

      if(matches.size() < 4 or homography.empty()) {
        return 0;
      }

      return countNonZero(inlierMask);
}
```

The next step is to perform this operation on all pairs of image views in our bundle and sort them based on the ratio of homography inliers to outliers:

```
//sort pairwise matches to find the lowest Homography inliers
map<float, ImagePair>pairInliersCt;
const size_t numImages = mImages.size();

//scan all possible image pairs (symmetric)
for (size_t i = 0; i < numImages - 1; i++) {
  for (size_t j = i + 1; j < numImages; j++) {

    if (mFeatureMatchMatrix[i][j].size() < MIN_POINT_CT) {
      //Not enough points in matching
      pairInliersCt[1.0] = {i, j};
      continue;
    }

    //Find number of homography inliers
    const int numInliers = findHomographyInliers(
      mImageFeatures[i],
      mImageFeatures[j],
      mFeatureMatchMatrix[i][j]);

    const float inliersRatio =
              (float)numInliers /
              (float)(mFeatureMatchMatrix[i][j].size());

    pairInliersCt[inliersRatio] = {i, j};
  }
}
```

Note that `std::map<float, ImagePair>` will internally sort the pairs based on the map's key: the inliers ratio. We then simply need to traverse this map from the beginning to find the image pair with least inlier ratio, and if that pair cannot be used, we can easily skip ahead to the next pair. The next section will reveal how we use these cameras pair to obtain a 3D structure of the scene.

Reconstructing the scene

Next, we look into the matter of recovering the 3D structure of the scene from the information we have acquired so far. As we had done before, we should look at the tools and information we have at hand to achieve this. In the preceding section, we obtained two camera matrices from the essential matrix; we already discussed how these tools would be useful for obtaining the 3D position of a point in space. Then, we can go back to our matched point pairs to fill in our equations with numerical data. The point pairs will also be useful in calculating the error we get from all our approximate calculations.

This is the time to see how we can perform triangulation using OpenCV. Luckily, OpenCV supplies us with a number of functions that make this process easy to implement: `triangulatePoints`, `undistortPoints`, and `convertPointsFromHomogeneous`.

Remember we had two key equations arising from the 2D point matching and P matrices: $x=PX$ and $x'=P'X$, where x and x' are matching 2D points and X is a real-world 3D point imaged by the two cameras. If we examine these equations, we will see that the x vector that represents a 2D point should be of size ($3x1$) and X that represents a 3D point should be ($4x1$). Both points received an extra entry in the vector; this is called **Homogeneous Coordinates**. We use these coordinates to streamline the triangulation process.

The equation $x = PX$ (where x is a 2D image point, X is a world 3D point, and P is a camera matrix) is missing a crucial element: the camera calibration parameters matrix, K. The matrix K is used to transform 2D image points from pixel coordinates to **normalized coordinates** (in the [-1, 1] range) removing the dependency on the size of the image in pixels, which is absolutely necessary. For example, a 2D point $x_1 = (160, 120)$ in a 320x240 image, may transform to $x_1' = (0, 0)$ under certain circumstances. To that end, we use the `undistortPoints` function:

```
Vector<Point2f> points2d; //in 2D coordinates (x, y)
Mat normalizedPts;        //in homogeneous coordinates (x', y', 1)

undistortPoints(points2d, normalizedPts, K, Mat());
```

We are now ready to triangulate the normalized 2D image points into 3D world points:

```
Matx34f Pleft, Pright;
//... findCameraMatricesFromMatch

Mat normLPts;
Mat normRPts;
//... undistortPoints

//the result is a set of 3D points in homogeneous coordinates (4D)
```

```
Mat pts3dHomog;
triangulatePoints(Pleft, Pright, normLPts, normRPts, pts3dHomog);

//convert from homogeneous to 3D world coordinates
Mat points3d;
convertPointsFromHomogeneous(pts3dHomog.t(), points3d);
```

In the following image, we can see a triangulation result of two images out of the Fountain P-11 sequence at `http://cvlabwww.epfl.ch/data/multiview/denseMVS.html`. The two images at the top are the original two views of the scene, and the bottom pair is the view of the reconstructed point cloud from the two views, including the estimated cameras looking at the fountain. We can see how the right-hand side section of the red brick wall was reconstructed, and also the fountain that protrudes from the wall:

However, as we discussed earlier, we have an issue with the reconstruction being only up to scale. We should take a moment to understand what up to scale means. The motion we obtained between our two cameras is going to have an arbitrary unit of measurement that is, it is not in centimeters or inches, but simply a given unit of scale. Our reconstructed cameras we will be one unit of scale distance apart. This has big implications, should we decide to recover more cameras later, as each pair of cameras will have their own units of scale, rather than a common one.

We will now discuss how the error measure that we set up may help us in finding a more robust reconstruction. First, we should note that reprojection means we simply take the triangulated 3D point and reimage it on a camera to get a reprojected 2D point, we then compare the distance between the original 2D point and the reprojected 2D point. If this distance is large, this means we may have an error in triangulation, so we may not want to include this point in the final result. Our global measure is the average reprojection distance and may give us a hint to how our triangulation performed overall. High average reprojection rates may point to a problem with the P matrices, and therefore a possible problem with the calculation of the essential matrix or the matched feature points. To reproject points, OpenCV offers the `projectPoints` function:

```
Mat x34f P; //camera pose matrix
Mat points3d;      //triangulated points
Points2d imgPts; //2D image points that correspond to 3D points
Mat K;             //camera intrinsics matrix

// ... triangulate points

//get rotation and translation elements
Mat R;
Rodrigues(P.get_minor<3, 3>(0, 0), rvec);
Mat t = P.get_minor<3, 1>(0, 3);

//reproject 3D points back into image coordinates
Mat projPts;
projectPoints(points3d, R, t, K, Mat(),projPts);

//check individual reprojection error
for (size_t i = 0; i < points3d.rows; i++) {
  const double err = norm(projPts.at<Point2f>(i) - imgPts[i]);

  //check if point reprojection error is too big
  if (err > MIN_REPROJECTION_ERROR){
    // Point reprojection error is too big.
  }
}
```

Next, we will take a look at recovering more cameras looking at the same scene, and combining the 3D reconstruction results.

Reconstruction from many views

Now that we know how to recover the motion and scene geometry from two cameras, it would seem simple to get the parameters of additional cameras and more scene points simply by applying the same process. This matter is in fact not so simple, as we can only get a reconstruction that is upto scale, and each pair of pictures has a different scale.

There are a number of ways to correctly reconstruct the 3D scene data from multiple views. One way to achieve **camera pose estimation** or **camera resectioning**, is the **Perspective N-Point(PnP)** algorithm, where we try to solve for the position of a new camera using N 3D scene points, which we have already found and their respective 2D image points. Another way is to triangulate more points and see how they fit into our existing scene geometry; this will tell us the position of the new camera by means of **point cloud registration**. In this section, we will discuss using OpenCV's solvePnP functions that implements the first method.

The first step we choose in this kind of reconstruction, incremental 3D reconstruction with camera resection, is to get a baseline scene structure. As we will look for the position of any new camera based on a known structure of the scene, we need to find an initial structure to work with. We can use the method we previously discussed-for example, between the first and second frames, to get a baseline by finding the camera matrices (using the findCameraMatricesFromMatch function) and triangulate the geometry (using triangulatePoints).

Having found an initial structure, we may continue; however, our method requires quite a bit of bookkeeping. First we should note that the solvePnP function needs aligned vectors of 3D and 2D points. Aligned vectors mean that the ith position in one vector aligns with the ith position in the other. To obtain these vectors we need to find those points among the 3D points that we recovered earlier, which align with the 2D points in our new frame. A simple way to do this is to attach, for each 3D point in the cloud, a vector denoting the 2D points it came from. We can then use feature matching to get a matching pair.

Let's introduce a new structure for a 3D point as follows:

```
struct Point3DInMap {
  // 3D point.
  cv::Point3f p;

  // Mapping from image index to a 2D point in that image's
  // list of features that correspond to this 3D point.
  std::map<int, int> originatingViews;
};
```

It holds, on top of the 3D point, an index to the 2D point inside the vector of 2D points that each frame has, which had contributed to this 3D point. The information for `Point3DInMap::originatingViews` must be initialized when triangulating a new 3D point, recording which cameras were involved in the triangulation. We can then use it to trace back from our 3D point cloud to the 2D point in each frame.

Let's add some convenience definitions:

```
struct Image2D3DMatch { //Aligned vectors of 2D and 3D points
  Points2f points2D;
  Points3f points3D;
};

//A mapping between an image and its set of 2D-3D aligned points
typedef std::map<int, Image2D3DMatch> Images2D3DMatches;
```

Now, let's see how to get aligned 2D-3D point vectors to use with `solvePnP`. The following code segment illustrates the process of finding 2D points in a new image from the existing 3D point cloud augmented with the originating 2D views. Simply put, the algorithm scans the existing 3D points in the cloud, looks at their originating 2D points, and tries to find a match (via the feature descriptors) to 2D points in the new image. If such a match is found, it may indicate that this 3D point also appears in the new image at a specific 2D point:

```
Images2D3DMatches matches;

//scan all pending new views
for (size_tnewView = 0; newView<images.size(); newView++) {
  if (doneViews.find(newView) != doneViews.end()) {
    continue; //skip done views
  }

Image2D3DMatch match2D3D;

//scan all current cloud's 3D points
for (const Point3DInMap&p : currentCloud) {
```

```
                 //scan all originating views for that 3D cloud point
                 for (const auto& origViewAndPoint : p.originatingViews) {

                   //check for 2D-2D matching via the match matrix
                   int origViewIndex        = origViewAndPoint.first;
                   int origViewFeatureIndex = origViewAndPoint.second;

                   //match matrix is upper-triangular (not symmetric)
                   //so the left index must be the smaller one
                   bool isLeft = (origViewIndex <newView);
                   int leftVIdx = (isLeft) ? origViewIndex: newView;
                   int rightVIdx = (isLeft) ? newView : origViewIndex;

                   //scan all 2D-2D matches between originating and new views
                   for (const DMatch& m : matchMatrix[leftVIdx][rightVIdx]) {
                     int matched2DPointInNewView = -1;

                       //find a match for this new view with originating view
                       if (isLeft) {
                         //originating view is 'left'
                         if (m.queryIdx == origViewFeatureIndex) {
                           matched2DPointInNewView = m.trainIdx;
                         }
                       } else {
                         //originating view is 'right'
                         if (m.trainIdx == origViewFeatureIndex) {
                           matched2DPointInNewView = m.queryIdx;
                         }
                       }

                     if (matched2DPointInNewView >= 0) {
                       //This point is matched in the new view
                       const Features& newFeat = imageFeatures[newView];

                       //Add the 2D point form the new view
                       match2D3D.points2D.push_back(
                         newFeat.points[matched2DPointInNewView]
                       );

                       //Add the 3D point
                       match2D3D.points3D.push_back(cloudPoint.p);

                       break; //look no further
                     }
                   }
                 }
               }
               matches[viewIdx] = match2D3D;
```

```
    }
```

Now we have aligned the pairing of 3D points in the scene to the 2D points in a new frame, and we can use them to recover the camera position as follows:

```
Image2D3DMatch match;
//... find 2D-3D match

//Recover camera pose using 2D-3D correspondence
Mat rvec, tvec;
Mat inliers;
solvePnPRansac(
  match.points3D,     //3D points
  match.points2D,     //2D points
  K,                    //Calibration intrinsics matrix
  distortion,         //Calibration distortion coefficients
  rvec,//Output extrinsics: Rotation vector
  tvec,                 //Output extrinsics: Translation vector
  false,                //Don't use initial guess
  100,                  //Iterations
  RANSAC_THRESHOLD, //Reprojection error threshold
  0.99,                 //Confidence
  inliers               //Output: inliers indicator vector
);

//check if inliers-to-points ratio is too small
const float numInliers   = (float)countNonZero(inliers);
const float numPoints    = (float)match.points2D.size();
const float inlierRatio = numInliers / numPoints;

if (inlierRatio < POSE_INLIERS_MINIMAL_RATIO) {
  cerr << "Inliers ratio is too small: "
       << numInliers<< " / " <<numPoints<< endl;
  //perhaps a 'return;' statement
}

Mat_<double>R;
Rodrigues(rvec, R); //convert to a 3x3 rotation matrix

P(0, 0) = R(0, 0); P(0, 1) = R(0, 1); P(0, 2) = R(0, 2);
P(1, 0) = R(1, 0); P(1, 1) = R(1, 1); P(1, 2) = R(1, 2);
P(2, 0) = R(2, 0); P(2, 1) = R(2, 1); P(2, 2) = R(2, 2);
P(0, 3) = tvec.at<double>(0, 3);
P(1, 3) = tvec.at<double>(1, 3);
P(2, 3) = tvec.at<double>(2, 3);
```

Note that we are using the `solvePnPRansac` function rather than the `solvePnP` function as it is more robust to outliers. Now that we have a new P matrix, we can simply use the `triangulatePoints` function as we did earlier and populate our point cloud with more 3D points.

In the following image, we see an incremental reconstruction of the Fountain-P11 scene at `http://cvlabwww.epfl.ch/data/multiview/denseMVS.html`, starting from the fourth image. The top-left image is the reconstruction after four images were used; the participating cameras are shown as red pyramids with a white line showing the direction. The other images show how more cameras add more points to the cloud:

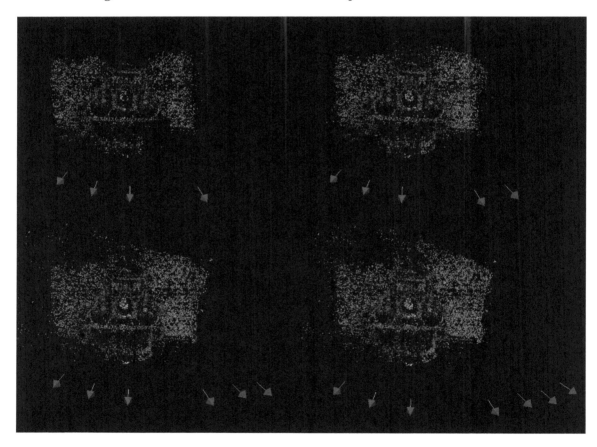

Refinement of the reconstruction

One of the most important parts of an SfM method is refining and optimizing the reconstructed scene, also known as the process of **Bundle Adjustment** (**BA**). This is an optimization step where all the data we gathered is fitted to a monolithic model. Both the position of the recovered 3D points and the positions of the cameras are optimized, so re-projection errors are minimized. In other words, recovered 3D points that are re-projected on the image are expected to lie close to the position of originating 2D feature points that generated them. The BA process we use will try to minimize this error for all 3D points together, making for a very big system of simultaneous linear equations with on the order of thousands of parameters.

We will implement a BA algorithm using the **Ceres** library, a well-known optimization package from Google. Ceres has built-in tools to help with BA, such as automatic differentiation and many flavors of linear and nonlinear optimization schemes, which result in less code and more flexibility.

To make things simple and easy to implement, we will make a few assumptions, whereas in a real SfM system, these things cannot be neglected. Firstly, we will assume a simple intrinsic model for our cameras, specifically that the focal length in x and y is the same and the center of projection is exactly the middle of the image. We further assume that all cameras share the same intrinsic parameters, meaning that the same camera takes all the images in the bundle with the exact configuration (for example, zoom). These assumptions greatly reduce the number of parameters to optimize, which in turn makes the optimization not only easier to code but also faster to converge.

To start, we will model the *error function*, sometimes also called the **cost function**, which is, simply put, the way the optimization knows how good the new parameters are and also which way to go to get even better parameters. We can write the following functor that makes use of Ceres' Auto Differentiation mechanism:

```
// The pinhole camera is parameterized using 7 parameters:
// 3 for rotation, 3 for translation, 1 for focal length.
// The principal point is not modeled (assumed be located at the
// image center, and already subtracted from 'observed'),
// and focal_x = focal_y.
struct SimpleReprojectionError {
  using namespace ceres;

  SimpleReprojectionError(double observed_x, double observed_y) :
  observed_x(observed_x), observed_y(observed_y) {}

  template<typenameT>
  bool operator()(const T* const camera,
```

```cpp
                     const T* const point,
                     const T* const focal,
                     T* residuals) const {
    T p[3];
    // Rotate: camera[0,1,2] are the angle-axis rotation.
    AngleAxisRotatePoint(camera, point, p);

    // Translate: camera[3,4,5] are the translation.
    p[0] += camera[3];
    p[1] += camera[4];
    p[2] += camera[5];

    // Perspective divide
    const T xp = p[0] / p[2];
    const T yp = p[1] / p[2];

    // Compute projected point position (sans center of
    // projection)
    const T predicted_x = *focal * xp;
    const T predicted_y = *focal * yp;

    // The error is the difference between the predicted
    // and observed position.
    residuals[0] = predicted_x - T(observed_x);
    residuals[1] = predicted_y - T(observed_y);
    return true;
  }

  // A helper construction function
  static CostFunction* Create(const double observed_x,
  const double observed_y) {
    return (newAutoDiffCostFunction<SimpleReprojectionError,
    2, 6, 3, 1>(
    newSimpleReprojectionError(observed_x,
    observed_y)));
  }
  double observed_x;
  double observed_y;
};
```

This functor calculates the deviation a 3D point has from its originating 2D point by re-projecting it using simplified extrinsic and intrinsic camera parameters. The error in x and y is saved as the residual, which guides the optimization.

There is quite a bit of additional code that goes into the BA implementation, but it primarily handles bookkeeping of cloud 3D points, originating 2D points, and their respective cameras. The readers may wish to review how this is done in the code attached to the book.

The following image shows the effects of BA. The two images on the left are the points of the point cloud before adjustment from two perspectives, and the images on the right show the optimized cloud. The change is quite dramatic, and many misalignments between points triangulated from different views are now mostly consolidated. We can also notice how the adjustment created a far better reconstruction of flat surfaces:

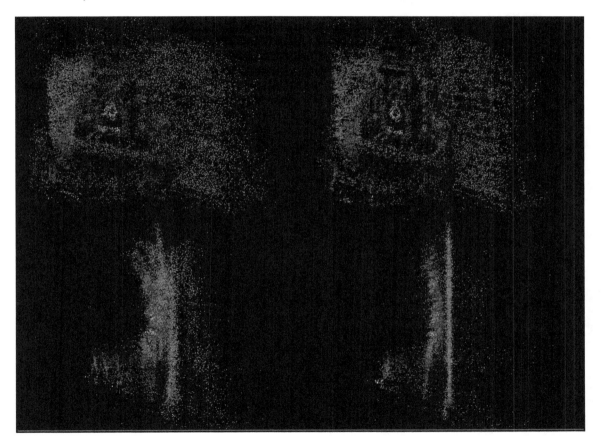

Using the example code

We can find the example code for SfM with the supporting material of this book. We will now see how we can build, run, and make use of it. The code makes use of **CMake**, a cross-platform build environment similar to Maven or SCons. We should also make sure that we have all the following prerequisites to build the application:

- OpenCV v3.0 or higher
- Ceres v1.11 or higher
- Boost v1.54 or higher

First, we must set up the build environment. To that end, we may create a folder named build in which all build-related files will go; we will now assume that all command-line operations are within the build/ folder, although the process is similar (up to the locations of the files) even if not using the build folder. We should also make sure that CMake can find boost and Ceres.

If we are using Windows as the operating system, we can use Microsoft Visual Studio to build; therefore, we should run the following command:

```
cmake -G "Visual Studio 10"
```

If we are using Linux, Mac OS, or another Unix-like operating system, we execute the following command:

```
cmake -G "Unix Makefiles"
```

If we prefer to use XCode on Mac OS, execute the following command:

```
cmake -G Xcode
```

CMake also has the ability to build macros for Eclipse, Codeblocks, and more.

After CMake is done creating the environment, we are ready to build. If we are using a Unix-like system, we can simply execute the make utility, else we should use our development environment's building process.

After the build has finished, we should be left with an executable named ExploringSfM, which runs the SfM process. Running it with no arguments will result in the following:

```
USAGE ./build/ExploringSfM [options] <input-directory>
-h [ --help ]                  Produce help message
-d [ --console-debug ] arg (=2) Debug output to console log level
(0 = Trace, 4 = Error).
```

```
-v [ --visual-debug ] arg (=3)   Visual debug output to screen log
    level
(0 = All, 4 = None).
-s [ --downscale ] arg (=1)      Downscale factor for input images.
-p [ --input-directory ] arg     Directory to find input images.
-o [ --output-prefix ] arg (=output) Prefix for output files.
```

To execute the process over a set of images, we should supply a location on the drive to find image files. If a valid location is supplied, the process should start and we should see the progress and debug information on the screen. If no errors arise, the process will end with a message stating that the point cloud that arises from the images was saved to PLY files, which can be opened in most 3D editing software.

Summary

In this chapter, we saw how OpenCV v3 can help us approach Structure from Motion in a manner that is both simple to code and simple to understand. OpenCV v3's new API contains a number of useful functions and data structures that make our lives easier and also assist in a cleaner implementation.

However, the state-of-the-art SfM methods are far more complex. There are many issues we choose to disregard in favor of simplicity, and plenty more error examinations that are usually in place. Our chosen methods for the different elements of SfM can also be revisited. For one, H&Z propose a highly accurate triangulation method that minimizes the reprojection error in the image domain. Some methods even use the N-view triangulation once they understand the relationship between the features in multiple images.

If we would like to extend and deepen our familiarity with SfM, we will certainly benefit from looking at other open source SfM libraries. One particularly interesting project is libMV, which implements a vast array of SfM elements that may be interchanged to get the best results. There is a great body of work from University of Washington that provides tools for many flavors of SfM (Bundler and VisualSfM). This work inspired an online product from Microsoft called **PhotoSynth** and **123D Catch** from Adobe. There are many more implementations of SfM readily available online, and one must only search to find quite a lot of them.

Another important relationship we have not discussed in depth is that of SfM and Visual Localization and Mapping, better known as **Simultaneous Localization and Mapping (SLAM)** methods. In this chapter, we dealt with a given dataset of images and a video sequence, and using SfM is practical in those cases; however, some applications have no prerecorded dataset and must bootstrap the reconstruction on the fly. This process is better known as **Mapping,** and it is done while we are creating a 3D map of the world, using feature matching and tracking in 2D, and after triangulation.

In the next chapter, we will see how OpenCV can be used for extracting license plate numbers from images, using various techniques in machine learning.

References

- *Hartley, Richard, and Andrew Zisserman, Multiple View Geometry in Computer Vision, Cambridge University Press, 2003*
- *Hartley, Richard I., and Peter Sturm; Triangulation, Computer Vision and image understanding 68.2 (1997): 146-157*
- *Snavely, Noah, Steven M. Seitz, and Richard Szeliski; Photo Tourism: Exploring Photo Collections in 3D, ACM Transactions on Graphics (TOG). Vol. 25. No. 3. ACM, 2006*
- *Strecha, Christoph, et al, On Benchmarking Camera Calibration and Multi-view Stereo for High Resolution Imagery, IEEE Conference on Computer Vision and Pattern Recognition (CVPR) 2008*
- `http://cvlabwww.epfl.ch/data/multiview/denseMVS.htmlhttps://developer.blender.org/tag/libmv/`
- `http://ccwu.me/vsfm/`
- `http://www.cs.cornell.edu/~snavely/bundler/`
- `http://photosynth.net`
- `http://en.wikipedia.org/wiki/Simultaneous_localization_and_mapping`
- `http://www.cmake.org`
- `http://ceres-solver.org`
- `http://www.123dapp.com/catch`

3

Number Plate Recognition using SVM and Neural Network

This chapter introduces us to the steps needed to create an application for **Automatic Number Plate Recognition** (**ANPR**). There are different approaches and techniques based on different situations, for example, IR camera, fixed car position, light conditions, and so on. We can proceed to construct an ANPR application to detect automobile license plates in a photograph taken between 2 or 3 meters from a car, in ambiguous light condition and with non-parallel ground with minor perspective distortions in the automobile's plate.

The main purpose of this chapter is to introduce us to image segmentation and feature extraction, pattern recognition basics, and two important pattern recognition algorithms: that are **Support Vector Machine** (**SVM**) and **Artificial Neural Network** (**ANN**). In this chapter, we will cover the following topics:

- ANPR
- Plate detection
- Plate recognition

Introduction to ANPR

Automatic Number Plate Recognition, or known by other terms such as **Automatic License-Plate Recognition** (**ALPR**), **Automatic Vehicle Identification** (**AVI**), or **Car Plate Recognition** (**CPR**), is a surveillance method that uses **Optical Character Recognition** (**OCR**) and other methods such as segmentations and detection to read vehicle registration plates.

The best results in an ANPR system can be obtained with an **Infrared** (**IR**) camera, because the segmentation steps for detection and OCR segmentation are easy, and clean, and they minimize errors. This is due to the laws of light, the basic one being that the angle of incidence equals the angle of reflection. We can see this basic reflection when we see a smooth surface such as a plane mirror. Reflection off of rough surfaces such as paper, leads to a type of reflection known as diffuse or scatter reflection. However, the majority of country plates have special characteristics named retro-reflection, that is, the surface of the plate is made with a material that is covered with thousands of tiny hemispheres that cause light to be reflected back to the source, as we can see in the following figure:

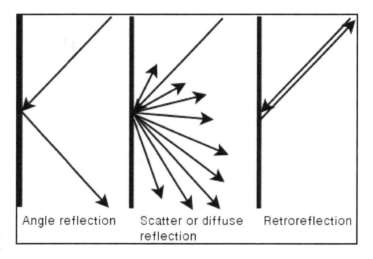

If we use a camera with filter-coupled, structured infrared light projector, we can retrieve just the Infrared light, and then, we have a very high quality image to segment, with which we can subsequently detect and recognize the plate number that is independent of any light environment, as shown in the following image:

We will not use IR photographs in this chapter; we will use regular photographs so that we do not obtain the best results, and we get a higher level of detection errors and higher false recognition rate, as opposed to if we used an IR camera. However, the steps for both are the same.

Each country has different license plate sizes and specifications. It is useful to know these specifications in order to get the best results and reduce errors. Algorithms used in every chapter are designed for explaining the basics of ANPR and concrete for license plates used in Spain, but we can extend it to any country or specification.

In this chapter, we will work with license plates from Spain. In Spain, there are three different sizes and shapes of license plates, but we will only use the most common (large) license plate, which has a 520 mm width by a 110 mm height. Two groups of characters are separated by a 41 mm space, and a 14 mm width separates each individual character. The first group of characters have four numeric digits, and the second group has three letters without the vowels A, E, I, O, U, or the letters N or Q. All characters have dimensions of 45 mm by 77 mm.

This data is important for character segmentation since we can check both the character and blank spaces to verify that we get a character and no other image segment:

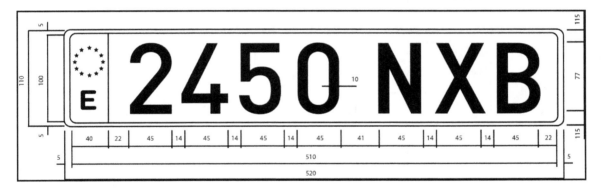

ANPR algorithm

Before explaining the ANPR code, we need to define the main steps and tasks in the ANPR algorithm. ANPR is divided in two main steps: plate detection and plate recognition. Plate detection has the purpose of detecting the location of the plate in the whole camera frame. When a plate is detected in an image, the plate segment is passed to the second step (plate recognition), which uses an OCR algorithm to determine the alphanumeric characters on the plate.

In the following diagram, we can see the two main algorithm steps: plate detection and plate recognition. After these steps, the program draws over the camera frame the plate's characters that have been detected. The algorithms can return bad results or may not return any result:

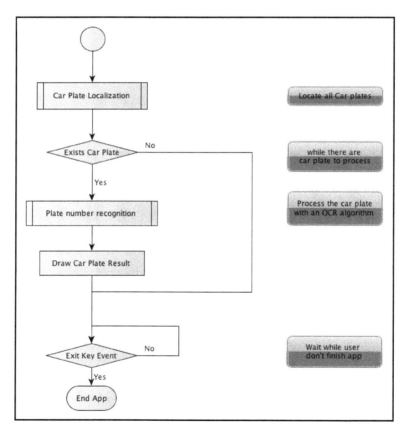

In each step shown in the previous figure, we will define three additional steps that are commonly used in pattern recognition algorithms. These steps are as follows:

1. **Segmentation**: This step detects and removes each patch/region of interest in the image.
2. **Feature extraction**: This step extracts from each patch a set of characteristics.
3. **Classification**: This step extracts each character from the plate recognition-step or classifies each image patch into *plate* or *no plate* in the plate-detection step.

In the following diagram, we can see these pattern recognition steps in the whole algorithm application:

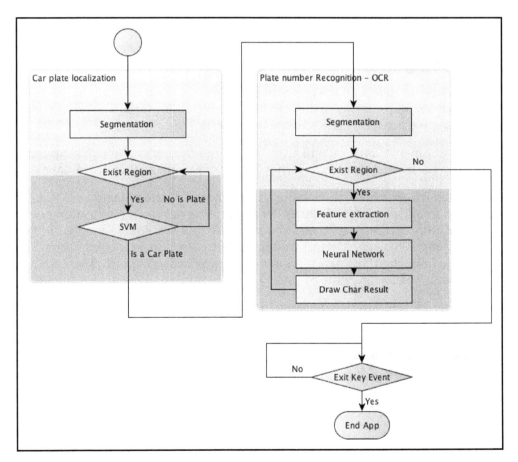

Aside from the main application, whose purpose is to detect and recognize a car plate number, we will briefly explain two more tasks that are usually not explained:

- How to train a pattern recognition system
- How to evaluate it

These tasks, however, can be more important than the main application, because if we do not train the pattern recognition system correctly, our system can fail and not work correctly; different patterns need different training's and evaluation. We need to evaluate our system in different environments, conditions, and features to get the best results. These two tasks are sometimes used together, since different features can produce different results that we can see in the evaluation section.

Plate detection

In this step, we have to detect all the plates in a current camera frame. To do this task, we divide it in two main steps: segmentation and segment classification. The feature step is not explained because we use the image patch as a vector feature.

In the first step (segmentation), we will apply different filters, morphological operations, contour algorithms, and validations to retrieve parts of the image that could have a plate.

In the second step (classification), we will apply a **Support Vector Machine** (**SVM**) classifier to each image patch, our feature. Before creating our main application, we will train with two different classes: *plate* and *non-plate*. We will work with parallel frontal view color images having 800 pixels of width and taken between 2 and 4 meters from a car. These requirements are important for correct segmentations. We can get perform detection if we create a multi-scale image algorithm.

In the next image, we will shown all process involved in plate detection:

- Sobel filter
- Threshold operation
- Close morphologic operation
- Mask of one of filled area
- In red possible detected plates (features images)

- Detected plates after SVM classifier

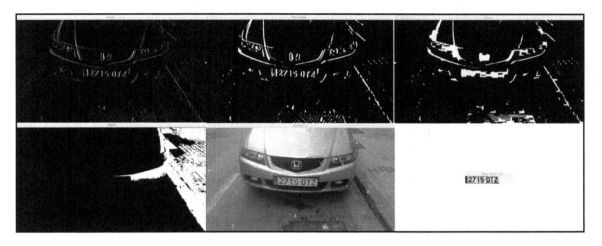

Segmentation

Segmentation is the process of dividing an image into multiple segments. This process is to simplify the image for analysis and make feature extraction easier.

One important feature of plate segmentation is the high number of vertical edges in a license plate, assuming that the image was taken frontally and the plate is not rotated and without perspective distortion. This feature can be exploited during the first segmentation step to eliminate regions that don't have any vertical edges.

Before finding vertical edges, we need to convert the color image to a grayscale image (because color can't help us in this task) and remove possible noise generated from the camera or other ambient noise. We will apply a 5x5 Gaussian blur and remove noise. If we don't apply a noise removal method, we can get a lot of vertical edges that produce fail detection:

```
//convert image to gray
Mat img_gray;
cvtColor(input, img_gray, CV_BGR2GRAY);
blur(img_gray, img_gray, Size(5,5));
```

To find the vertical edges, we will use a Sobel filter and find the first horizontal derivate. The derivate is a mathematic function that allows us to find vertical edges on an image. The definition of Sobel function in OpenCV is as follows:

```
void Sobel(InputArray src, OutputArray dst, int ddepth, int
xorder, int yorder, int ksize=3, double scale=1, double delta=0,
int borderType=BORDER_DEFAULT )
```

Here, ddepth is the destination image depth; xorder is the order of the derivate by x; yorder is the order of the derivate by y; ksize is the kernel size of 1, 3, 5, or 7; scale is an optional factor for computed derivative values; delta is an optional value added to the result; and borderType is the pixel interpolation method.

Then, for our case, we can use xorder=1, yorder=0, and ksize=3:

```
//Find vertical lines. Car plates have high density of vertical
lines
Mat img_sobel;
Sobel(img_gray, img_sobel, CV_8U, 1, 0, 3, 1, 0);
```

After applying a Sobel filter, we will apply a threshold filter to obtain a binary image with a threshold value obtained through Otsu's method. Otsu's algorithm needs an 8-bit input image, and Otsu's method automatically determines the optimal threshold value:

```
//threshold image
Mat img_threshold;
threshold(img_sobel, img_threshold, 0, 255,
CV_THRESH_OTSU+CV_THRESH_BINARY);
```

To define Otsu's method in threshold function, we will combine the type parameter with the CV_THRESH_OTSU value and the threshold value parameter is ignored.

 When the CV_THRESH_OTSU value is defined, the threshold function returns the optimal threshold value obtained by Otsu's algorithm.

By applying a close morphological operation, we can remove blank spaces between each vertical edge line and connect all regions that have a high number of edges. In this step, we have possible regions that can contain plates.

First, we will define our structural element to use in our morphological operation. We will use the `getStructuringElement` function to define a structural rectangular element with a 17x3 dimension size in our case; this may be different in other image sizes:

```
Mat element = getStructuringElement(MORPH_RECT, Size(17, 3));
```

Then, we will use this structural element in a close morphological operation using the `morphologyEx` function:

```
morphologyEx(img_threshold, img_threshold, CV_MOP_CLOSE,
element);
```

After applying these functions, we have regions in the image that could contain a plate; however, most of the regions do not contain license plates. These regions can be split with a connected component analysis or using the `findContours` function. This last function retrieves the contours of a binary image with different methods and results. We only need to get the external contours with any hierarchical relationship and any polygonal approximation results:

```
//Find contours of possibles plates
vector< vector< Point>> contours;
findContours(img_threshold,
            contours,            // a vector of contours
            CV_RETR_EXTERNAL,    // retrieve the external contours
            CV_CHAIN_APPROX_NONE); // all pixels of each contours
```

For each contour detected, extract the bounding rectangle of minimal area. OpenCV brings up the `minAreaRect` function for this task. This function returns a rotated `RotatedRect` rectangle class. Then, using a vector iterator over each contour, we can get the rotated rectangle and make some preliminary validations before we classify each region:

```
//Start to iterate to each contour founded
vector<vector<Point>>::iterator itc= contours.begin();
vector<RotatedRect> rects;

//Remove patch that has no inside limits of aspect ratio and
area.
while (itc!=contours.end()) {
  //Create bounding rect of object
    RotatedRect mr= minAreaRect(Mat(*itc));
    if(!verifySizes(mr)){
    itc= contours.erase(itc);
    }else{
    ++itc;
    rects.push_back(mr);
  }
```

```
    }
```

We make basic validations about the regions detected based on their area and aspect ratio. We will consider that a region can be a plate if the aspect ratio is approximately *520/110 = 4.727272* (plate width divided by plate height) with an error margin of 40 percent and an area based on a minimum of 15 pixels and maximum of 125 pixels for the height of plate. These values are calculated depending on the image size and camera position:

```cpp
bool DetectRegions::verifySizes(RotatedRect candidate ){

float error=0.4;
  //Spain car plate size: 52x11 aspect 4,7272
const float aspect=4.7272;
  //Set a min and max area. All other patchs are discarded
int min= 15*aspect*15; // minimum area
int max= 125*aspect*125; // maximum area
  //Get only patches that match to a respect ratio.
float rmin= aspect-aspect*error;
float rmax= aspect+aspect*error;

int area= candidate.size.height * candidate.size.width;
float r= (float)candidate.size.width /
(float)candidate.size.height;
if(r<1)
    r= 1/r;

if(( area < min || area > max ) || ( r < rmin || r > rmax )){
    return false;
}else{
    return true;
  }
}
```

We can make even more improvements using the license plate's white background property. All plates have the same background color, and we can use a flood fill algorithm to retrieve the rotated rectangle for precise cropping.

The first step to crop the license plate is to get several seeds near the last rotated rect center. Then, we will get the minimum size of plate between the width and height, and use it to generate random seeds near the patch center.

We want to select the white region, and we need several seeds to touch at least one white pixel. Then, for each seed, we use a `floodFill` function to draw a new mask image to store the new closest cropping region:

```cpp
for(int i=0; i< rects.size(); i++){
//For better rect cropping for each possible box
```

```
//Make floodfill algorithm because the plate has white background
//And then we can retrieve more clearly the contour box
   ircle(result, rects[i].center, 3, Scalar(0,255,0), -1);
//get the min size between width and height
   float minSize=(rects[i].size.width < rects[i].size.height)?
rects[i].size.width:rects[i].size.height;
minSize=minSize-minSize*0.5;
//initialize rand and get 5 points around center for floodfill
algorithm
srand ( time(NULL) );
//Initialize floodfill parameters and variables
Mat mask;
mask.create(input.rows + 2, input.cols + 2, CV_8UC1);
mask= Scalar::all(0);
int loDiff = 30;
int upDiff = 30;
int connectivity = 4;
int newMaskVal = 255;
int NumSeeds = 10;
Rect ccomp;
int flags = connectivity + (newMaskVal << 8 ) +
CV_FLOODFILL_FIXED_RANGE + CV_FLOODFILL_MASK_ONLY;
for(int j=0; j<NumSeeds; j++){
Point seed;
seed.x=rects[i].center.x+rand()%(int)minSize-(minSize/2);
seed.y=rects[i].center.y+rand()%(int)minSize-(minSize/2);
circle(result, seed, 1, Scalar(0,255,255), -1);
int area = floodFill(input, mask, seed, Scalar(255,0,0), &ccomp,
Scalar(loDiff, loDiff, loDiff), Scalar(upDiff, upDiff, upDiff),
flags);
```

The floodfill function fills a connected component with a color into a mask image starting from a point seed, and sets maximal lower and upper brightness/color difference between the pixel to fill and the pixel neighbors or pixel seed:

```
intfloodFill(InputOutputArray image, InputOutputArray mask, Point
seed, Scalar newVal, Rect* rect=0, Scalar loDiff=Scalar(), Scalar
upDiff=Scalar(), int flags=4 )
```

The newval parameter is the new color we want to put into the image when filling. Parameters loDiff and upDiff are the maximal lower and maximal upper brightness/color difference between the pixel to fill and the pixel neighbors or pixel seed.

The parameter `flag` is a combination of the following bits:

- **Lower bits**: These bits contain connectivity value, 4 (by default) or 8, used within the function. Connectivity determines which neighbors of a pixel are considered
- **Upper bits**: These can be 0 or a combination of the following values- CV_FLOODFILL_FIXED_RANGE and CV_FLOODFILL_MASK_ONLY.

CV_FLOODFILL_FIXED_RANGE sets the difference between the current pixel and the seed pixel. CV_FLOODFILL_MASK_ONLY will only fill the image mask and not change the image itself.

Once we have a crop mask, we will get a minimal area rectangle from the image mask points and check the validity size again. For each mask, a white pixel gets the position and uses the `minAreaRect` function for retrieving the closest crop region:

```
//Check new floodfill mask match for a correct patch.
//Get all points detected for get Minimal rotated Rect
vector<Point> pointsInterest;
Mat_<uchar>::iterator itMask= mask.begin<uchar>();
Mat_<uchar>::iterator end= mask.end<uchar>();
for( ; itMask!=end; ++itMask)
  if(*itMask==255)
    pointsInterest.push_back(itMask.pos());
RotatedRect minRect = minAreaRect(pointsInterest);
if(verifySizes(minRect)){
```

The segmentation process is finished, and we have valid regions. Now, we can crop each detected region, remove possible rotation, crop the image region, resize the image, and equalize the light of the cropped image regions.

First, we need to generate the transform matrix with `getRotationMatrix2D` to remove possible rotations in the detected region. We need to pay attention to height, because `RotatedRect` can be returned and rotated at 90 degrees. So, we have to check the rectangle aspect, and if it is less than 1, we need to rotate it by 90 degrees:

```
//Get rotation matrix
float r= (float)minRect.size.width / (float)minRect.size.height;
float angle=minRect.angle;
if(r<1)
angle=90+angle;
Mat rotmat= getRotationMatrix2D(minRect.center, angle,1);
```

With the transform matrix, we now can rotate the input image by an affine transformation (affine transformation in geometry is a transformation that takes parallel lines to parallel lines) with the warpAffine function where we set the input and destination images, the transform matrix, the output size (same as input in our case), and the interpolation method to use. We can define the border method and border value if needed:

```
//Create and rotate image
Mat img_rotated;
warpAffine(input, img_rotated, rotmat, input.size(),
CV_INTER_CUBIC);
```

After we rotate the image, we will crop the image with getRectSubPix which crops and copies an image portion of width and height centered in a point. If the image is rotated, we need to change the width and height sizes with the C++ swap function:

```
//Crop image
Size rect_size=minRect.size;
if(r < 1)
swap(rect_size.width, rect_size.height);
Mat img_crop;
getRectSubPix(img_rotated, rect_size, minRect.center,
img_crop);
```

Cropped images are not good for use in training and classification since they do not have the same size. Also, each image contains different light conditions, making them more different. To resolve this, we resize all the images to same width and height, and apply a light histogram equalization:

```
Mat resultResized;
resultResized.create(33,144, CV_8UC3);
resize(img_crop, resultResized, resultResized.size(), 0, 0,
INTER_CUBIC);
//Equalize croped image
Mat grayResult;
cvtColor(resultResized, grayResult, CV_BGR2GRAY);
blur(grayResult, grayResult, Size(3,3));
equalizeHist(grayResult, grayResult);
```

For each detected region, we store the cropped image and its position in a vector:

```
output.push_back(Plate(grayResult,minRect.boundingRect()));
```

Classification

After we preprocess and segment all possible parts of an image, we now need to decide whether each segment is (or is not) a license plate. To do this, we will use a **Support Vector Machine (SVM)** algorithm.

A Support Vector Machine is a pattern recognition algorithm included in a family of supervised learning algorithms that was originally created for binary classification. Supervised learning is the machine learning algorithm technique that is trained with labeled data. We need to train the algorithm with an amount of data that is labeled; each data set needs to have a class.

The SVM creates one or more hyperplanes, which is used to discriminate each class of data.

A classic example is a 2D point set that defines two classes; the SVM searches the optimal line that differentiates each class:

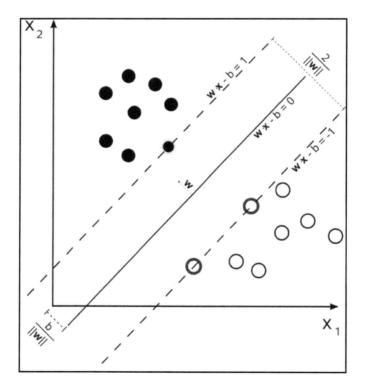

The first task before any classification is to train our classifier; this is a job before the main application and it's named "offline training". This is not an easy job because it requires a sufficient amount of data to train the system, but a bigger dataset does not always imply the best results. In our case, we do not have enough data due to the fact that there are no public license plate databases. Because of this, we need to take hundreds of car photos, and then preprocess and segment all of it.

We trained our system with 75 license plate images and 35 images without license plates, containing a 144x33 pixel resolution. We can see a sample of this data in the following image. This is not a large dataset, but sufficient enough to get decent results for our chapter. In a real application, we would need to train with more data:

To easily understand how machine learning works, we will proceed to use image pixel features of the classifier algorithm (keep in mind that there are better methods and features to train an SVM, such as **Principal Components Analysis (PCA)**, Fourier transform, texture analysis, and so on).

We need to create the images to train our system using the `DetectRegions` class and set the `savingRegions` variable to "true" in order to save the images. We can use the `segmentAllFiles.sh` bash script to repeat the process on all image files under a folder. This can be taken from the source code of the book:

To make this easier, we will store all image training data that is processed and prepared into an XML file for use directly with the SVM function. The `trainSVM.cpp` application creates this file using the folders and number of image files.

Training data for a machine learning OpenCV algorithm is stored in an *NxM* matrix, with *N* samples and *M* features. Each dataset is saved as a row in the training matrix.

The classes are stored in another matrix with *n*x1 size, where each class is identified by a float number.

OpenCV has an easy way to manage a data file in the XML or YAML format with the `FileStorage` class. This class lets us store and read OpenCV variables and structures or our custom variables. With this function, we can read the training data matrix and training classes and save it in `SVM_TrainingData` and `SVM_Classes`:

```
FileStorage fs;
fs.open("SVM.xml", FileStorage::READ);
Mat SVM_TrainingData;
Mat SVM_Classes;
fs["TrainingData"] >>SVM_TrainingData;
fs["classes"] >>SVM_Classes;
```

Now, we have the training data in the `SVM_TrainingData` variable and labels in `SVM_Classes`. Then, we only have to create the training data object that connects data and labels to use in our machine learning algorithm. To do this, we will use the `TrainData` class as a OpenCV pointer `Ptr` class as follows:

```
Ptr<TrainData> trainData = TrainData::create(SVM_TrainingData,
ROW_SAMPLE, SVM_Classes);
```

We will create the classifier object using the `SVM` class using the `Ptr`OpenCV class:

```
Ptr<SVM> svmClassifier = SVM::create()
```

Now, we need to set the SVM parameters that define the basic parameters to use in an SVM algorithm. To do this, we only have to change some object variables. After different experiments, we will choose the next parameter's setup:

```
svmClassifier-
>setTermCriteria(TermCriteria(TermCriteria::MAX_ITER, 1000,
0.01));
svmClassifier->setC(0.1);
svmClassifier->setKernel(SVM::LINEAR);
```

We chose a 1000 iterations for training, a C param variable optimization of 0.1, and finally, a kernel function.

We only need train our classifier with the `train` function and the train data:

```
svmClassifier->train(trainData);
```

Our classifier is ready to predict a possible cropped image using the `predict` function of our SVM class; this function returns the class identifier `i`. In our case, we will label a plate class with 1 and no plate class with 0. Then, for each detected region that can be a plate, we will use SVM to classify it as plate or no plate, and save only the correct responses. The following code is a part of a main application called online processing:

```
vector<Plate> plates;
for(int i=0; i< posible_regions.size(); i++)
{
Mat img=posible_regions[i].plateImg;
Mat p= img.reshape(1, 1);//convert img to 1 row m features
p.convertTo(p, CV_32FC1);
int response = (int)svmClassifier.predict( p );
if(response==1)
plates.push_back(posible_regions[i]);
}
```

Plate recognition

The second step in License Plate Recognition aims to retrieve the characters of the license plate with Optical Character Recognition. For each detected plate, we proceed to segment the plate for each character and use an Artificial Neural Network machine learning algorithm to recognize the character. Also, in this section, you will learn how to evaluate a classification algorithm.

OCR segmentation

First, we will obtain a plate image patch as an input to the OCR segmentation function with an equalized histogram. We then need to apply only a threshold filter and use this threshold image as the input of a Find Contours algorithm. We can observe this process in the following image:

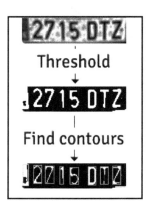

This segmentation process is coded as follows:

```
Mat img_threshold;
threshold(input, img_threshold, 60, 255, CV_THRESH_BINARY_INV);
if(DEBUG)
imshow("Threshold plate", img_threshold);
Mat img_contours;
img_threshold.copyTo(img_contours);
//Find contours of possibles characters
vector< vector< Point>> contours;
findContours(img_contours,
    contours, // a vector of contours
    CV_RETR_EXTERNAL, // retrieve the external contours
    CV_CHAIN_APPROX_NONE); // all pixels of each contours
```

We used the CV_THRESH_BINARY_INV parameter to invert the threshold output by turning the white input values black and the black input values white. This is needed to get the contours of each character, because the contours algorithm looks for white pixels.

For each detected contour, we can make a size verification and remove all regions where the size is smaller or the aspect is not correct. In our case, the characters have a 45/77 aspect, and we can accept a 35 percent error of aspect for rotated or distorted characters. If an area is higher than 80 percent, we will consider that region to be a black block and not a character. For counting the area, we can use the `countNonZero` function that counts the number of pixels with a value higher than 0:

```
bool OCR::verifySizes(Mat r){
  //Char sizes 45x77
float aspect=45.0f/77.0f;
float charAspect= (float)r.cols/(float)r.rows;
float error=0.35;
float minHeight=15;
float maxHeight=28;
  //We have a different aspect ratio for number 1, and it can be
  ~0.2
  float minAspect=0.2;
float maxAspect=aspect+aspect*error;
  //area of pixels
float area=countNonZero(r);
  //bb area
float bbArea=r.cols*r.rows;
  //% of pixel in area
float percPixels=area/bbArea;
if(percPixels < 0.8 && charAspect > minAspect && charAspect <
maxAspect && r.rows >= minHeight && r.rows < maxHeight)
  return true;
 else
  return false;
}
```

If a segmented character is verified, we have to preprocess it to set the same size and position for all characters, and save it in a vector with the auxiliary `CharSegment` class. This class saves the segmented character image and the position that we need to order the characters, because the Find Contour algorithm does not return the contours in the correct and needed order.

Feature extraction

The next step for each segmented character is to extract the features for training and classify the Artificial Neural Network algorithm.

Unlike plate detection, the feature extraction step used in SVM doesn't use all of the image pixels. We will apply more common features used in OCR that contain horizontal and vertical accumulation histograms and low-resolution image samples. We can see this feature more graphically in the next image, as each image has a low resolution 5x5 image and the histogram accumulations:

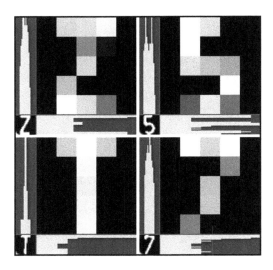

For each character, we will count the number of pixels in a row or column with a nonzero value using the `countNonZero` function and store it in a new data matrix called `mhist`. We will normalize it by looking for the maximum value in the data matrix using the `minMaxLoc` function and divide all elements of `mhist` by the maximum value with the `convertTo` function. We will create the `ProjectedHistogram` function to create the accumulation histograms that have a binary image and a type of histogram that we need, horizontal or vertical, as input:

```
Mat OCR::ProjectedHistogram(Mat img, int t)
{
int sz=(t)?img.rows:img.cols;
Mat mhist=Mat::zeros(1,sz,CV_32F);

for(int j=0; j<sz; j++){
Mat data=(t)?img.row(j):img.col(j);
mhist.at<float>(j)=countNonZero(data);
}

//Normalize histogram
double min, max;
minMaxLoc(mhist, &min, &max);
```

```
if(max>0)
mhist.convertTo(mhist,-1 , 1.0f/max, 0);

return mhist;
}
```

Other features use a low-resolution sample image. Instead of using the whole character image, we will create a low-resolution character, for example, a character of 5x5. We will train the system with 5x5, 10x10, 15x15, and 20x20 characters and then evaluate which one returns the best result to use it in our system. Once we have all features, we will create a matrix of *M* columns by one row where the columns are the features:

```
Mat OCR::features(Mat in, int sizeData){
  //Histogram features
Mat vhist=ProjectedHistogram(in,VERTICAL);Mat
hhist=ProjectedHistogram(in,HORIZONTAL);
  //Low data feature
Mat lowData;resize(in, lowData, Size(sizeData, sizeData) );
int numCols=vhist.cols + hhist.cols + lowData.cols *
lowData.cols;
Mat out=Mat::zeros(1,numCols,CV_32F);
  //Asign values to feature
int j=0;
for(int i=0; i<vhist.cols; i++){
  out.at<float>(j)=vhist.at<float>(i); j++;}
for(int i=0; i<hhist.cols; i++){
  out.at<float>(j)=hhist.at<float>(i);
  j++;}
for(int x=0; x<lowData.cols; x++){
  for(int y=0; y<lowData.rows; y++){
    out.at<float>(j)=(float)lowData.at<unsigned char>(x,y);
    j++;
    }
  }
return out;
}
```

OCR classification

In the classification step, we used an Artificial Neural Network machine learning algorithm, more specifically, a **Multi-Layer Perceptron (MLP)** which is the most commonly used ANN algorithm.

MLP consists of a network of neurons with an input layer, output layer, and one or more hidden layers. Each layer has one or more neurons connected with the previous and next layers.

The following example represents a three-layer perceptron (is a binary classifier that maps a real-valued vector input to a single binary value output) with three inputs, two outputs, and the hidden layer including five neurons:

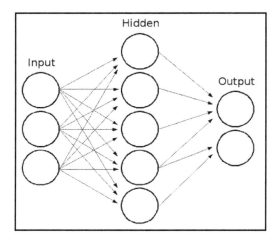

All neurons in an MLP are similar, and each one has several inputs (the previous linked neurons) and several output links with the same value (the next linked neurons). Each neuron calculates the output value as a sum of the weighted inputs plus a bias term and is transformed by a selected activation function:

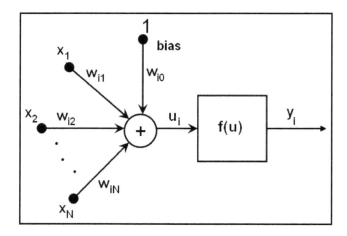

There are three widely used activation functions: Identity, Sigmoid, and Gaussian. The most common and default activation function is the Sigmoid function; it has an alpha and beta value set to 1:

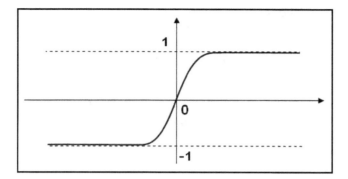

An ANN-trained network has a vector of input with features; it passes the values to the hidden layer and computes the results with the weights and activation function. It passes outputs further downstream until it gets the output layer that has the number of neurons classes.

The weight of each layer, synapses, and neuron is computed and learned by training the ANN algorithm. To train our classifier, we will create two matrices of data, as we did in the SVM training, but the training labels are a bit different. Instead of an $Nx1$ matrix, where N stands for training data rows and 1 is the column, we will use the label number identifier. We have to create an NxM matrix, where N is the training/samples data and M are the classes (10 digits + 20 letters in our case), and set 1 in a position i, j if the data row i is classified with class j:

$$
\begin{vmatrix}
1 & 0 & 0 & \cdots & 0 & 0 \\
1 & 0 & 0 & \cdots & 0 & 0 \\
0 & 1 & 0 & \cdots & 0 & 0 \\
0 & 1 & 0 & \cdots & 0 & 0 \\
0 & 1 & 0 & \cdots & 0 & 0 \\
\cdots & \cdots & \cdots & \cdots & \cdots & \cdots \\
0 & 0 & 0 & \cdots & 0 & 1 \\
0 & 0 & 0 & \cdots & 0 & 1 \\
0 & 0 & 0 & \cdots & 0 & 1
\end{vmatrix}
$$

We will create an OCR::train function to create all needed matrix and train our system, with the training data matrix, classes matrix, and the number of hidden neurons in the hidden layers. The training data is loaded from an XML file, just as we did in SVM training.

We have to define the number of neurons in each layer to initialize the ANN class. For our sample, we will use only one hidden layer. Then, we will define a matrix of one row and three columns. The first column position is the number of features, the second column position is the number of hidden neurons on the hidden layer, and the third column position is the number of classes.

OpenCV defines an ANN_MLP class for ANN. With the create function, we can initiate the class pointer and later define the number of layers and neurons and the activation function. We can thencreate the training data like SVM, and alpha and beta parameters of training method:

```
void OCR::train(Mat TrainData, Mat classes, int nlayers){
Mat_<int> layerSizes(1, 3);
layerSizes(0, 0) = data.cols;
layerSizes(0, 1) = nlayers;
layerSizes(0, 2) = numCharacters;
ann= ANN_MLP::create();
ann->setLayerSizes(layerSizes);
ann->setActivationFunction(ANN_MLP::SIGMOID_SYM, 0, 0);
ann->setTrainMethod(ANN_MLP::BACKPROP, 0.0001, 0.0001);

//Prepare trainClases
//Create a mat with n trained data by m classes
Mat trainClasses;
trainClasses.create( TrainData.rows, numCharacters, CV_32FC1 );
for( int i = 0; i <trainClasses.rows; i++ )
{
    for( int k = 0; k < trainClasses.cols; k++ )
    {
      //If class of data i is same than a k class
    if( k == classes.at<int>(i) )
       trainClasses.at<float>(i,k) = 1;
         else
              trainClasses.at<float>(i,k) = 0;
     }
    }

  Ptr<TrainData> trainData = TrainData::create(data, ROW_SAMPLE,
 trainClasses);
   //Learn classifier
    ann->train( trainData );
```

```
    }
```

After training, we can classify any segmented plate features using the `OCR::classify` function:

```
int OCR::classify(Mat f){
int result=-1;
Mat output;
ann.predict(f, output);
Point maxLoc;
double maxVal;
minMaxLoc(output, 0, &maxVal, 0, &maxLoc);
//We need know where in output is the max val, the x (cols) is
the class.
return maxLoc.x;
}
```

The `ANN_MLP` class uses the `predict` function for classifying a feature vector in a class. Unlike the SVM `classify` function, the ANN predict function returns a row with the size of equal to the number of classes, with the probability of belonging the input feature to each class.

To get the best result, we can use the `minMaxLoc` function to get the max and min response, and the position in the matrix. The class of our character is specified by the *x* position of higher value:

To finish each plate detected, we order its characters and return a string with the `str()` function of the `Plate` class, and we can draw it on the original image:

```
string licensePlate=plate.str();
rectangle(input_image, plate.position, Scalar(0,0,200));
putText(input_image, licensePlate, Point(plate.position.x,
plate.position.y), CV_FONT_HERSHEY_SIMPLEX, 1,
Scalar(0,0,200),2);
```

Evaluation

Our project is finished. However, when we train a machine learning algorithm like OCR, for example, we need to know the best features and parameters to use and how to correct the classification, recognition, and detection errors in our system.

We need to evaluate our system with different situations and parameters and evaluate the errors produced in order to get the best parameters that minimize those errors.

In this chapter, we evaluated the OCR task with variables: size of low-level resolution image feature and the number of hidden neurons in the hidden layer.

We created the `evalOCR.cpp` application where we uses the XML training data file generated by the `trainOCR.cpp` application. The `OCR.xml` file contains the training data matrix for 5x5, 10x10, 15x15, and 20x20 downsampled image features:

```
Mat classes;
Mat trainingData;
//Read file storage.
FileStorage fs;
fs.open("OCR.xml", FileStorage::READ);
fs[data] >> trainingData;
fs["classes"] >> classes;
```

The evaluation application gets each downsampled matrix feature and gets 100 random rows for traning, as well as other rows for testing the ANN algorithm and checking the error.

Before training the system, we will test each random sample and check whether the response is correct. If the response is not correct, we increment the error counter variable and then divide by the number of samples to evaluate. This indicates the error ratio between 0 and 1 for training with random data:

```
float test(Mat samples, Mat classes){
float errors=0;
```

```
for(int i=0; i<samples.rows; i++){
  int result= ocr.classify(samples.row(i));
  if(result!= classes.at<int>(i))
  errors++;
}
return errors/samples.rows;
}
```

The application returns output command-line error ratio for each sample size. For a good evaluation, we need to train the application with different random training rows. This produces different test error values. Then, we can add up all the errors and obtain an average. To do this task, we will create the bash UNIX script to automate it:

```
#!/bin/bash
echo "#ITS t 5 t 10 t 15 t 20">data.txt
folder=$(pwd)

for numNeurons in 10 20 30 40 50 60 70 80 90 100 120 150 200 500
do
s5=0;
s10=0;
s15=0;
s20=0;
for j in {1..100}
do
echo $numNeurons $j
a=$($folder/build/evalOCR $numNeurons TrainingDataF5)
s5=$(echo "scale=4; $s5+$a" | bc -q 2>/dev/null)

a=$($folder/build/evalOCR $numNeurons TrainingDataF10)
s10=$(echo "scale=4; $s10+$a" | bc -q 2>/dev/null)

a=$($folder/build/evalOCR $numNeurons TrainingDataF15)
s15=$(echo "scale=4; $s15+$a" | bc -q 2>/dev/null)

a=$($folder/build/evalOCR $numNeurons TrainingDataF20)
s20=$(echo "scale=4; $s20+$a" | bc -q 2>/dev/null)
done

echo "$i t $s5 t $s10 t $s15 t $s20"
echo "$i t $s5 t $s10 t $s15 t $s20">>data.txt
done
```

This script saves a `data.txt` file that contains all results for each size and neuron hidden layer number. This file can be used for plotting with *gnuplot*. We can see the result in the following image:

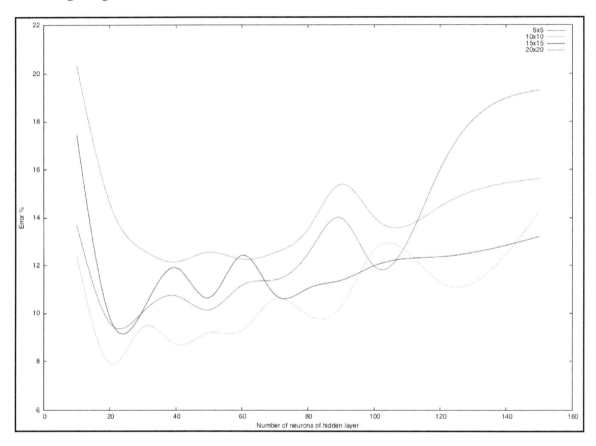

We can see that the lowest error is over 8 percent and is using 20 neurons in hidden layer and character's features extracted from a downscaled to 10x10 image patch.

Summary

In this chapter, you learned how an Automatic Plate License Recognition program works and its two important steps: plate localization and plate recognition.

In the first step, you learned how to segment an image looking for patches where we can have a plate, and use a simple heuristics and SVM algorithm to make a binary classification for patches with *plates* and *no plates*.

In the second step, you learned how to segment with the Find Contours algorithm, extract feature vector from each character, and use an ANN to classify each feature in a character class.

You also learned how to evaluate a machine algorithm with training with random samples, and using different parameters and features.

In the next chapter, you will learn how to create a face-recognition application using eigenfaces.

4
Non-Rigid Face Tracking

Non-rigid face tracking, which is the estimation of a quasi-dense set of facial features in each frame of a video stream, is a difficult problem for which modern approaches borrow ideas from a number of related fields, including Computer Vision, computational geometry, machine learning, and image processing. Non-rigidity here refers to the fact that relative distances between facial features vary between facial expression and across the population, and is distinct from face detection and tracking, which aims only to find the location of the face in each frame, rather than the configuration of facial features. Non-rigid face tracking is a popular research topic that has been pursued for over two decades, but it is only recently that various approaches have become robust enough, and processors fast enough, which makes the building of commercial applications possible.

Although commercial-grade face tracking can be highly sophisticated and pose a challenge even for experienced Computer Vision scientists, in this chapter we will see that a face tracker that performs reasonably well under constrained settings can be devised using modest mathematical tools and OpenCV's substantial functionality in linear algebra, image processing, and visualization. This is particularly the case when the person to be tracked is known ahead of time, and training data in the form of images and landmark annotations are available. The techniques described henceforth will act as a useful starting point and a guide for further pursuits towards a more elaborate face-tracking system.

An outline of this chapter is as follows:

- **Overview**: This section covers a brief history of face tracking.
- **Utilities**: This section outlines the common structures and conventions used in this chapter. It includes object-oriented design, data storage and representation, and a tool for data collection and annotation.

- **Geometrical constraints**: This section describes how facial geometry and its variations are learned from the training data and utilized during tracking to constrain the solution. This includes modeling the face as a linear shape model and how global transformations can be integrated into its representation.
- **Facial feature detectors**: This section describes how to learn the appearance of facial features in order to detect them in an image where the face is to be tracked.
- **Face detection and initialization**: This section describes how to use face detection to initialize the tracking process.
- **Face tracking**: This section combines all components described previously into a tracking system through the process of image alignment. Discussion on the settings in which the system can be expected to work best.

The following block diagram illustrates the relationships between the various components of the system:

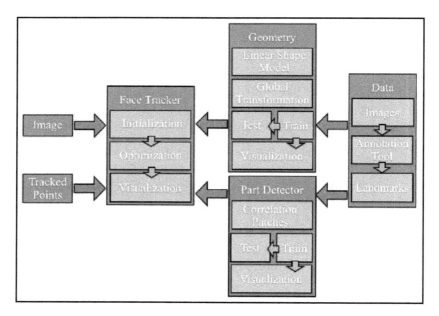

Note that all methods employed in this chapter follow a data-driven paradigm whereby all models used are learned from data rather than designed by hand in a rule-based setting. As such, each component of the system will involve two components: training and testing. Training builds the models from data and testing employs these models on new unseen data.

Overview

Non-rigid face tracking was first popularized in the early to mid-1990s with the advent of **Active Shape Models** (**ASM**) by Cootes and Taylor. Since then, a tremendous amount of research has been dedicated to solving the difficult problem of generic face tracking with many improvements over the original method that ASM proposed. The first milestone was the extension of ASM to **Active Appearance Models** (**AAM**) in 2001, also by Cootes and Taylor. This approach was later formalized though the principled treatment of image warps by Baker and colleges in the mid-2000s. Another strand of work along these lines was the **3D morphable model** (**3DMM**) by Blanz and Vetter, which like AAM, not only modeled image textures as opposed to profiles along object boundaries as in ASM, but took it one step further by representing the models with a highly dense 3D data learned from laser scans of faces. From the mid- to late 2000s, the focus of research on face tracking shifted away from how the face was parameterized to how the objective of the tracking algorithm was posed and optimized. Various techniques from the machine-learning community were applied with various degrees of success. Since the turn of the century, the focus has shifted once again, this time towards joint parameter and objective design strategies that guarantee global solutions.

Despite the continued intense research into face tracking, there have been relatively few commercial applications that use it. There has also been a lag in uptake by hobbyists and enthusiasts, despite there being a number of freely available source code packages for a number of common approaches. Nonetheless, in the past 2 years there has been a renewed interest in the public domain for the potential use of face tracking and commercial-grade products are beginning to emerge.

Utilities

Before diving into the intricacies of face tracking, a number of book-keeping tasks and conventions common to all face-tracking methods must first be introduced. The rest of this section will deal with these issues. An interested reader may want to skip this section at the first reading and go straight to the section on geometrical constraints.

Object-oriented design

As with face detection and recognition, programmatically, face tracking consists of two components: data and algorithms. The algorithms typically perform some kind of operation on the incoming (that is, online) data by referencing prestored (that is, offline) data as a guide. As such, an object-oriented design that couples algorithms with the data they rely on is a convenient design choice.

In OpenCV v2.x, a convenient XML/YAML file storage class was introduced that greatly simplifies the task of organizing offline data for use in the algorithms. To leverage this feature, all classes described in this chapter will implement read-and write-serialization functions. An example of this is shown as follows for an imaginary class foo:

```
#include <opencv2/opencv.hpp>
using namespace cv;
class foo {
  public:
  Mat a;
  type_b b;
  void write(FileStorage &fs) const{
    assert(fs.isOpened());
    fs<< "{" << "a"  << a << "b"  << b << "}";
  }
  void read(const FileNode& node){
    assert(node.type() == FileNode::MAP);
    node["a"] >> a; node["b"] >> b;
  }
};
```

Here, Mat is OpenCV's matrix class and type_b is a (imaginary) user-defined class that also has the serialization functionality defined. The I/O functions read and write implement the serialization. The FileStorage class supports two types of data structures that can be serialized. For simplicity, in this chapter all classes will only utilize mappings, where each stored variable creates a FileNode object of type FileNode::MAP. This requires a unique key to be assigned to each element. Although the choice for this key is arbitrary, we will use the variable name as the label for consistency reasons. As illustrated in the preceding code snippet, the read and write functions take on a particularly simple form, whereby the streaming operators (<< and >>) are used to insert and extract data to the FileStorage object. Most OpenCV classes have implementations of the read and write functions, allowing the storage of the data that they contain to be done with ease.

In addition to defining the serialization functions, one must also define two additional functions for the serialization in the `FileStorage` class to work, as follows:

```
void write(FileStorage& fs, const string&, const foo& x) {
  x.write(fs);
}
void read(const FileNode& node, foo& x,const foo& default){
  if(node.empty())x = d; else x.read(node);
}
```

As the functionality of these two functions remains the same for all classes we describe in this section, they are templated and defined in the `ft.hpp` header file found in the source code pertaining to this chapter. Finally, to easily save and load user-defined classes that utilize the serialization functionality, templated functions for these are also implemented in the header file as follows:

```
template<class T>
T load_ft(const char* fname){
  T x; FileStorage f(fname,FileStorage::READ);
  f["ft object"] >> x; f.release(); return x;
}
template<class T>
void save_ft(const char* fname,const T& x){
  FileStorage f(fname,FileStorage::WRITE);
  f << "ft object" << x; f.release();
}
```

Note that the label associated with the object is always the same (that is, `ft object`). With these functions defined, saving and loading object data is a painless process. This is shown with the help of the following example:

```
#include "opencv_hotshots/ft/ft.hpp"
#include "foo.hpp"
int main() {
  ...
  foo A; save_ft<foo>("foo.xml",A);
  ...
  foo B = load_ft<foo>("foo.xml");
  ...
}
```

Note that the `.xml` extension results in an XML-formatted data file. For any other extension, it defaults to the (more human-readable) YAML format.

Data collection - image and video annotation

Modern face-tracking techniques are almost entirely data driven, that is, the algorithms used to detect the locations of facial features in the image rely on models of the appearance of the facial features and the geometrical dependencies between their relative locations from a set of examples. The larger the set of examples, the more robust the algorithms behave, as they become more aware of the gamut of variability that faces can exhibit. Thus, the first step in building a face-tracking algorithm is to create an image/video annotation tool, where the user can specify the locations of the desired facial features in each example image.

Training data types

The data for training face tracking algorithms generally consists of four components:

- **Images**: This component is a collection of images (still images or video frames) that contain an entire face. For best results, this collection should be specialized to the types of conditions (that is, identity, lighting, distance from camera, capturing device, among others) in which the tracker is later deployed. It is also crucial that the faces in the collection exhibit the range of head poses and facial expressions that the intended application expects.

- **Annotations**: This component has ordered hand-labeled locations in each image that correspond to every facial feature to be tracked. More facial features often lead to a more robust tracker as the tracking algorithm can use their measurements to reinforce each other. The computational cost of common tracking algorithms typically scales linearly with the number of facial features.

- **Symmetry indices**: This component has an index for each facial feature point that defines its bilaterally symmetrical feature. This can be used to mirror the training images, effectively doubling the training set size and symmetrizing the data along the y axis.

- **Connectivity indices**: This component has a set of index pairs of the annotations that define the semantic interpretation of the facial features. These connections are useful for visualizing the tracking results.

A visualization of these four components is shown in the following image, where from left to right we have the raw image, facial feature annotations, color-coded bilateral symmetry points, mirrored image, and annotations and facial feature connectivity:

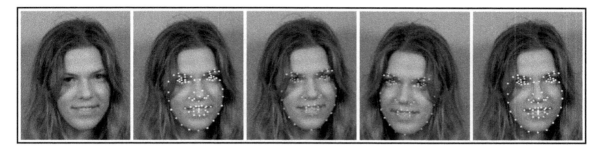

To conveniently manage such data, a class that implements storage and access functionality is a useful component. The CvMLData class in the ml module of OpenCV has the functionality for handling general data often used in machine-learning problems. However, it lacks the functionality required from the face-tracking data. As such, in this chapter, we will use the ft_data class, declared in the ft_data.hpp header file, which is designed specifically with the peculiarity of face-tracking data in mind. All data elements are defined as public members of the class, as follows:

```
class ft_data{
  public:
  vector<int> symmetry;
  vector<Vec2i> connections;
  vector<string> imnames;
  vector<vector<Point2f>> points;
  ...
}
```

The Vec2i and Point2f types are OpenCV classes for vectors of two integers and 2D floating-point coordinates respectively. The symmetry vector has as many components as there are feature points on the face (as defined by the user). Each of the connections define a zero-based index pair of connected facial features. As the training set can potentially be very large, rather than storing the images directly, the class stores the filenames of each image in the imnames member variable (note that this requires the images to be located in the same relative path for the filenames to remain valid). Finally, for each training image, a collection of facial feature locations are stored as vectors of floating-point coordinates in the points member variable.

The `ft_data` class implements a number of convenience methods for accessing the data. To access an image in the dataset, the `get_image` function loads the image at the specified index, `idx`, and optionally mirrors it around the y axis as follows:

```
Mat
ft_data::get_image(
  const int idx,    //index of image to load from file
  const int flag) { //0=gray,1=gray+flip,2=rgb,3=rgb+flip
    if((idx < 0) || (idx >= (int)imnames.size()))return Mat();
    Mat img,im;
    if(flag < 2) img = imread(imnames[idx],0);
    else         img = imread(imnames[idx],1);
    if(flag % 2 != 0) flip(img,im,1);
    else              im = img;
    return im;
  }
```

The (0,1) flag passed to OpenCV's `imread` function specifies whether the image is loaded as a three-channel color image or as a single-channel grayscale image. The flag passed to OpenCV's `flip` function specifies the mirroring around the *y* axis.

To access a point set corresponding to an image at a particular index, the `get_points` function returns a vector of floating-point coordinates with the option of mirroring their indices as follows:

```
vector<Point2f>
ft_data::get_points(
const int idx,          //index of image corresponding to points
const bool flipped) { //is the image flipped around the y-axis?
  if((idx < 0) || (idx >= (int)imnames.size()))
  return vector<Point2f>();
  vector<Point2f> p = points[idx];
  if(flipped){
    Mat im = this->get_image(idx,0); int n = p.size();
    vector<Point2f> q(n);
    for(int i = 0; i < n; i++){
      q[i].x = im.cols-1-p[symmetry[i]].x;
      q[i].y = p[symmetry[i]].y;
    } return q;
  } else return p;
}
```

Note that when the mirroring flag is specified, this function calls the `get_image` function. This is required to determine the width of the image in order to correctly mirror the facial feature coordinates. A more efficient method could be devised by simply passing the image width as a variable. Finally, the utility of the `symmetry` member variable is illustrated in this function. The mirrored feature location of a particular index is simply the feature location at the index specified in the `symmetry` variable with its *x* coordinate flipped and biased.

Both the `get_image` and `get_points` functions return empty structures if the specified index is outside the one that exists for the dataset. It is also possible that not all images in the collection are annotated. Face-tracking algorithms can be designed to handle missing data; however, these implementations are often quite involved and are outside the scope of this chapter. The `ft_data` class implements a function for removing samples from its collection that do not have corresponding annotations, as follows:

```
void ft_data::rm_incomplete_samples(){
  int n = points[0].size(),N = points.size();
  for(int i = 1; i < N; i++)n = max(n,int(points[i].size()));
  for(int i = 0; i < int(points.size()); i++){
    if(int(points[i].size()) != n){
      points.erase(points.begin()+i);
      imnames.erase(imnames.begin()+i); i--;
    } else {
      int j = 0;
      for(; j < n; j++) {
        if((points[i][j].x <= 0) ||
        (points[i][j].y <= 0))break;
      }
      if(j < n) {
        points.erase(points.begin()+i);
        imnames.erase(imnames.begin()+i); i--;
      }
    }
  }
}
```

The sample instance that has the most number of annotations is assumed to be the canonical sample. All data instances that have a point set with less than that number of points are removed from the collection using the vector's `erase` function. Also notice that points with (*x*, *y*) coordinates less than 1 are considered missing in their corresponding image (possibly due to occlusion, poor visibility, or ambiguity).

The `ft_data` class implements the serialization functions `read` and `write`, and can thus be stored and loaded easily. For example, saving a dataset can be done as simply as:

```
ft_data D;                          //instantiate data structure
...                                 //populate data
save_ft<ft_data>("mydata.xml",D);   //save data
```

For visualizing the dataset, `ft_data` implements a number of drawing functions. Their use is illustrated in the `visualize_annotations.cpp` file. This simple program loads annotation data stored in the file specified in the command-line, removes the incomplete samples, and displays the training images with their corresponding annotations, symmetry, and connections superimposed. A few notable features of OpenCV's `highgui` module are demonstrated here. Although quite rudimentary and not well suited for complex user interfaces, the functionality in OpenCV's `highgui` module is extremely useful for loading and visualizing data and algorithmic outputs in Computer Vision applications. This is perhaps one of OpenCV's distinguishing qualities compared to other Computer Vision libraries.

Annotation tool

To aid in generating annotations for use with the code in this chapter, a rudimentary annotation tool can be found in the `annotate.cpp` file. The tool takes as input a video stream, either from a file or from the camera. The procedure for using the tool is listed in the following four steps:

1. **Capture images**: In this first step, the image stream is displayed on the screen and the user chooses the images to annotate by pressing the S key. The best set of features to annotate are those that maximally span the range of facial behaviors that the face-tracking system will be required to track.

2. **Annotate first image**: In this second step, the user is presented with the first image selected in the previous stage. The user then proceeds to click on the image at the locations pertaining to the facial features that require tracking.

3. **Annotate connectivity**: In this third step, to better visualize a shape, the connectivity structure of points needs to be defined. Here, the user is presented with the same image as in the previous stage, where the task now is to click a set of point pairs, one after the other, to build the connectivity structure for the face model.

4. **Annotate symmetry**: In this step, still with the same image, the user selects pairs of points that exhibit bilateral symmetry.

5. **Annotate remaining images**: In this final step, the procedure here is similar to that of *step 2*, except that the user can browse through the set of images and annotate them asynchronously.

An interested reader may want to improve on this tool by improving its usability or may even integrate an incremental learning procedure, whereby a tracking model is updated after each additional image is annotated and is subsequently used to initialize the points to reduce the burden of annotation.

Although some publicly available datasets are available for use with the code developed in this chapter (see for example, the description in the following section), the annotation tool can be used to build person-specific face-tracking models, which often perform far better than their generic, person-independent, counterparts.

Pre-annotated data (the MUCT dataset)

One of the hindering factors of developing face-tracking systems is the tedious and error-prone process of manually annotating a large collection of images, each with a large number of points. To ease this process for the purpose of following the work in this chapter, the publicly available MUCT dataset can be downloaded from `http://www/milbo.org/muct`.

The dataset consists of 3,755 face images annotated with 76 point landmarks. The subjects in the dataset vary in age and ethnicity and are captured under a number of different lighting conditions and head poses.

To use the MUCT dataset with the code in this chapter, perform the following steps:

1. **Download the image set**: In this step, all the images in the dataset can be obtained by downloading the files `muct-a-jpg-v1.tar.gz` to `muct-e-jpg-v1.tar.gz` and uncompressing them. This will generate a new folder in which all the images will be stored.
2. **Download the annotations**: In this step, download the file containing the annotations `muct-landmarks-v1.tar.gz`. Save and uncompress this file in the same folder as the one in which the images were downloaded.

3. **Define connections and symmetry using the annotation tool**: In this step, from the command-line, issue the command `./annotate -m $mdir -d $odir`, where `$mdir` denotes the folder where the MUCT dataset was saved and `$odir` denotes the folder to which the `annotations.yaml` file, containing the data stored as an `ft_data` object, will be written.

Usage of the MUCT dataset is encouraged to get a quick introduction to the functionality of the face-tracking code described in this chapter.

Geometrical constraints

In face tracking, geometry refers to the spatial configuration of a predefined set of points that correspond to physically consistent locations on the human face (such as eye corners, nose tips, and eyebrow edges). A particular choice of these points is application dependent, with some applications requiring a dense set of over 100 points and others requiring only a sparser selection. However, the robustness of face-tracking algorithms generally improves with an increased number of points, as their separate measurements can reinforce each other through their relative spatial dependencies. For example, the location of an eye corner is a good indication of where to expect the nose to be located. However, there are limits to improvements in robustness gained by increasing the number of points, where performance typically plateaus after around 100 points. Furthermore, increasing the point set used to describe a face carries with it a linear increase in computational complexity. Thus, applications with strict constraints on computational load may fare better with fewer points.

It is also the case that faster tracking often leads to more accurate tracking in the online setting. This is because, when frames are dropped, the perceived motion between frames increases, and the optimization algorithm used to find the configuration of the face in each frame has to search a larger space of possible configurations of feature points; a process that often fails when displacement between frames becomes too large. In summary, although there are general guidelines on how to best design the selection of facial feature points, to get an optimal performance, this selection should be specialized to the application's domain.

Facial geometry is often parameterized as a composition of two elements: a **global transformation** (rigid) and a **local deformation** (non-rigid). The global transformation accounts for the overall placement of the face in the image, which is often allowed to vary without constraint (that is, the face can appear anywhere in the image). This includes the (x, y) location of the face in the image, the in-plane head rotation, and the size of the face in the image. Local deformations, on the other hand, account for differences between facial shapes across identities and between expressions. In contrast to the global transformation, these local deformations are often far more constrained largely due to the highly structured configuration of facial features. Global transformations are generic functions of 2D coordinates, applicable to any type of object, whereas local deformations are object specific and must be learned from a training dataset.

In this section, we will describe the construction of a geometrical model of a facial structure, hereby referred to as the shape model. Depending on the application, it can capture expression variations of a single individual, differences between facial shapes across a population, or a combination of both. This model is implemented in the shape_model class which can be found in the shape_model.hpp and shape_model.cpp files. The following code snippet is a part of the header of the shape_model class that highlights its primary functionality:

```
class shape_model { //2d linear shape model
  public:
  Mat p; //parameter vector (kx1) CV_32F
  Mat V; //linear subspace (2nxk) CV_32F
  Mat e; //parameter variance (kx1) CV_32F
  Mat C; //connectivity (cx2) CV_32S
  ...
  void calc_params(
  const vector<Point2f>&pts,   //points to compute parameters
  const Mat &weight = Mat(),    //weight/point (nx1) CV_32F
  const float c_factor = 3.0); //clamping factor
  ...
  vector<Point2f>                //shape described by parameters
  calc_shape();
  ...
  void train(
  const vector<vector<Point2f>>&p, //N-example shapes
  const vector<Vec2i>&con = vector<Vec2i>(),//connectivity
  const float frac = 0.95, //fraction of variation to retain
  const int kmax = 10);   //maximum number of modes to retain
  ...
}
```

The model that represents variations in face shapes is encoded in the subspace matrix `V` and variance vector `e`. The parameter vector `p` stores the encoding of a shape with respect to the model. The connectivity matrix `C` is also stored in this class as it pertains only to visualizing instances of the face's shape. The three functions of primary interest in this class are `calc_params`, `calc_shape`, and `train`. The `calc_params` function projects a set of points onto the space of plausible face shapes. It optionally provides separate confidence weights for each of the points to be projected. The `calc_shape` function generates a set of points by decoding the parameter vector `p` using the face model (encoded by `V` and `e`). The `train` function learns the encoding model from a dataset of face shapes, each of which consists of the same number of points. The parameters `frac` and `kmax` are parameters of the training procedure that can be specialized for the data at hand.

The functionality of this class will be elaborated in the sections that follow, where we begin by describing **Procrustes analysis**, a method for rigidly registering a point set, followed by the linear model used to represent local deformations. The programs in the `train_shape_model.cpp` and `visualize_shape_model.cpp` files train and visualize the shape model respectively. Their usage will be outlined at the end of this section.

Procrustes analysis

In order to build a deformation model of face shapes, we must first process the raw annotated data to remove components pertaining to global rigid motion. When modeling geometry in 2D, a rigid motion is often represented as a similarity transform; this includes the scale, in-plane rotation, and translation. The following image illustrates the set of permissible motion types under a similarity transform. The process of removing global rigid motion from a collection of points is called **Procrustes analysis**.

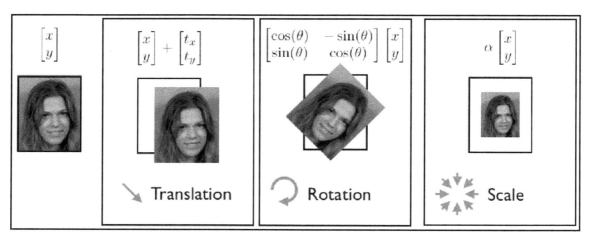

Mathematically, the objective of Procrustes analysis is to simultaneously find a canonical shape and similarity, and transform each data instance that brings them into alignment with the canonical shape. Here, alignment is measured as the least-squares distance between each transformed shape with the canonical shape. An iterative procedure for fulfilling this objective is implemented in the `shape_model` class as follows:

```
#define fl at<float>
Mat shape_model::procrustes (
const Mat &X,         //interleaved raw shape data as columns
const int itol,       //maximum number of iterations to try
const float ftol)     //convergence tolerance
{
  int N = X.cols,n = X.rows/2; Mat Co,P = X.clone();//copy
  for(int i = 0; i < N; i++){
    Mat p = P.col(i);             //i'th shape
    float mx = 0,my = 0;          //compute centre of mass...
    for(int j = 0; j < n; j++) { //for x and y separately
      mx += p.fl(2*j); my += p.fl(2*j+1);
    }
    mx /= n; my /= n;
    for(int j = 0; j < n; j++) {  //remove center of mass
      p.fl(2*j) -= mx; p.fl(2*j+1) -= my;
    }
  }
  for(int iter = 0; iter < itol; iter++) {
    Mat C = P*Mat::ones(N,1,CV_32F)/N; //compute normalized...
    normalize(C,C);                    //canonical shape
    if(iter > 0) { if(norm(C,Co) < ftol) break; } //converged?
    Co = C.clone();                             //remember current
estimate
    for(int i = 0; i < N; i++){
      Mat R = this->rot_scale_align(P.col(i),C);
      for(int j = 0; j < n; j++) { //apply similarity transform
        float x = P.fl(2*j,i), y = P.fl(2*j+1,i);
        P.fl(2*j  ,i) = R.fl(0,0)*x + R.fl(0,1)*y;
        P.fl(2*j+1,i) = R.fl(1,0)*x + R.fl(1,1)*y;
      }
    }
  } return P; //returned procrustes aligned shapes
}
```

The algorithm begins by subtracting the center of mass of each shape's instance followed by an iterative procedure that alternates between computing the canonical shape, as the normalized average of all shapes, and rotating and scaling each shape to best match the canonical shape. The normalization step of the estimated canonical shape is necessary to fix the scale of the problem and prevent it from shrinking all the shapes to zero. The choice of this anchor scale is arbitrary; here, we have chosen to enforce the length of the canonical shape vector C to 1.0, as is the default behavior of OpenCV's `normalize` function. Computing the in-plane rotation and scaling that best aligns each shape's instance to the current estimate of the canonical shape is effected through the `rot_scale_align` function as follows:

```
Mat shape_model::rot_scale_align(
  const Mat &src, //[x1;y1;...;xn;yn] vector of source shape
  const Mat &dst) //destination shape
  {
    //construct linear system
    int n = src.rows/2;
    float a=0, b=0, d=0;
    for(int i = 0; i < n; i++) {
      d+= src.fl(2*i)*src.fl(2*i  )+src.fl(2*i+1)*src.fl(2*i+1);
      a+= src.fl(2*i)*dst.fl(2*i  )+src.fl(2*i+1)*dst.fl(2*i+1);
      b+= src.fl(2*i)*dst.fl(2*i+1)-src.fl(2*i+1)*dst.fl(2*i  );
    }
    a /= d; b /= d;//solve linear system
    return (Mat_<float>(2,2) << a,-b,b,a);

  }
```

This function minimizes the following least squares difference between the rotated and canonical shapes. Mathematically this can be written as:

$$
\min_{a,b} \sum_{i=1}^{n} \left\| \begin{bmatrix} a & -b \\ b & a \end{bmatrix} \begin{bmatrix} x_i \\ y_i \end{bmatrix} - \begin{bmatrix} c_x \\ c_y \end{bmatrix} \right\|^2 \rightarrow \begin{bmatrix} a \\ b \end{bmatrix} = \frac{1}{\sum_i (x_i^2 + y_i^2)} \sum_{i=1}^{n} \begin{bmatrix} x_i c_x + y_i c_y \\ x_i c_y - y_i c_x \end{bmatrix}
$$

Here the solution to the least-squares problem takes on the closed-form solution shown in the following image on the right-hand side of the equation. Note that rather than solving for the scaling and in-plane rotation, which are nonlinearly related in the scaled 2D rotation matrix, we solve for the variables (a, b). These variables are related to the scale and rotation matrix as follows:

$$\begin{bmatrix} a & -b \\ b & a \end{bmatrix} = \begin{bmatrix} k\cos(\theta) & -k\sin(\theta) \\ k\sin(\theta) & k\cos(\theta) \end{bmatrix}$$

A visualization of the effects of Procrustes analysis on raw annotated shape data is illustrated in the following image. Each facial feature is displayed with a unique color. After translation normalization, the structure of the face becomes apparent, where the locations of facial features cluster around their average locations. After the iterative scale and rotation normalization procedure, the feature clustering becomes more compact and their distribution becomes more representative of the variation induced by facial deformation. This last point is important as it is these deformations that we will attempt to model in the following section. Thus, the role of Procrustes analysis can be thought of as a preprocessing operation on the raw data that will allow better local deformation models of the face to be learned:

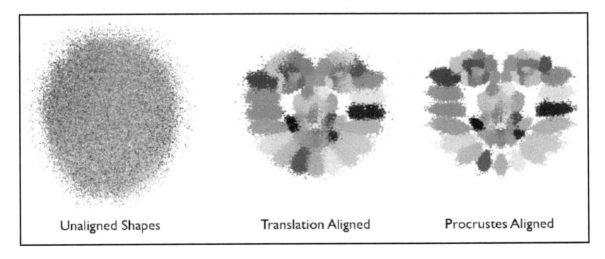

Unaligned Shapes   Translation Aligned   Procrustes Aligned

Linear shape models

The aim of facial-deformation modeling is to find a compact parametric representation of how the face's shape varies across identities and between expressions. There are many ways of achieving this goal with various levels of complexity. The simplest of these is to use a linear representation of facial geometry. Despite its simplicity, it has been shown to accurately capture the space of facial deformations, particularly when the faces in the dataset are largely in a frontal pose. It also has the advantage that inferring the parameters of its representation is an extremely simple and cheap operation, in contrast to its nonlinear counterparts. This plays an important role when deploying it to constrain the search procedure during tracking.

The main idea of linearly modeling facial shapes is illustrated in the following image. Here, a face shape, which consists of N facial features, is modeled as a single point in a $2N$-dimensional space. The aim of linear modeling is to find a low-dimensional hyperplane embedded within this $2N$-dimensional space in which all the face shape points lie (that is, the green points in the image). As this hyperplane spans only a subset of the entire $2N$-dimensional space, it is often referred to as the subspace. The lower the dimensionality of the subspace, the more compact the representation of the face is and the stronger the constraint that it places on the tracking procedure becomes. This often leads to more robust tracking. However, care should be taken in selecting the subspace's dimension so that it has enough capacity to span the space of all faces, but not so much that non-face shapes lie within its span (that is, the red points in the image). It should be noted that when modeling data from a single person, the subspace that captures the face's variability is often far more compact than the one that models multiple identities. This is one of the reasons why person-specific trackers perform much better than generic ones.

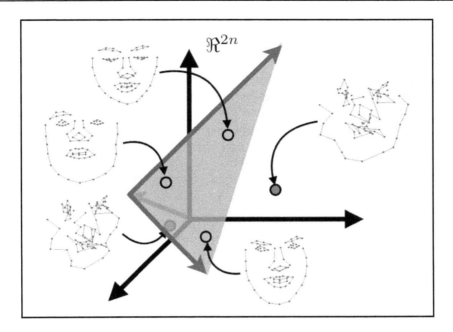

The procedure for finding the best low-dimensional subspace that spans a dataset is called **Principal Component Analysis (PCA)**. OpenCV implements a class for computing PCA; however, it requires the number of preserved subspace dimensions to be prespecified. As this is often difficult to determine a priori, a common heuristic is to choose it based on the fraction of the total amount of variation it accounts for. In the `shape_model::train` function, PCA is implemented as follows:

```
SVD svd(dY*dY.t());
int m = min(min(kmax,N-1),n-1);
float vsum = 0; for(int i = 0; i < m; i++)vsum += svd.w.fl(i);
float v = 0; int k = 0;
for(k = 0; k < m; k++){
  v += svd.w.fl(k); if(v/vsum >= frac){k++; break;}
}
if(k > m)k = m;
Mat D = svd.u(Rect(0,0,k,2*n));
```

Here, each column of the `dY` variable denotes the mean-subtracted Procrustes-aligned shape. Thus, **Singular Value Decomposition (SVD)** is effectively applied to the covariance matrix of the shape data (that is, `dY.t()*dY`). The `w` member of OpenCV's `SVD` class stores the variance in the major directions of variability of the data, ordered from largest to smallest. A common approach to choose the dimensionality of the subspace is to choose the smallest set of directions that preserve a fraction `frac` of the total energy of the data, which is represented by the entries of `svd.w`. As these entries are ordered from largest to smallest, it suffices to enumerate the subspace selection by greedily evaluating the energy in the top `k` directions of variability. The directions themselves are stored in the `u` member of the `SVD` class. The `svd.w` and `svd.u` components are generally referred to as the eigen spectrum and eigen vectors respectively. A visualization of these two components is shown in the following figure:

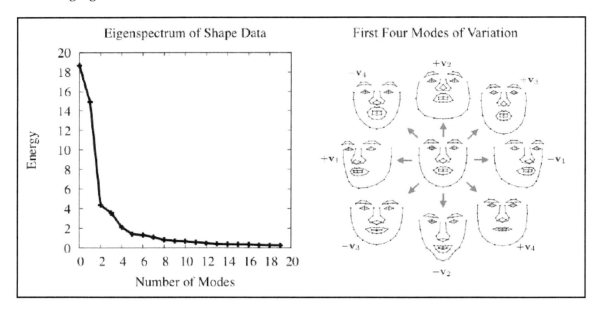

 Note that the eigen spectrum decreases rapidly, which suggests that most of the variation contained in the data can be modeled with a low-dimensional subspace.

A combined local-global representation

A shape in the image frame is generated by the composition of a local deformation and a global transformation. Mathematically, this parameterization can be problematic, as the composition of these transformations results in a nonlinear function that does not admit a closed-form solution. A common way to circumvent this problem is to model the global transformation as a linear subspace and append it to the deformation subspace. For a fixed shape, a similarity transform can be modeled with a subspace as follows:

$$
\begin{bmatrix} \begin{bmatrix} a & -b \\ b & a \end{bmatrix} \begin{bmatrix} x_1 \\ y_1 \end{bmatrix} + \begin{bmatrix} t_x \\ t_y \end{bmatrix} \\ \vdots \\ \begin{bmatrix} a & -b \\ b & a \end{bmatrix} \begin{bmatrix} x_n \\ y_n \end{bmatrix} + \begin{bmatrix} t_x \\ t_y \end{bmatrix} \end{bmatrix} = \begin{bmatrix} x_1 & -y_1 & 1 & 0 \\ y_1 & x_1 & 0 & 1 \\ \vdots & \vdots & \vdots & \vdots \\ x_n & -y_n & 1 & 0 \\ y_n & x_n & 0 & 1 \end{bmatrix} \begin{bmatrix} a \\ b \\ t_x \\ t_y \end{bmatrix}
$$

In the `shape_model` class, this subspace is generated using the `calc_rigid_basis` function. The shape from which the subspace is generated (that is, the x and y components in the preceding equation) is the mean shape over the Procustes-aligned shape (that is, the canonical shape). In addition to constructing the subspace in the aforementioned form, each column of the matrix is normalized to unit length. In the `shape_model::train` function, the variable dY described in the previous section is computed by projecting out the components of the data that pertain to rigid motion, as follows:

```
Mat R = this->calc_rigid_basis(Y); //compute rigid subspace
Mat P = R.t()*Y; Mat dY = Y - R*P; //project-out rigidity
```

Note that this projection is implemented as a simple matrix multiplication. This is possible because the columns of the rigid subspace have been length normalized. This does not change the space spanned by the model, and means only that `R.t()*R` equals the identity matrix.

As the directions of variability stemming from rigid transformations have been removed from the data before learning the deformation model, the resulting deformation subspace will be orthogonal to the rigid transformation subspace. Thus, concatenating the two subspaces results in a combined local-global linear representation of facial shapes that is also orthonormal. Concatenation here can be performed by assigning the two subspace matrices to submatrices of the combined subspace matrix through the ROI extraction mechanism implemented in OpenCV's `Mat` class as follows:

```
V.create(2*n,4+k,CV_32F);                    //combined subspace
Mat Vr = V(Rect(0,0,4,2*n)); R.copyTo(Vr); //rigid subspace
Mat Vd = V(Rect(4,0,k,2*n)); D.copyTo(Vd); //nonrigid subspace
```

The orthonormality of the resulting model means that the parameters describing a shape can be computed easily, as is done in the `shape_model::calc_params` function:

```
p = V.t()*s;
```

Here `s` is a vectorized face shape and `p` stores the coordinates in the face subspace that represents it.

A final point to note about linearly modeling facial shapes is how to constrain the subspace coordinates such that shapes generated using it remain valid. In the following image, instances of face shapes that lie within the subspace are shown for an increasing value of the coordinates in one of the directions of variability in increments of four standard deviations. Notice that for small values, the resulting shape remains face-like, but deteriorates as the values become too large.

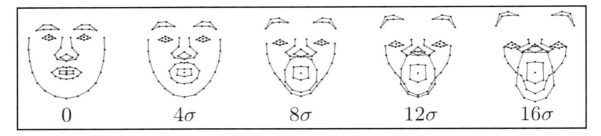

A simple way to prevent such deformation is to clamp the subspace coordinate values to lie within a permissible region as determined from the dataset. A common choice for this is a box constraint within ±3 standard deviations of the data, which accounts for 99.7 percent of variation in the data. These clamping values are computed in the `shape_model::train` function after the subspace is found, as follows:

```
Mat Q = V.t()*X;                   //project raw data onto subspace
for(int i = 0; i < N; i++) {       //normalize coordinates w.r.t scale
  float v = Q.fl(0,i); Mat q = Q.col(i); q /= v;
}
e.create(4+k,1,CV_32F); multiply(Q,Q,Q);
for(int i = 0; i < 4+k; i++) {
  if(i < 4)   e.fl(i) = -1;        //no clamping for rigid coefficients
  else        e.fl(i) = Q.row(i).dot(Mat::ones(1,N,CV_32F))/(N-1);
}
```

Notice that the variance is computed over the subspace coordinate Q after normalizing with respect to the coordinate of the first dimension (that is, scale). This prevents data samples that have relatively large scale from dominating the estimate. Also, notice that a negative value is assigned to the variance of the coordinates of the rigid subspace (that is, the first four columns of V). The clamping function `shape_model::clamp` checks to see if the variance of a particular direction is negative and only applies clamping if it is not, as follows:

```
void shape_model::clamp(const float c) {
  //clamping as fraction of standard deviation
  double scale = p.fl(0);          //extract scale
  for(int i = 0; i < e.rows; i++) {
    if(e.fl(i) < 0)continue;       //ignore rigid components
    float v = c*sqrt(e.fl(i));     //c*standard deviations box
    if(fabs(p.fl(i)/scale) > v) {  //preserve sign of coordinate
      if(p.fl(i) > 0) p.fl(i) =  v*scale; //positive threshold
      else            p.fl(i) = -v*scale; //negative threshold
    }
  }
}
```

The reason for this is that the training data is often captured under contrived settings where the face is upright and centered in the image at a particular scale. Clamping the rigid components of the shape model to adhere to the configurations in the training set would then be too restrictive. Finally, as the variance of each deformable coordinate is computed in the scale-normalized frame, the same scaling must be applied to the coordinates during clamping.

Training and visualization

An example program for training a shape model from the annotation data can be found in `train_shape_model.cpp`. With the command-line argument `argv[1]` containing the path to the annotation data, training begins by loading the data into memory and removing incomplete samples, as follows:

```
ft_data data = load_ft<ft_data>(argv[1]);
data.rm_incomplete_samples();
```

The annotations for each example, and optionally their mirrored counterparts, are then stored in a vector before passing them to the training function as follows:

```
vector<vector<Point2f>> points;
for(int i = 0; i < int(data.points.size()); i++) {
  points.push_back(data.get_points(i,false));
  if(mirror)points.push_back(data.get_points(i,true));
}
```

The shape model is then trained by a single function call to `shape_model::train` as follows:

```
shape_model smodel;
smodel.train(points,data.connections,frac,kmax);
```

Here, `frac` (that is, the fraction of variation to retain) and `kmax` (that is, the maximum number of eigen vectors to retain) can be optionally set through command-line options, although the default settings of 0.95 and 20, respectively, tend to work well in most cases. Finally, with the command-line argument `argv[2]` containing the path to save the trained shape model to, saving can be performed by a single function call as follows:

```
save_ft(argv[2],smodel);
```

The simplicity of this step results from defining the `read` and `write` serialization functions for the `shape_model` class.

To visualize the trained shape model, the `visualize_shape_model.cpp` program animates the learned non-rigid deformations of each direction in turn. It begins by loading the shape model into memory as follows:

```
shape_model smodel = load_ft<shape_model>(argv[1]);
```

The rigid parameters that place the model at the center of the display window are computed as follows:

```
int n = smodel.V.rows/2;
float scale = calc_scale(smodel.V.col(0),200);
float tranx =
  n*150.0/smodel.V.col(2).dot(Mat::ones(2*n,1,CV_32F));
float trany =
  n*150.0/smodel.V.col(3).dot(Mat::ones(2*n,1,CV_32F));
```

Here, the `calc_scale` function finds the scaling coefficient that would generate face shapes with a width of 200 pixels. The translation components are computed by finding the coefficients that generate a translation of 150 pixels (that is, the model is mean-centered and the display window is 300x300 pixels in size).

 Note that the first column of `shape_model::V` corresponds to scale and the third and fourth columns to x and y translations respectively.

A trajectory of parameter values is then generated, which begins at zero, moves to the positive extreme, moves to the negative extreme, and then back to zero, as follows:

```
vector<float> val;
for(int i = 0; i < 50; i++)val.push_back(float(i)/50);
for(int i = 0; i < 50; i++)val.push_back(float(50-i)/50);
for(int i = 0; i < 50; i++)val.push_back(-float(i)/50);
for(int i = 0; i < 50; i++)val.push_back(-float(50-i)/50);
```

Here, each phase of the animation is composed of 50 increments. This trajectory is then used to animate the face model and render the results in a display window as follows:

```
Mat img(300,300,CV_8UC3); namedWindow("shape model");
while(1) {
  for(int k = 4; k < smodel.V.cols; k++){
    for(int j = 0; j < int(val.size()); j++){
      Mat p = Mat::zeros(smodel.V.cols,1,CV_32F);
      p.at<float>(0) = scale;
      p.at<float>(2) = tranx;
      p.at<float>(3) = trany;
      p.at<float>(k) = scale*val[j]*3.0*
      sqrt(smodel.e.at<float>(k));
      p.copyTo(smodel.p); img = Scalar::all(255);
      vector<Point2f> q = smodel.calc_shape();
      draw_shape(img,q,smodel.C);
      imshow("shape model",img);
      if(waitKey(10) == 'q')return 0;
    }
  }
}
```

Note that the rigid coefficients (that is, those corresponding to the first four columns of `shape_model::V`) are always set to the values computed previously, to place the face at the center of the display window.

Facial feature detectors

Detecting facial features in images bares a strong resemblance to general object detection. OpenCV has a set of sophisticated functions for building general object detectors, the most well-known of which is the cascade of Haar-based feature detectors used in their implementation of the well-known **Viola-Jones face detector**. There are, however, a few distinguishing factors that make facial feature detection unique. These are as follows:

- **Precision versus robustness**: In generic object detection, the aim is to find the coarse position of the object in the image; facial feature detectors are required to give highly precise estimates of the location of the feature. An error of a few pixels is considered inconsequential in object detection but it can mean the difference between a smile and a frown in facial expression estimation through feature detections.

- **Ambiguity from limited spatial support**: It is common to assume that the object of interest in generic object detection exhibits sufficient image structure such that it can be reliably discriminated from image regions that do not contain the object. This is often not the case for facial features, which typically have limited spatial support. This is because image regions that do not contain the object can often exhibit a very similar structure to facial features. For example, a feature on the periphery of the face, seen from a small bounding box centered at the feature, can be easily confused with any other image patch that contains a strong edge through its center.

- **Computational complexity**: Generic object detection aims to find all instances of the object in an image. Face tracking, on the other hand, requires the locations of all facial features, which often ranges from around 20 to 100 features. Thus, the ability to evaluate each feature detector efficiently is paramount in building a face tracker that can run in real time.

Due to these differences, the facial feature detectors used in face tracking are often specifically designed with that purpose in mind. There are, of course, many instances of generic object-detection techniques being applied to facial feature detectors in face tracking. However, there does not appear to be a consensus in the community about which representation is best suited for the problem.

In this section, we will build facial feature detectors using a representation that is perhaps the simplest model one would consider: a linear image patch. Despite its simplicity, with due care in designing its learning procedure, we will see that this representation can in fact give reasonable estimates of facial feature locations for use in a face-tracking algorithm. Furthermore, their simplicity enables an extremely rapid evaluation that makes real-time face tracking possible. Due to their representation as an image patch, the facial feature detectors are hereby referred to as patch models. This model is implemented in the `patch_model` class that can be found in the `patch_model.hpp` and `patch_model.cpp` files. The following code snippet is of the header of the `patch_model` class that highlights its primary functionality:

```
class patch_model{
  public:
  Mat P; //normalized patch
  ...
  Mat                          //response map
  calc_response(
  const Mat &im,               //image patch of search region
  const bool sum2one = false); //normalize to sum-to-one?
  ...
  void train(const vector<Mat>&images, //training image patches
  const Size psize,             //patch size
  const float var = 1.0,        //ideal response variance
  const float lambda = 1e-6,    //regularization weight
  const float mu_init = 1e-3,   //initial step size
  const int nsamples = 1000,    //number of samples
  const bool visi = false);     //visualize process?
  ...
};
```

The patch model used to detect a facial feature is stored in the matrix P. The two functions of primary interest in this class are `calc_response` and `train`. The `calc_response` function evaluates the patch model's response at every integer displacement over the search region im. The `train` function learns the patch model P of size `psize` that, on an average, yields response maps over the training set that is as close as possible to the ideal response map. The parameters var, lambda, mu_init, and nsamples are parameters of the training procedure that can be tuned to optimize performance for the data at hand.

The functionality of this class will be elaborated in this section. We begin by discussing the correlation patch and its training procedure, which will be used to learn the patch model. Next, the `patch_models` class, which is a collection of the patch models for each facial feature and has functionality that accounts for global transformations will be described. The programs in `train_patch_model.cpp` and `visualize_patch_model.cpp` train and visualize the patch models, respectively, and their usage will be outlined at the end of this section on facial feature detectors.

Correlation-based patch models

In learning detectors, there are two primary competing paradigms: generative and discriminative. Generative methods learn an underlying representation of image patches that can best generate the object appearance in all its manifestations. Discriminative methods, on the other hand, learn a representation that best discriminates instances of the object from other objects that the model will likely encounter when deployed. Generative methods have the advantage that the resulting model encodes properties specific to the object, allowing novel instances of the object to be visually inspected. A popular approach that falls within the paradigm of generative methods is the famous `Eigenfaces` method. Discriminative methods have the advantage that the full capacity of the model is geared directly towards the problem at hand; discriminating instances of the object from all others. Perhaps the most well-known of all discriminative methods is the support vector machine. Although both paradigms can work well in many situations, we will see that when modeling facial features as an image patch, the discriminative paradigm is far superior.

 Note that the `Eigenfaces` and support vector machine methods were originally developed for classification rather than detection or image alignment. However, their underlying mathematical concepts have been shown to be applicable to the face-tracking domain.

Learning discriminative patch models

Given an annotated dataset, the feature detectors can be learned independently from each other. The learning objective of a discriminative patch model is to construct an image patch that, when cross-correlated with an image region containing the facial feature, yields a strong response at the fease. Mathematically, this can be expressed as:

$$\min_{\mathbf{P}} \sum_{i=1}^{N} \sum_{x,y} \left[\mathbf{R}(x,y) - \mathbf{P} \cdot \mathbf{I}_i \left(x - \frac{w}{2} : x + \frac{w}{2}, y - \frac{h}{2} : y + \frac{h}{2} \right) \right]^2$$

Here, **P** denotes the patch model, **I** denotes the ith training image, **I**(*a:b, c:d*) denotes the rectangular region whose top-left and bottom-right corners are located at *(a, c)* and *(b, d)*, respectively. The period symbol denotes the inner product operation and **R** denotes the ideal response map. The solution to this equation is a patch model that generates response maps that are, on average, closest to the ideal response map as measured using the least-squares criterion. An obvious choice for the ideal response map, **R**, is a matrix with zeros everywhere except at the center (assuming the training image patches are centered at the facial feature of interest). In practice, since the images are hand-labeled, there will always be an annotation error. To account for this, it is common to describe R as a decaying function of distance from the center. A good choice is the 2D-Gaussian distribution, which is equivalent to assuming the annotation error is Gaussian distributed. A visualization of this setup is shown in the following figure for the left outer eye corner:

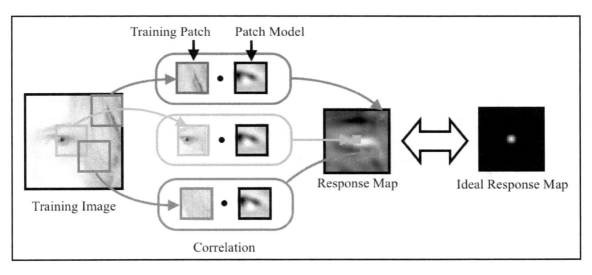

The learning objective as written previously is in a form commonly referred to as linear least squares. As such, it affords a closed-form solution. However, the degrees of freedom of this problem; that is, the number of ways the variables can vary to solve the problem, is equal to the number of pixels in the patch. Thus, the computational cost and memory requirements of solving for the optimal patch model can be prohibitive, even for a moderately sized patch; for example, a 40x40 patch model has 1,600 degrees of freedom.

An efficient alternative to solving the learning problem as a linear system of equations is a method called stochastic gradient descent. By visualizing the learning objective as an error terrain over the degrees of freedom of the patch model, stochastic gradient descent iteratively makes an approximate estimate of the gradient direction of the terrain and takes a small step in the opposite direction. For our problem, the approximation to gradient can be computed by considering only the gradient of the learning objective for a single, randomly chosen image from the training set:

$$\mathbf{D} = -\sum_{x,y} (\mathbf{R}(x,y) - \mathbf{P} \cdot \mathbf{W}) \ \mathbf{W} \ ; \ \ \mathbf{W} = \mathbf{I} \left(x - \frac{w}{2} : x + \frac{w}{2}, y - \frac{h}{2} : y + \frac{h}{2} \right)$$

In the `patch_model` class, this learning process is implemented in the `train` function:

```
void patch_model::train(
  const vector<Mat>&images, //featured centered training images
  const Size psize,          //desired patch model size
  const float var,           //variance of annotation error
  const float lambda,        //regularization parameter
  const float mu_init,       //initial step size
  const int nsamples,        //number of stochastic samples
  const bool visi) {         //visualise training process
    int N = images.size(),n = psize.width*psize.height;
    int dx = wsize.width-psize.width;        //center of response map
    int dy = wsize.height-psize.height;      //...
    Mat F(dy,dx,CV_32F);                     //ideal response map
    for(int y = 0; y < dy; y++) {
      float vy = (dy-1)/2 - y;
      for(int x = 0; x < dx; x++) {
        float vx = (dx-1)/2 - x;
        F.fl(y,x) = exp(-0.5*(vx*vx+vy*vy)/var); //Gaussian
      }
    }
    normalize(F,F,0,1,NORM_MINMAX); //normalize to [0:1] range

    //allocate memory
    Mat I(wsize.height,wsize.width,CV_32F);
    Mat dP(psize.height,psize.width,CV_32F);
    Mat O = Mat::ones(psize.height,psize.width,CV_32F)/n;
    P = Mat::zeros(psize.height,psize.width,CV_32F);

    //optimise using stochastic gradient descent
    RNG rn(getTickCount()); //random number generator
    double mu=mu_init,step=pow(1e-8/mu_init,1.0/nsamples);
    for(int sample = 0; sample < nsamples; sample++){
      int i = rn.uniform(0,N); //randomly sample image index
```

```
I = this->convert_image(images[i]); dP = 0.0;
for(int y = 0; y < dy; y++) { //compute stochastic gradient
  for(int x = 0; x < dx; x++){
    Mat Wi=I(Rect(x,y,psize.width,psize.height)).clone();
    Wi -= Wi.dot(O); normalize(Wi,Wi); //normalize
    dP += (F.fl(y,x) - P.dot(Wi))*Wi;
  }
}
P += mu*(dP - lambda*P); //take a small step
mu *= step;                 //reduce step size
...
} return;
}
```

The first highlighted code snippet in the preceding code is where the ideal response map is computed. Since the images are centered on the facial feature of interest, the response map is the same for all samples. In the second highlighted code snippet, the decay rate, `step`, of the step sizes is determined such that after `nsamples` iterations, the step size would have decayed to a value close to zero. The third highlighted code snippet is where the stochastic gradient direction is computed and used to update the patch model. There are two things to note here. First, the images used in training are passed to the `patch_model::convert_image` function, which converts the image to a single-channel image (if it is a color image) and applies the natural logarithm to the image pixel intensities:

```
I += 1.0; log(I,I);
```

A bias value of 1 is added to each pixel before applying the logarithm since the logarithm of zero is undefined. The reason for performing this pre-processing on the training images is because log-scale images are more robust against differences in contrast and changes in illumination conditions. The following figure shows images of two faces with different degrees of contrast in the facial region. The difference between the images is much less pronounced in the log-scale images than it is in the raw images.

Raw   Log Scale

The second point to note about the update equation is the subtraction of `lambda*P` from the update direction. This effectively regularizes the solution from growing too large; a procedure that is often applied in machine-learning algorithms to promote generalization to unseen data. The scaling factor `lambda` is user defined and is usually problem dependent. However, a small value typically works well for learning patch models for facial feature detection.

Generative versus discriminative patch models

Despite the ease of which discriminative patch models can be learned as described previously, it is worth considering whether generative patch models and their corresponding training regimes are simple enough to achieve similar results. The generative counterpart of the correlation patch model is the average patch. The learning objective for this model is to construct a single image patch that is as close as possible to all examples of the facial feature as measured via the least-squares criterion:

$$\min_{\mathbf{P}} \sum_{i=1}^{N} \|\mathbf{P} - \mathbf{I}_i\|_F^2$$

The solution to this problem is exactly the average of all the feature-centered training image patches. Thus, in a way, the solution afforded by this objective is far simpler.

In the following figure, a comparison is shown for the response maps obtained by cross-correlating the average and correlation patch models with an example image. The respective average and correlation patch models are also shown, where the range of pixel values is normalized for visualization purposes. Although the two patch model types exhibit some similarities, the response maps they generate differ substantially. While the correlation patch model generates response maps that are highly peaked around the feature location, the response map generated by the average patch model is overly smooth and does not strongly distinguish the feature location from those close by. Inspecting the patch models' appearance, the correlation patch model is mostly gray, which corresponds to zero in the un-normalized pixel range, with strong positive and negative values strategically placed around prominent areas of the facial feature. Thus, it preserves only those components of the training patches, useful for discriminating it from misaligned configuration, which leads to highly peaked responses. In contrast, the average patch model encodes no knowledge of misaligned data. As a result, it is not well suited to the task of facial feature localization, where the task is to discriminate an aligned image patch from locally shifted versions of itself:

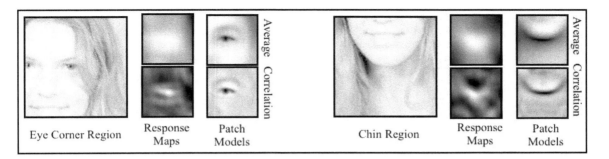

| Eye Corner Region | Response Maps | Patch Models | Average Correlation | | Chin Region | Response Maps | Patch Models | Average Correlation |

Accounting for global geometric transformations

So far, we have assumed that the training images are centered at the facial feature and are normalized with respect to global scale and rotation. In practice, the face can appear at any scale and rotation within the image during tracking. Thus, a mechanism must be devised to account for this discrepancy between the training and testing conditions. One approach is to synthetically perturb the training images in scale and rotation within the ranges one expects to encounter during deployment. However, the simplistic form of the detector as a correlation patch model often lacks the capacity to generate useful response maps for that kind of data. On the other hand, the correlation patch model does exhibit a degree of robustness against small perturbations in scale and rotation. Since motion between consecutive frames in a video sequence is relatively small, one can leverage the estimated global transformation of the face in the previous frame to normalize the current image with respect to scale and rotation. All that is needed to enable this procedure is to select a reference frame in which the correlation patch models are learned.

The `patch_models` class stores the correlation patch models for each facial feature as well as the reference frame in which they are trained. It is the `patch_models` class, rather than the `patch_model` class, that the face tracker code interfaces with directly, to obtain the feature detections. The following code snippet of the declaration of this class highlights its primary functionality:

```
class patch_models {
  public:
  Mat reference;        //reference shape [x1;y1;...;xn;yn]
  vector<patch_model> patches; //patch model/facial feature
  ...
  void train(ft_data &data,        //annotated image and shape data
    const vector<Point2f>&ref,      //reference shape
    const Size psize,              //desired patch size
    const Size ssize,              //training search window size
    const bool mirror = false,     //use mirrored training data
```

```
        const float var = 1.0,      //variance of annotation error
        const float lambda = 1e-6,  //regularisation weight
        const float mu_init = 1e-3, //initial step size
        const int nsamples = 1000,  //number of samples
        const bool visi = false);   //visualise training procedure?
        ...
        vector<Point2f>//location of peak responses/feature in image
    calc_peaks(
        const Mat &im,      //image to detect features in
        const vector<Point2f>&points, //current estimate of shape
        const Size ssize = Size(21,21)); //search window size
        ...
    };
```

The `reference` shape is stored as an interleaved set of (x, y) coordinates that are used to normalize the scale and rotation of the training images, and later, during deployment, that of the test images. In the `patch_models::train` function, this is done by first computing the similarity transform between the `reference` shape and the annotated shape for a given image using the `patch_models::calc_simil` function, which solves a similar problem to that in the `shape_model::procrustes` function, albeit for a single pair of shapes. Since the rotation and scale is common across all facial features, the image normalization procedure only requires adjusting this similarity transform to account for the centers of each feature in the image and the center of the normalized image patch. In `patch_models::train`, this is implemented as follows:

```
Mat S = this->calc_simil(pt),A(2,3,CV_32F);
A.fl(0,0) = S.fl(0,0); A.fl(0,1) = S.fl(0,1);
A.fl(1,0) = S.fl(1,0); A.fl(1,1) = S.fl(1,1);
A.fl(0,2) = pt.fl(2*i  ) - (A.fl(0,0)*(wsize.width -1)/2 +
A.fl(0,1)*(wsize.height-1)/2);
A.fl(1,2) = pt.fl(2*i+1) - (A.fl(1,0)*(wsize.width -1)/2 +
A.fl(1,1)*(wsize.height-1)/2);
Mat I; warpAffine(im,I,A,wsize,INTER_LINEAR+WARP_INVERSE_MAP);
```

Here, `wsize` is the total size of the normalized training image, which is the sum of the patch size and the search region size. As just mentioned, the top-left (2x2) block of the similarity transform from the reference shape to the annotated shape `pt`, which corresponds to the scale and rotation component of the transformation, is preserved in the affine transform passed to OpenCV's `warpAffine` function. The last column of the affine transform `A` is an adjustment that will render the ith facial feature location centered in the normalized image after warping (that is, the normalizing translation). Finally, the `cv::warpAffine` function has the default setting of warping from the image to the reference frame. Since the similarity transform was computed for transforming the `reference` shape to the image-space annotations, the `pt`, the `WARP_INVERSE_MAP` flag needs to be set to ensure the function applies the warp in the desired direction. Exactly the same procedure is performed in the `patch_models::calc_peaks` function, with the additional step that the computed similarity transform between the reference and the current shape in the image-frame is re-used to un-normalize the detected facial features, placing them appropriately in the image:

```
vector<Point2f>
patch_models::calc_peaks(const Mat &im,
const vector<Point2f>&points,const Size ssize){
int n = points.size(); assert(n == int(patches.size()));
Mat pt = Mat(points).reshape(1,2*n);
Mat S = this->calc_simil(pt);
Mat Si = this->inv_simil(S);
vector<Point2f> pts = this->apply_simil(Si,points);
for(int i = 0; i < n; i++){
  Size wsize = ssize + patches[i].patch_size();
  Mat A(2,3,CV_32F),I;
  A.fl(0,0) = S.fl(0,0); A.fl(0,1) = S.fl(0,1);
  A.fl(1,0) = S.fl(1,0); A.fl(1,1) = S.fl(1,1);
  A.fl(0,2) = pt.fl(2*i  ) - (A.fl(0,0)*(wsize.width -1)/2 +
  A.fl(0,1)*(wsize.height-1)/2);
  A.fl(1,2) = pt.fl(2*i+1) - (A.fl(1,0)*(wsize.width -1)/2 +
  A.fl(1,1)*(wsize.height-1)/2);
  warpAffine(im,I,A,wsize,INTER_LINEAR+WARP_INVERSE_MAP);
  Mat R = patches[i].calc_response(I,false);
  Point maxLoc; minMaxLoc(R,0,0,0,&maxLoc);
  pts[i] = Point2f(pts[i].x + maxLoc.x - 0.5*ssize.width,
  pts[i].y + maxLoc.y - 0.5*ssize.height);
} return this->apply_simil(S,pts);
```

In the first highlighted code snippet in the preceding code, both the forward and inverse similarity transforms are computed. The reason why the inverse transform is required here is so that the peaks of the response map for each feature can be adjusted according to the normalized locations of the current shape estimate. This must be performed before reapplying the similarity transform to place the new estimates of the facial feature locations back into the image frame using the
`patch_models::apply_simil` function.

Training and visualization

An example program for training the patch models from the annotation data can be found in `train_patch_model.cpp`. With the command-line argument `argv[1]` containing the path to the annotation data, training begins by loading the data into memory and removing incomplete samples:

```
ft_data data = load_ft<ft_data>(argv[1]);
data.rm_incomplete_samples();
```

The simplest choice for the reference shape in the `patch_models` class is the average shape of the training set, scaled to a desired size. Assuming that a shape model has previously been trained for this dataset, the reference shape is computed by first loading the shape model stored in `argv[2]` as follows:

```
shape_model smodel = load_ft<shape_model>(argv[2]);
```

This is followed by the computation of the scaled-centered average shape:

```
smodel.p = Scalar::all(0.0);
smodel.p.fl(0) = calc_scale(smodel.V.col(0),width);
vector<Point2f> r = smodel.calc_shape();
```

The `calc_scale` function computes the scaling factor to transform the average shape (that is, the first column of `shape_model::V`) to one with a width of `width`. Once the reference shape `r` is defined, training the set of patch models can be done with a single function call:

```
patch_models pmodel;
pmodel.train(data,r,Size(psize,psize),Size(ssize,ssize));
```

The optimal choices for the parameters `width`, `psize`, and `ssize` are application dependent; however, the default values of 100, 11, and 11, respectively, give reasonable results in general.

Although the training process is quite simple, it can still take some time to complete. Depending on the number of facial features, the size of the patches, and the number of stochastic samples in the optimization algorithm, the training process can take anywhere from between a few minutes to over an hour. However, since the training of each patch can be performed independently of all others, this process can be sped up substantially by parallelizing the training process across multiple processorcores or machines.

Once training has been completed, the program in `visualize_patch_model.cpp` can be used to visualize the resulting patch models. As with the `visualize_shape_model.cpp` program, the aim here is to visually inspect the results to verify if anything went wrong during the training process. The program generates a composite image of all the patch models, `patch_model::P`, each centered at their respective feature location in the reference shape, `patch_models::reference`, and displaying a bounding rectangle around the patch whose index is currently active. The `cv::waitKey` function is used to get user input for selecting the activee patch index and terminating the program. The following image shows three examples of composite patch images learned for patch models with varying spatial support. Despite using the same training data, modifying the spatial support of the patch model appears to change the structure of the patch models substantially. Visually inspecting the results in this way can lend intuition into how to modify the parameters of the training process, or even the training process itself, in order to optimize results for a particular application:

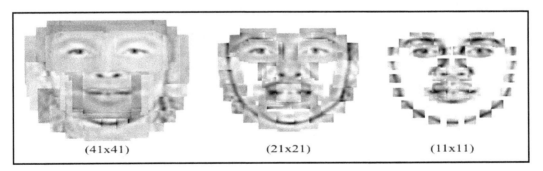

(41x41)　　　　　(21x21)　　　　　(11x11)

Face detection and initialization

The method for face tracking described thus far has assumed that the facial features in the image are located within a reasonable proximity to the current estimate. Although this assumption is reasonable during tracking, where face motion between frames is often quite small, we are still faced with the dilemma of how to initialize the model in the first frame of the sequence. An obvious choice for this is to use OpenCV's in-built cascade detector to find the face. However, the placement of the model within the detected bounding box will depend on the selection made for the facial features to track. In keeping with the data-driven paradigm we have followed so far in this chapter, a simple solution is to learn the geometrical relationship between the face detection's bounding box and the facial features.

The `face_detector` class implements exactly this solution. A snippet of its declaration that highlights its functionality is given as follows:

```
class face_detector{ //face detector for initialisation
  public:
  string detector_fname; //file containing cascade classifier
  Vec3f detector_offset; //offset from center of detection
  Mat reference;         //reference shape
  CascadeClassifier detector; //face detector

  vector<Point2f>  //points describing detected face in image
  detect(const Mat &im,          //image containing face
    const float scaleFactor = 1.1,//scale increment
    const int minNeighbours = 2,  //minimum neighborhood size
  const Size minSize = Size(30,30));//minimum window size

  void train(ft_data &data,          //training data
    const string fname,              //cascade detector
    const Mat &ref,                  //reference shape
    const bool mirror = false,       //mirror data?
    const bool visi = false,         //visualize training?
    const float frac = 0.8,          //fraction of points in detection
    const float scaleFactor = 1.1,   //scale increment
    const int minNeighbours = 2,     //minimum neighbourhood size
  const Size minSize = Size(30,30)); //minimum window size
  ...
};
```

The class has four public member variables: the path to an object of type
`cv::CascadeClassifier` called `detector_fname`, a set of offsets from a detection
bounding box to the location and scale of the face in the image `detector_offset`, a
reference shape to place in the bounding box `reference`, and a face detector `detector`.
The primary function of use to a face-tracking system is `face_detector::detect`, which
takes an image as the input, along with standard options for the `cv::CascadeClassifier`
class, and returns a rough estimate of the facial feature locations in the image. Its
implementation is as follows:

```
Mat gray; //convert image to grayscale and histogram equalize
if(im.channels() == 1)   gray = im;
else                     cvtColor(im,gray,CV_RGB2GRAY);
Mat eqIm; equalizeHist(gray,eqIm);
vector<Rect> faces; //detect largest face in image
detector.detectMultiScale(eqIm,faces,scaleFactor, minNeighbours,0
  |CV_HAAR_FIND_BIGGEST_OBJECT
  |CV_HAAR_SCALE_IMAGE,minSize);
if(faces.size() < 1) { return vector<Point2f>(); }

Rect R = faces[0]; Vec3f scale = detector_offset*R.width;
  int n = reference.rows/2; vector<Point2f> p(n);
  for(int i = 0; i < n; i++){ //predict face placement
    p[i].x = scale[2]*reference.fl(2*i  ) + R.x + 0.5 * R.width  +
    scale[0];
    p[i].y = scale[2]*reference.fl(2*i+1) + R.y + 0.5 * R.height +
    scale[1];
  } return p;
```

The face is detected in the image in the usual way, except that the
`CV_HAAR_FIND_BIGGEST_OBJECT` flag is set so as to enable tracking the most prominent
face in the image. The highlighted code is where the reference shape is placed in the image
in accordance with the detected face's bounding box. The `detector_offset` member
variable consists of three components: an (x, y) offset of the center of the face from the
center of the detection's bounding box, and the scaling factor that resizes the reference
shape to best fit the face in the image. All three components are a linear function of the
bounding box's width.

The linear relationship between the bounding box's width and the `detector_offset` variable is learned from the annotated dataset in the `face_detector::train` function. The learning process is started by loading the training data into memory and assigning the reference shape:

```
detector.load(fname.c_str()); detector_fname = fname; reference =
ref.clone();
```

As with the reference shape in the `patch_models` class, a convenient choice for the reference shape is the normalized average face shape in the dataset. The `cv::CascadeClassifier` is then applied to each image (and optionally its mirrored counterpart) in the dataset and the resulting detection is checked to ensure that enough annotated points lie within the detected bounding box (see the figure towards the end of this section) to prevent learning from misdetections:

```
if(this->enough_bounded_points(pt,faces[0],frac)){
  Point2f center = this->center_of_mass(pt);
  float w = faces[0].width;
  xoffset.push_back((center.x -
    (faces[0].x+0.5*faces[0].width ))/w);
  yoffset.push_back((center.y -
    (faces[0].y+0.5*faces[0].height))/w);
  zoffset.push_back(this->calc_scale(pt)/w);
}
```

If more than a fraction of `frac` of the annotated points lie within the bounding box, the linear relationship between its width and the offset parameters for that image are added as a new entry in an STL `vector` class object. Here, the `face_detector::center_of_mass` function computes the center of mass of the annotated point set for that image and the `face_detector::calc_scale` function computes the scaling factor for transforming the reference shape to the centered annotated shape. Once all images have been processed, the `detector_offset` variable is set to the median over all of the image-specific offsets:

```
Mat X = Mat(xoffset),Xsort,Y = Mat(yoffset),Ysort,Z =
  Mat(zoffset),Zsort;
cv::sort(X,Xsort,CV_SORT_EVERY_COLUMN|CV_SORT_ASCENDING);
int nx = Xsort.rows;
cv::sort(Y,Ysort,CV_SORT_EVERY_COLUMN|CV_SORT_ASCENDING);
int ny = Ysort.rows;
cv::sort(Z,Zsort,CV_SORT_EVERY_COLUMN|CV_SORT_ASCENDING);
int nz = Zsort.rows;
detector_offset =
  Vec3f(Xsort.fl(nx/2),Ysort.fl(ny/2),Zsort.fl(nz/2));
```

As with the *shape and patch* models, the simple program in `train_face_detector.cpp` is an example of how a `face_detector` object can be built and saved for later use in the tracker. It first loads the annotation data and the shape model, and sets the reference shape as the mean-centered average of the training data (that is, the identity shape of the `shape_model` class):

```
ft_data data = load_ft<ft_data>(argv[2]);
shape_model smodel = load_ft<shape_model>(argv[3]);
smodel.set_identity_params();
vector<Point2f> r = smodel.calc_shape();
Mat ref = Mat(r).reshape(1,2*r.size());
```

Training and saving the face detector, then, consists of two function calls:

```
face_detector detector;
detector.train(data,argv[1],ref,mirror,true,frac);
save_ft<face_detector>(argv[4],detector);
```

To test the performance of the resulting shape-placement procedure, the program in `visualize_face_detector.cpp` calls the `face_detector::detect` function for each image in the video or camera input stream and draws the results on screen. An example of the results using this approach is shown in the following figure. Although the placed shape does not match the individual in the image, its placement is close enough so that face tracking can proceed using the approach described in the following section:

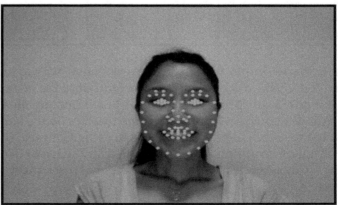

Training Image   Test Image

Face tracking

The problem of face tracking can be posed as that of finding an efficient and robust way to combine the independent detections of various facial features with the geometrical dependencies they exhibit in order to arrive at an accurate estimate of facial feature locations in each image of a sequence. With this in mind, it is perhaps worth considering whether geometrical dependencies are at all necessary. In the following figure, the results of detecting the facial features with and without geometrical constraints are shown. These results clearly highlight the benefit of capturing the spatial inter-dependencies between facial features. The relative performance of these two approaches is typical, whereby relying strictly on the detections leads to overly noisy solutions. The reason for this is that the response maps for each facial feature cannot be expected to always peak at the correct location. Whether due to image noise, lighting changes, or expression variation, the only way to overcome the limitations of facial feature detectors is by leveraging the geometrical relationship they share with each other:

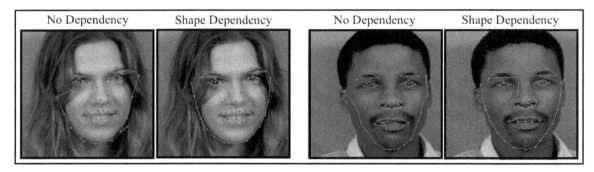

A particularly simple, but surprisingly effective, way to incorporate facial geometry into the tracking procedure is by projecting the output of the feature detections onto the linear shape model's subspace. This amounts to minimizing the distance between the original points and their closest plausible shape that lies on the subspace. Thus, when the spatial noise in the feature detections is close to being Gaussian distributed, the projection yields the most likely solution. In practice, the distribution of detection errors on occasion does not follow a Gaussian distribution and additional mechanisms need to be introduced to account for this.

Face tracker implementation

An implementation of the face-tracking algorithm can be found in the `face_tracker` class (see `face_tracker.cpp` and `face_tracker.hpp`). The following code is a snippet of its header that highlights its primary functionality:

```
class face_tracker{
  public:
  bool tracking;          //are we in tracking mode?
  fps_timer timer;        //frames/second timer
  vector<Point2f> points; //current tracked points
  face_detector detector; //detector for initialisation
  shape_model smodel;     //shape model
  patch_models pmodel;    //feature detectors

  face_tracker(){tracking = false;}

  int                         //0 = failure
  track(const Mat &im,        //image containing face
  const face_tracker_params &p =  //fitting parameters
  face_tracker_params());     //default tracking parameters

  void
  reset(){
    //reset tracker
    tracking = false; timer.reset();
  }
  ...
  protected:
  ...
  vector<Point2f>    //points for fitted face in image
  fit(const Mat &image,//image containing face
  const vector<Point2f>&init,    //initial point estimates
  const Size ssize = Size(21,21),//search region size
  const bool robust = false,     //use robust fitting?
  const int itol = 10,     //maximum number of iterations
  const float ftol = 1e-3);      //convergence tolerance
};
```

The class has public member instances of the `shape_model`, `patch_models`, and `face_detector` classes. It uses the functionality of these three classes to effect tracking. The `timer` variable is an instance of the `fps_timer` class that keeps track of the frame rate at which the `face_tracker::track` function is called and is useful for analyzing the effects patch and shape model configurations on the computational complexity of the algorithm. The `tracking` member variable is a flag to indicate the current state of the tracking procedure. When this flag is set to `false`, as it is in the constructor and the `face_tracker::reset` function, the tracker enters a detection mode whereby the `face_detector::detect` function is applied to the next incoming image to initialize the model. When in the tracking mode, the initial estimate used for inferring facial feature locations in the next incoming image is simply their location in the previous frame. The complete tracking algorithm is implemented simply as follows:

```
int face_tracker::
track(const Mat &im,const face_tracker_params &p) {
  Mat gray; //convert image to grayscale
  if(im.channels()==1)  gray=im;
  else                  cvtColor(im,gray,CV_RGB2GRAY);
  if(!tracking) //initialize
  points = detector.detect(gray,p.scaleFactor,
    p.minNeighbours,p.minSize);
  if((int)points.size() != smodel.npts()) return 0;
  for(int level = 0; level < int(p.ssize.size()); level++)
  points = this->fit(gray,points,p.ssize[level],
    p.robust,p.itol,p.ftol);
  tracking = true; timer.increment();  return 1;
}
```

Other than bookkeeping operations, such as setting the appropriate `tracking` state and incrementing the tracking time, the core of the tracking algorithm is the multi-level fitting procedure, which is highlighted in the preceding code snippet. The fitting algorithm, implemented in the `face_tracker::fit` function, is applied multiple times with the different search window sizes stored in `face_tracker_params::ssize`, where the output of the previous stage is used as input to the next. In its simplest setting, the `face_tracker_params::ssize` function performs the facial feature detection around the current estimate of the shape in the image:

```
smodel.calc_params(init);
vector<Point2f> pts = smodel.calc_shape();
vector<Point2f> peaks = pmodel.calc_peaks(image,pts,ssize);
```

It also projects the result onto the face shape's subspace:

```
smodel.calc_params(peaks);
pts = smodel.calc_shape();
```

To account for gross outliers in the facial features' detected locations, a robust model's fitting procedure can be employed instead of a simple projection by setting the robust flag to true. However, in practice, when using a decaying search window size (that is, as set in face_tracker_params::ssize), this is often unnecessary as gross outliers typically remain far from its corresponding point in the projected shape, and will likely lie outside the search region of the next level of the fitting procedure. Thus, the rate at which the search region size is reduced acts as an incremental outlier rejection scheme.

Training and visualization

Unlike the other classes detailed in this chapter, training a face_tracker object does not involve any learning process. It is implemented in train_face_tracker.cpp simply as:

```
face_tracker tracker;
tracker.smodel = load_ft<shape_model>(argv[1]);
tracker.pmodel = load_ft<patch_models>(argv[2]);
tracker.detector = load_ft<face_detector>(argv[3]);
save_ft<face_tracker>(argv[4],tracker);
```

Here arg[1] to argv[4] contain the paths to the shape_model, patch_model, face_detector, and face_tracker objects, respectively. The visualization for the face tracker in visualize_face_tracker.cpp is equally simple. Obtaining its input image stream either from a camera or video file, through the cv::VideoCapture class, the program simply loops until the end of the stream or until the user presses the Q key, tracking each frame as it comes in. The user also has the option of resetting the tracker by pressing the D key at any time.

Generic versus person-specific models

There are a number of variables in the training and tracking process that can be tweaked to optimize the performance for a given application. However, one of the primary determinants of tracking quality is the range of shape and appearance variability the tracker has to model. As a case in point, consider the generic versus person-specific case. A generic model is trained using annotated data from multiple identities, expressions, lighting conditions, and other sources of variability. In contrast, person-specific models are trained specifically for a single individual. Thus, the amount of variability it needs to account for is far smaller. As a result, person-specific tracking is often more accurate than its generic counter part by a large magnitude.

An illustration of this is shown in the following image. Here the generic model was trained using the MUCT dataset. The person-specific model was learned from data generated using the annotation tool described earlier in this chapter. The results clearly show a substantially better tracking offered by the person-specific model, capable of capturing complex expressions and head-pose changes, whereas the generic model appears to struggle even for some of the simpler expressions:

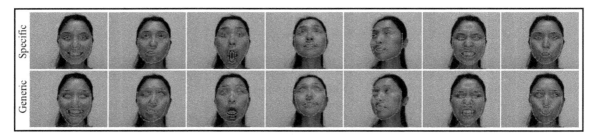

It should be noted that the method for face tracking described in this chapter is a bare-bones approach that serves to highlight the various components utilized in most non-rigid face-tracking algorithms. The numerous approaches to remedy some of the drawbacks of this method are beyond the scope of this book and require specialized mathematical tools that are not yet supported by OpenCV's functionality. The relatively few commercial-grade face-tracking software packages available are testament to the difficulty of this problem in the general setting. Nonetheless, the simple approach described in this chapter can work remarkably well in constrained settings.

Summary

In this chapter, we have built a simple face tracker that can work reasonably in constrained settings using only modest mathematical tools and OpenCV's substantial functionality for basic image processing and linear algebraic operations. Improvements to this simple tracker can be achieved by employing more sophisticated techniques in each of the three components of the tracker: the shape model, the feature detectors, and the fitting algorithm. The modular design of the tracker described in this section should allow these three components to be modified without substantial disruptions to the functionality of the others.

References

- *Procrustes Problems, Gower, John C. and Dijksterhuis, Garmt B, Oxford University Press, 2004.*

5

3D Head Pose Estimation Using AAM and POSIT

A good computer vision algorithm can't be complete without great, robust capabilities, as well as wide generalization and a solid math foundation. All these features accompany the work mainly developed by Timothy Cootes with Active Appearance Models. This chapter will teach you how to create an **Active Appearance Model (AAM)** of your own using OpenCV as well as how to use it to search for the closest position your model is located at in a given frame. Besides, you will learn how to use the POSIT algorithm and how to fit your 3D model in the *posed* image. With all these tools, you will be able to track a 3D model in a video, in real time--ain't it great? Although the examples focus on head pose, virtually any deformable model could use the same approach.

This chapter will cover the following topics:

- Active Appearance Models overview
- Active Shape Models overview
- Model instantiation--playing with the Active Appearance Model
- AAM search and fitting
- POSIT

The following list has an explanation of the terms that you will come across in the chapter:

- **Active Appearance Model (AAM)**: This is an object model containing statistical information of its shape and texture. It is a powerful way of capturing shape and texture variation from objects.
- **Active Shape Model (ASM)**: This is a statistical model of the shape of an object. It is very useful for learning shape variation.

- **Principal Component Analysis** (**PCA**): This is an orthogonal linear transformation that transforms the data to a new coordinate system, such that the greatest variance by any projection of the data comes to lie on the first coordinate (called the first principal component), the second greatest variance on the second coordinate, and so on. This procedure is often used in dimensionality reduction. When reducing the dimension of the original problem, one can use a faster fitting algorithm.

- **Delaunay Triangulation (DT)**: For a set of P points in a plane, it is a triangulation such that no point in P is inside the circumcircle of any triangle in the triangulation. It tends to avoid skinny triangles. The triangulation is required for texture mapping.

- **Affine transformation**: This is any transformation that can be expressed in the form of a matrix multiplication followed by a vector addition. This can be used for texture mapping.

- **Pose from Orthography and Scaling with Iterations** (**POSIT**): This is a computer vision algorithm that performs 3D pose estimation.

Active Appearance Models overview

In few words, Active Appearance Models are a nice model parameterization of combined texture and shape, coupled to an efficient search algorithm that can tell exactly where and how a model is located in a picture frame. In order to do this, we will start with the *Active Shape Models* section and see that they are more closely related to landmark positions. A Principal Component Analysis and some hands-on experience will be better described in the following sections. Then, we will be able to get some help from OpenCV's Delaunay functions and learn some triangulation. From that, we will evolve to applying piecewise affine warps in the triangle texture warping section, where we can get information from an object's texture.

As we get enough background to build a good model, we can play with the techniques in the model instantiation section. We will then be able to solve the inverse problem through AAM search and fitting. These, by themselves, are already very useful algorithms for 2D and maybe even 3D image matching. However, when one is able to get it to work, why not bridge it to **POSIT** (**Pose from Orthography and Scaling with Iterations**), another rock-solid algorithm for 3D model fitting? Diving into the POSIT section will give us enough background to work with it in OpenCV, and you will then learn how to couple a head model to it, in the following section. This way, we can use a 3D model to fit the already matched 2D frame.

If you want to know where this will take us, it is just a matter of combining AAM and POSIT in a frame-by-frame fashion to get real-time 3D tracking by detection for deformable models! These details will be covered in the tracking from the webcam or video file section.

It is said that a picture is worth a thousand words; imagine if we get N pictures. This way, what we previously mentioned is easily tracked in the following screenshot:

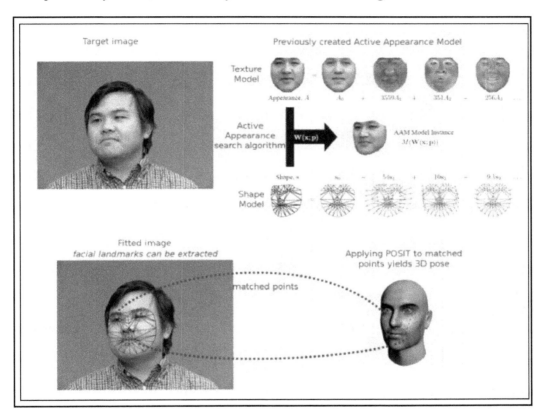

Overview of the chapter algorithms

Given an image (upper-left image in the preceding screenshot), we can use an Active Appearance search algorithm to find the 2D pose of the human head. The top-right figure in the screenshot shows a previously trained Active Appearance model used in the search algorithm. After a pose has been found, POSIT can be applied to extend the result to a 3D pose. If the procedure is applied to a video sequence, 3D tracking by detection will be obtained.

Active Shape Models

As mentioned earlier, AAMs require a shape model, and this role is played by Active Shape Models (ASMs). In the upcoming sections, we will create an ASM that is a statistical model of shape variation. The shape model is generated through the combination of shape variations. A training set of labeled images is required, as described in the article *Active Shape Models--Their Training and Application*, by Timothy Cootes. In order to build a face-shape model, several images marked with points on key positions of a face are required to outline the main features. The following screenshot shows such an example:

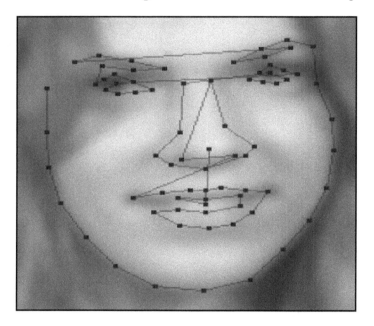

There are 76 landmarks on a face, which are taken from the **MUCT** dataset. These landmarks are usually marked up by hand, and they outline several face features such as mouth contour, nose, eyes, eyebrows, and face shape, since they are easier to track.

 Procrustes Analysis: A form of statistical shape analysis used to analyze the distribution of a set of shapes. Procrustes superimposition is performed by optimally translating, rotating, and uniformly scaling the objects.

If we have the previously mentioned set of images, we can generate a statistical model of shape variation. Since the labeled points on an object describe the shape of that object, we will first align all the sets of points into a coordinate frame using Procrustes Analysis, if required, and represent each shape by a vector, *x*. Then, we will apply Principal Component Analysis to the data. We can then approximate any example using the following formula:

$x = x + Ps\ bs$

In the preceding formula, *x* is the mean shape, *Ps* is a set of orthogonal modes of variation, and *bs* is a set of shape parameters. Well, in order to understand this better, we will create a simple application in the rest of this section, which will show us how to deal with PCA and shape models.

Why use PCA at all? Because PCA is going to really help us when it comes to reducing the number of parameters of our model. We will also see how much that helps when searching for it in a given image later in this chapter. The following is said about PCA (http://en.wikipedia.org/wiki/Principal_component_analysis):

> *PCA can supply the user with a lower-dimensional picture, a shadow of this object when viewed from its (in some sense) most informative viewpoint. This is done by using only the first few principal components so that the dimensionality of the transformed data is reduced.*

This becomes clear when we see the following figure:

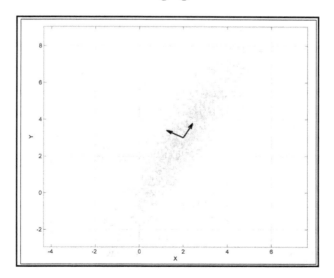

Image source: http://en.wikipedia.org/wiki/File:GaussianScatterPCA.png

The preceding figure shows the PCA of a multivariate Gaussian distribution centered at *(2,3)*. The vectors shown are the eigenvectors of the covariance matrix, shifted so their tails are at the mean.

This way, if we wanted to represent our model with a single parameter, taking the direction from the eigenvector that points to the upper-right part of the screenshot would be a good idea. Besides, by varying the parameter a bit, we can extrapolate data and get values similar to the ones we are looking for.

Getting the feel of PCA

In order to get a feeling of how PCA could help us with our face model, we will start with an Active Shape Model and test some parameters.

Since face detection and tracking have been studied for a while, several face databases are available online for research purposes. We will use a couple of samples from the IMM database.

First, let's understand how the PCA class works in OpenCV. We can conclude from the documentation that the PCA class is used to compute a special basis for a set of vectors, which consist of eigenvectors of the covariance matrix computed from the input set of vectors. This class can also transform vectors to and from the new coordinate space, using project and **backproject** methods. This new coordinate system can be quite accurately approximated by taking just the first few of its components. This means, we can represent the original vector from a high-dimensional space with a much shorter vector consisting of the projected vector's coordinates in the subspace.

Since we want a parameterization in terms of a few scalar values, the main method we will use from the class is the backproject method. It takes principal component coordinates of projected vectors and reconstructs the original ones. We could retrieve the original vectors if we retained all the components, but the difference will be very small if we just use a couple of components; that's one of the reasons for using PCA. Since we want some variability around the original vectors, our parameterized scalars will be able to extrapolate the original data.

Besides, the PCA class can transform vectors to and from the new coordinate space, defined by the basis. Mathematically, it means that we compute projection of the vector to a subspace formed by a few eigenvectors corresponding to the dominant eigenvalues of the covariance matrix, as one can see from the documentation.

Our approach will be annotating our face images with landmarks yielding a training set for our **Point Distribution Model** (PDM). If we have k-aligned landmarks in two dimensions, our shape description will look like this:

$X = \{ x1, y1, x2, y2, ..., xk, yk\}$

It's important to note that we need consistent labeling across all image samples. So, for instance, if the left part of the mouth is landmark number 3 in the first image, it will need to be number 3 in all other images.

These sequences of landmarks will now form the shape outlines, and a given training shape can be defined as a vector. We generally assume this scattering is Gaussian in this space, and we use PCA to compute normalized eigenvectors and eigenvalues of the covariance matrix across all training shapes. Using the top-center eigenvectors, we will create a matrix of dimensions $2k * m$, which we will call P. This way, each eigenvector describes a principal mode of variation along the set.

Now, we can define a new shape through the following equation:

$X' = X' + Pb$

Here, X' is the mean shape across all training images--we just average each of the landmarks--and b is a vector of scaling values for each principal component. This leads us to create a new shape modifying the value of b. It's common to set b to vary within three standard deviations so that the generated shape can fall inside the training set.

The following screenshot shows point-annotated mouth landmarks for three different pictures:

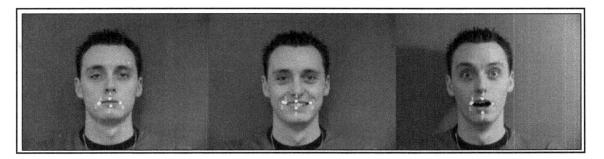

As can be seen in the preceding screenshot, the shapes are described by their landmark sequences. One could use a program such as *GIMP* or *ImageJ* as well as building a simple application in OpenCV in order to annotate the training images. We will assume the user has completed this process and saved the points as sequences of *x* and *y* landmark positions for all training images in a text file, which will be used in our PCA analysis. We will then add two parameters to the first line of this file, which is the number of training images and the number of read columns. So, for *k* 2D points, this number will be 2*k*.

In the following data, we have an instance of this file, which was obtained through the annotation of three images from IMM database, in which *k* is equal to 5:

```
3 10
265 311 303 321 337 310 302 298 265 311
255 315 305 337 346 316 305 309 255 315
262 316 303 342 332 315 298 299 262 316
```

Now that we have annotated images, let's turn this data into our shape model. First, load this data into a matrix. This will be achieved through the `loadPCA` function. The following code snippet shows the use of the `loadPCA` function:

```cpp
PCA loadPCA(char* fileName, int& rows, int& cols,Mat& pcaset){
    FILE* in = fopen(fileName,"r");
    int a;
    fscanf(in,"%d%d",&rows,&cols);

    pcaset = Mat::eye(rows,cols,CV_64F);
    int i,j;


    for(i=0;i<rows;i++){
        for(j=0;j<cols;j++){
            fscanf(in,"%d",&a);
            pcaset.at<double>(i,j) = a;
        }
    }


    PCA pca(pcaset, // pass the data
        Mat(), // we do not have a pre-computed mean vector,
        // so let the PCA engine compute it
        CV_PCA_DATA_AS_ROW, // indicate that the vectors
        // are stored as matrix rows
        // (use CV_PCA_DATA_AS_COL if the vectors are
        // the matrix columns)
        pcaset.cols// specify, how many principal components to retain
    );
    return pca;
```

```
        }
```

Note that our matrix is created in the `pcaset = Mat::eye(rows,cols,CV_64F)` line and that enough space is allocated for *2*k* values. After the two `for` loops load the data into the matrix, the PCA constructor is called with the data, an empty matrix, that could be our precomputed mean vector, if we wish to make it only once. We also indicate that our vectors will be stored as matrix rows and that we wish to keep the same number of given rows as the number of components, though we could use just a few ones.

Now that we have filled our PCA object with our training set, it has everything it needs to back project our shape according to the parameters. We do so by invoking `PCA.backproject`, passing the parameters as a row vector, and receiving the back projected vector into the second argument:

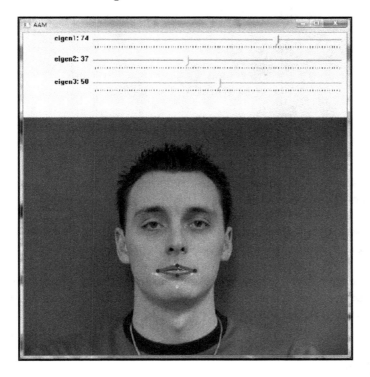

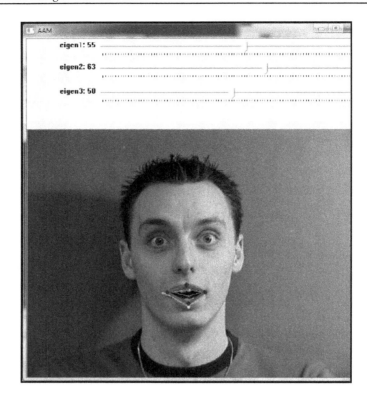

The two previous screenshots show two different shape configurations according to the selected parameters chosen from the slider. The yellow and green shapes show training data, while the red one reflects the shape generated from the chosen parameters. A sample program can be used to experiment with Active Shape Models, as it allows the user to try different parameters for the model. One is able to note that varying only the first two scalar values through the slider (which correspond to the first and second modes of variation), we can achieve a shape that is very close to the trained ones. This variability will help us when searching for a model in AAM, since it provides interpolated shapes. We will discuss triangulation, texturing, AAM, and AAM search in the following sections.

Triangulation

As the shape we are looking for might be distorted, such as an open mouth for instance, we are required to map our texture back to a mean shape and then apply PCA to this normalized texture. In order to do this, we will use triangulation. The concept is very simple: we will create triangles including our annotated points and then map from one triangle to another.

OpenCV comes with a handy class called `Subdiv2D`, which deals with Delaunay Triangulation. You can just consider this a good triangulation that will avoid skinny triangles.

 In mathematics and computational geometry, a Delaunay Triangulation for a set *P* of points in a plane is a triangulation DT(P) such that no point in *P* is inside the circumcircle of any triangle in DT(P). Delaunay Triangulations maximize the minimum angle of all the angles of the triangles in the triangulation; they tend to avoid skinny triangles. The triangulation is named after Boris Delaunay for his work on this topic from 1934 onwards.

After a Delaunay subdivision has been created, one will use the `insert` member function to populate points into the subdivision. The following lines of code will elucidate what a direct use of triangulation would be like:

```
Subdiv2D* subdiv;
CvRect rect = { 0, 0, 640, 480 };

subdiv = new Subdiv2D(rect);

std::vector<CvPoint> points;

//initialize points somehow
...

//iterate through points inserting them in the subdivision
for(int i=0;i<points.size();i++){
  float x = points.at(i).x;
  float y = points.at(i).y;
  Point2f fp(x, y);
  subdiv->insert(fp);
}
```

Note that our points are going to be inside a rectangular frame that is passed as a parameter to `Subdiv2D`. In order to create a subdivision, we need to instantiate the `Subdiv2D` class, as seen earlier. Then, in order to create the triangulation, we need to insert points using the insert method from `Subdiv2D`. This happens inside the `for` loop in the preceding code. Note that the points should already have been initialized, since they are the ones we'll usually be using as inputs.

The following diagram shows what the triangulation could look like:

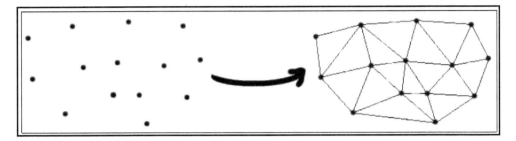

This diagram is the output of the preceding code for a set of points that yield the triangulation using Delaunay algorithm.

In order to iterate through all the triangles from a given subdivision, one can use the following code:

```
vector<Vec6f> triangleList;

subdiv->getTriangleList(triangleList);
vector<Point> pt(3);

for( size_t i = 0; i < triangleList.size(); i++ )
{
  Vec6f t = triangleList[i];
  pt[0] = Point(cvRound(t[0]), cvRound(t[1]));
  pt[1] = Point(cvRound(t[2]), cvRound(t[3]));
  pt[2] = Point(cvRound(t[4]), cvRound(t[5]));
}
```

Given a subdivision, we will initialize its `triangleList` through a `Vec6f` vector, which will save space for each set of three points, which can be obtained iterating `triangleList`, as shown in the preceding `for` loop.

Triangle texture warping

Now that we've been able to iterate through the triangles of a subdivision, we are able to warp one triangle from an original annotated image into a generated distorted one. This is useful for mapping the texture from the original shape to a distorted one.

The following piece of code will guide the process:

```
    void warpTextureFromTriangle(Point2f srcTri[3], Mat originalImage,
Point2f dstTri[3], Mat warp_final){

    Mat warp_mat(2, 3, CV_32FC1);
    Mat warp_dst, warp_mask;
    CvPoint trianglePoints[3];
    trianglePoints[0] = dstTri[0];
    trianglePoints[1] = dstTri[1];
    trianglePoints[2] = dstTri[2];
    warp_dst  = Mat::zeros(originalImage.rows, originalImage.cols,
originalImage.type());
    warp_mask = Mat::zeros(originalImage.rows, originalImage.cols,
originalImage.type());

    /// Get the Affine Transform
    warp_mat = getAffineTransform(srcTri, dstTri);

    /// Apply the Affine Transform to the src image
    warpAffine(originalImage, warp_dst, warp_mat, warp_dst.size());
    cvFillConvexPoly(new IplImage(warp_mask), trianglePoints, 3,
CV_RGB(255,255,255), CV_AA, 0);
    warp_dst.copyTo(warp_final, warp_mask);
    }
```

The preceding code assumes we have the triangle vertices packed in the `srcTri` array and the destination one packed in the `dstTri` array. The 2x3 `warp_mat` matrix is used to get the Affine transformation from the source triangles to the destination ones. More information can be quoted from OpenCV's *cvGetAffineTransform* documentation:

The `cvGetAffineTransform` function calculates the matrix of an affine transform in the following way:

$$\begin{bmatrix} x'_i \\ y'_i \end{bmatrix} = \texttt{mapMatrix} \cdot \begin{bmatrix} x_i \\ y_i \\ 1 \end{bmatrix}$$

In the preceding equation, destination *(i)* is equal to *(xi',yi')*, source *(i)* is equal to *(xi, yi)*, and *i* is equal to *0, 1, 2*.

After retrieving the affine matrix, we can apply the Affine transformation to the source image. This is done through the `warpAffine` function. Since we don't want to do it in the entire image, we want to focus on our triangle, a mask can be used for this task. This way, the last line copies only the triangle from our original image with the mask we just created, which was made through a `cvFillConvexPoly` call.

The following screenshot shows the result of applying this procedure to every triangle in an annotated image. Note that the triangles are mapped back to the alignment frame, which faces toward the viewer. This procedure is used to create the statistical texture of the AAM:

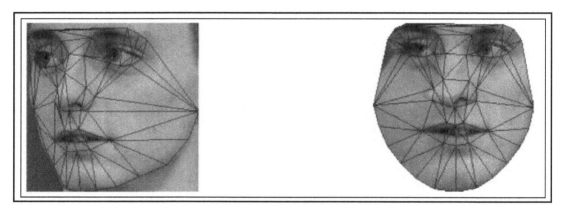

The preceding screenshot shows the result of warping all the mapped triangles in the left image to a mean reference frame.

Model Instantiation - playing with the AAM

An interesting aspect of AAMs is their ability to easily interpolate the model that we trained our images on. We can get used to their amazing representational power through the adjustment of a couple of shape or model parameters. As we vary shape parameters, the destination of our warp changes according to the trained shape data. On the other hand, while appearance parameters are modified, the texture on the base shape is modified. Our warp transforms will take every triangle from the base shape to the modified destination shape so that we can synthesize a closed mouth on top of an open mouth, as shown in the following screenshot:

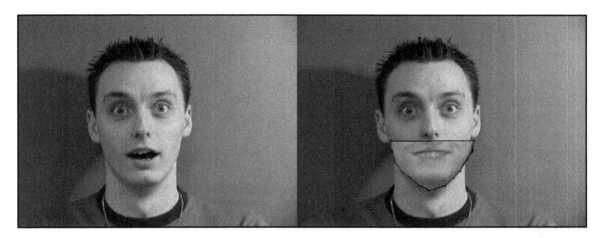

This preceding screenshot shows a synthesized closed mouth obtained through Active Appearance Model instantiation on top of another image. It shows how one could combine a smiling mouth with an admired face, extrapolating the trained images.

The preceding screenshot was obtained by changing only three parameters for shape and three for the texture, which is the goal of AAMs. A sample application has been developed and is available at http://www.packtpub.com/ for you to try out AAM. Instantiating a new model is just a question of sliding the equation parameters, as defined in the *Getting the feel of PCA* section. You should note that AAM search and fitting rely on this flexibility to find the best match for a given captured frame of our model in a different position from the trained ones. We will see this in the next section.

AAM search and fitting

With our fresh, new combined shape and texture model, we have found a nice way to describe how a face could change not only in shape, but also in appearance. Now, we want to find which set of p shape and λ appearance parameters will bring our model as close as possible to a given input image $I(x)$. We could naturally calculate the error between our instantiated model and the given input image in the coordinate frame of $I(x)$, or map the points back to the base appearance and calculate the difference there. We are going to use the latter approach. This way, we want to minimize the following function:

$$\sum_{\mathbf{x} \in s_0} \left[A_0(\mathbf{x}) + \sum_{i=1}^{m} \lambda_i A_i(\mathbf{x}) - I(\mathbf{W}(\mathbf{x}; \mathbf{p})) \right]^2$$

In the preceding equation, *S0* denotes the set of pixels *x* is equal to *(x,y)T* that lie inside the AAMs base mesh, *A0(x)* is our base mesh texture, *Ai(x)* is appearance images from PCA, and *W(x;p)* is the warp that takes pixels from the input image back to the base mesh frame.

Several approaches have been proposed for this minimization through years of studying. The first idea was to use an additive approach, in which Δpi and $\Delta \lambda i$ were calculated as linear functions of the error image and then the shape parameter *p* and appearance λ were updated as $pi \leftarrow pi + \Delta pi$ and $\lambda i \leftarrow \lambda i + \Delta \lambda i$, in the iteration. Although convergence can occur sometimes, the delta doesn't always depend on current parameters, and this might lead to divergence. Another approach, which was studied based on the gradient descent algorithms, was very slow, so another way of finding convergence was sought. Instead of updating the parameters, the whole warp could be updated. This way, a compositional approach was proposed by Ian Mathews and Simon Baker in a famous paper called *Active Appearance Models Revisited*. More details can be found in the paper, but the important contribution it gave to fitting was that it brought the most intensive computation to a **pre-compute** step, as seen in the following screenshot:

Pre-compute:

    (3) Evaluate the gradient ∇A_0 of the template $A_0(\mathbf{x})$

    (4) Evaluate the Jacobian $\frac{\partial \mathbf{W}}{\partial \mathbf{p}}$ at $(\mathbf{x}:0)$

    (5) Compute the modified steepest descent images using Equation (41)

    (6) Compute the Hessian matrix using modified steepest descent images

Iterate:

    (1) Warp I with $\mathbf{W}(\mathbf{x}:\mathbf{p})$ to compute $I(\mathbf{W}(\mathbf{x}:\mathbf{p}))$

    (2) Compute the error image $I(\mathbf{W}(\mathbf{x}:\mathbf{p})) - A_0(\mathbf{x})$

    (7) Compute dot product of modified steepest descent images with error image

    (8) Compute $\Delta \mathbf{p}$ by multiplying by inverse Hessian

    (9) Update the warp $\mathbf{W}(\mathbf{x}:\mathbf{p}) \leftarrow \mathbf{W}(\mathbf{x}:\mathbf{p}) \circ \mathbf{W}(\mathbf{x}:\Delta \mathbf{p})^{-1}$

Post-computation:

    (10) Compute λ_i using Equation (40). [Optional step]

Note that the update occurs in terms of a compositional step as seen in step **(9)** (see the previous screenshot). Equations (40) and (41) from the paper can be seen in the following screenshots:

$$\lambda_i = \sum_{\mathbf{x} \in s_0} A_i(\mathbf{x}) \cdot [I(\mathbf{W}(\mathbf{x}; \mathbf{p})) - A_0(\mathbf{x})], \tag{40}$$

$$SD_j(\mathbf{x}) = \nabla A_0 \frac{\partial \mathbf{W}}{\partial p_j} - \sum_{i=1}^{m} \left[\sum_{\mathbf{x} \in s_0} A_i(\mathbf{x}) \cdot \nabla A_0 \frac{\partial \mathbf{W}}{\partial p_j} \right] A_i(\mathbf{x}) \tag{41}$$

Although the algorithm just mentioned will mostly converge very well from a position near the final one, this might not be the case when there's a big difference in rotation, translation, or scale. We can bring more information to the convergence through the parameterization of a global 2D similarity transform. This is equation 42 in the paper and is shown as follows:

$$N(\mathbf{x}; \mathbf{q}) = \begin{pmatrix} (1+a) & -b \\ b & (1+a) \end{pmatrix} \begin{pmatrix} x \\ y \end{pmatrix} + \begin{pmatrix} t_x \\ t_y \end{pmatrix}$$

In the preceding equation, the four parameters $q = (a, b, t_x, t_y)$ have the following interpretations. The ﬁrst pair (a, b) is related to the scale k and rotation θ: a is equal to k $cos\ \theta$ - 1 and $b = k\ sin\ \theta$. The second pair (t_x, t_y) is the x and y translations, as proposed in the *Active Appearance Models Revisited* paper.

With a bit more of math transformations, you can finally use the preceding algorithm to find the best image fit with a global 2D transform.

As the warp compositional algorithm has several performance advantages, we will use the one described in the AAM Revisited paper: the *inverse compositional project-out algorithm*. Remember that in this method, the effect of appearance variation during fitting can be precomputed, or projected out, improving AAM fitting performance.

The following screenshot shows convergence for different images from the MUCT dataset using the inverse compositional project-out AAM fitting algorithm:

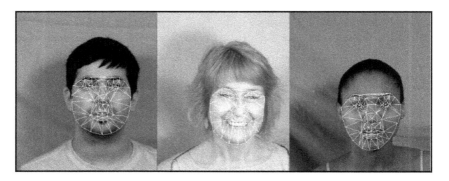

The preceding screenshot shows successful convergences, over faces outside the AAM training set-using the inverse compositional project, out AAM fitting algorithm.

POSIT

After we have found the 2D position of our landmark points, we can derive the 3D pose of our model using the POSIT. The pose P of a 3D object is defined as the 3 x 3 rotation matrix R and the 3D translation vector T; hence, P is equal to $[R \mid T]$.

 Most of this section is based on the *OpenCV POSIT* tutorial by Javier Barandiaran.

As the name implies, POSIT uses the **Pose from Orthography and Scaling** (**POS**) algorithm in several iterations, so it is an acronym for POS with iterations. The hypothesis for its working is that we can detect and match in the image four or more non-coplanar feature points of the object and that we know their relative geometry on the object.

The main idea of the algorithm is that we can find a good approximation to the object pose, supposing that all the model points are in the same plane, since their depths are not very different from one another if compared to the distance from the camera to a face. After the initial pose is obtained, the rotation matrix and translation vector of the object are found by solving a linear system. Then, the approximate pose is iteratively used to better compute scaled orthographic projections of the feature points, followed by POS application to these projections instead of the original ones. For more information, you can refer to the paper by DeMenton, *Model-Based Object Pose in 25 Lines of Code*.

Diving into POSIT

In order for POSIT to work, you need at least four non-coplanar 3D model points and their respective matchings in the 2D image. We will add a termination criteria to that, since POSIT is an iterative algorithm, which generally is a number of iterations or a distance parameter. We will then call the cvPOSIT function, included in calib3d_c.h, which yields the rotation matrix and the translation vector.

As an example, we will follow the tutorial from Javier Barandiaran, which uses POSIT to obtain the pose of a cube. The model is created with four points. It is initialized with the following code:

```
float cubeSize = 10.0;
std::vector<CvPoint3D32f> modelPoints;
modelPoints.push_back(cvPoint3D32f(0.0f, 0.0f, 0.0f));
modelPoints.push_back(cvPoint3D32f(0.0f, 0.0f, cubeSize));
modelPoints.push_back(cvPoint3D32f(cubeSize, 0.0f, 0.0f));
modelPoints.push_back(cvPoint3D32f(0.0f, cubeSize, 0.0f));
CvPOSITObject *positObject = cvCreatePOSITObject( &modelPoints[0],
    static_cast<int>(modelPoints.size()) );
```

Note that the model itself is created with the cvCreatePOSITObject method, which returns a CvPOSITObject method that will be used in the cvPOSIT function. Be aware that the pose will be calculated referring to the first model point, which makes it a good idea to put it at the origin.

We then need to put the 2D image points in another vector. Remember that they must be put in the array in the same order that the model points were inserted in; this way, the ith 2D image point matches the ith 3D model point. A catch here is that the origin for the 2D image points is located at the center of the image, which might require you to translate them. You can insert the following 2D image points (of course, they will vary according to the user's matching):

```
std::vector<CvPoint2D32f> srcImagePoints;
srcImagePoints.push_back( cvPoint2D32f( -48, -224 ) );
srcImagePoints.push_back( cvPoint2D32f( -287, -174 ) );
srcImagePoints.push_back( cvPoint2D32f( 132, -153 ) );
srcImagePoints.push_back( cvPoint2D32f( -52, 149 ) );
```

Now, you only need to allocate memory for the matrixes and create termination criteria, followed by a call to cvPOSIT, as shown in the following code snippet:

```
//Estimate the pose
float* rotation_matrix = new float[9];
float* translation_vector = new float[3];
```

```
CvTermCriteria criteria = cvTermCriteria(CV_TERMCRIT_EPS |
    CV_TERMCRIT_ITER, 100, 1.0e-4f);
cvPOSIT( positObject, &srcImagePoints[0], FOCAL_LENGTH, criteria,
    rotation_matrix, translation_vector );
```

After the iterations, `cvPOSIT` will store the results in `rotation_matrix` and `translation_vector`. The following screenshot shows the inserted `srcImagePoints` with white circles as well as a coordinate axis showing the rotation and translation results:

With reference to the preceding screenshot, let's see the following input points and results of running the POSIT algorithm:

- The white circles show input points, while the coordinate axes show the resulting model pose.
- Make sure you use the focal length of your camera as obtained through a calibration process. You might want to check one of the calibration procedures available in the *Camera calibration* section in Chapter 7, *Natural Feature Tracking for Augmented Reality*. The current implementation of POSIT will only allow square pixels, so there won't be room for focal length in the x and y axes.
- Expect the rotation matrix in the following format:
    - [rot[0] rot[1] rot[2]]
    - [rot[3] rot[4] rot[5]]
    - [rot[6] rot[7] rot[8]]

- The translation vector will be in the following format:
  - [trans[0]]
  - [trans[1]]
  - [trans[2]]

POSIT and head model

In order to use POSIT as a tool for head pose, you will need to use a 3D head model. There is one available from the Institute of Systems and Robotics of the University of Coimbra and can be found at

`http://aifi.isr.uc.pt/Downloads/OpenGL/glAnthropometric3DModel.cpp`. Note that the model can be obtained from where it says:

```
float Model3D[58][3]= {{-7.308957,0.913869,0.000000}, ...
```

The model can be seen in the following screenshot:

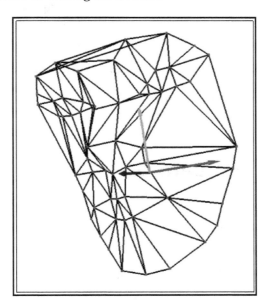

The preceding screenshot shows a 58-point 3D head model available for POSIT.

In order to get POSIT to work, the point corresponding to the 3D head model must be matched accordingly. Note that at least four non-coplanar 3D points and their corresponding 2D projections are required for POSIT to work, so these must be passed as parameters, pretty much as described in the *Diving into POSIT* section. Note that this algorithm is linear in terms of the number of matched points. The following screenshot shows how matching should be done:

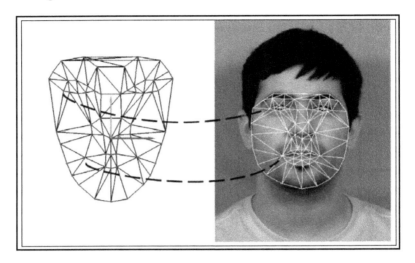

The preceding screenshot shows the correctly matched points of a 3D head model and an AAM mesh.

Tracking from webcam or video file

Now that all the tools have been assembled to get 6 degrees of freedom head tracking, we can apply it to a camera stream or video file. OpenCV provides the `VideoCapture` class that can be used in the following manner (see the *Accessing the webcam* section in `Chapter 1`, *Cartoonifier and Skin Changer for Raspberry Pi*, for more details):

```
#include "opencv2/opencv.hpp"

using namespace cv;

int main(int, char**)
{
  VideoCapture cap(0);// opens the default camera, could use a
                      // video file path instead
```

```
if(!cap.isOpened()) // check if we succeeded
  return -1;

AAM aam = loadPreviouslyTrainedAAM();
HeadModel headModel = load3DHeadModel();
Mapping mapping = mapAAMLandmarksToHeadModel();

Pose2D pose = detectFacePosition();


while(1)
{
  Mat frame;
  cap >> frame; // get a new frame from camera

  Pose2D new2DPose = performAAMSearch(pose, aam);
  Pose3D new3DPose = applyPOSIT(new2DPose, headModel, mapping);

  if(waitKey(30) >= 0) break;
}

// the camera will be deinitialized automatically in VideoCapture
// destructor
return 0;
}
```

The algorithm works like this. A video capture is initialized through `VideoCapture` `cap(0)` so that the default webcam is used. Now that we have video capture working, we also need to load our trained Active Appearance Model, which will occur in the `loadPreviouslyTrainedAAM` pseudocode mapping. We will also load the 3D head model for POSIT and the mapping of landmark points to 3D head points in our mapping variable.

After everything we need has been loaded, we will need to initialize the algorithm from a known pose, which is a known 3D position, known rotation, and a known set of AAM parameters. This could be made automatically through OpenCV's highly documented Haar features classifier face detector (more details in the *Face Detection* section of `Chapter 4`, *Nonrigid Face Tracking*, or in OpenCV's cascade classifier documentation), or we could manually initialize the pose from a previously annotated frame. A brute-force approach, which would be to run an AAM fitting for every rectangle, could also be used, since it would be very slow only during the first frame. Note that by initialization, we mean finding the 2D landmarks of the AAM through their parameters.

When everything is loaded, we can iterate through the main loop delimited by the `while` loop. In this loop, we first query the next grabbed frame, and we then run an Active Appearance Model fit so that we can find landmarks on the next frame. Since the current position is very important at this step, we pass it as a parameter to the pseudocode function `performAAMSearch(pose,aam)`. If we find the current pose, which is signaled through error image convergence, we will get the next landmark positions, so we can provide them to POSIT. This happens in the following line, `applyPOSIT(new2DPose, headModel, mapping)`, where the new 2D pose is passed as a parameter, as also our previously loaded `headModel` and the mapping. After that, we can render any 3D model in the obtained pose like a coordinate axis or an augmented reality model. As we have landmarks, more interesting effects can be obtained through model parameterization, such as opening a mouth or changing eyebrow position.

As this procedure relies on the previous pose for the next estimation, we could accumulate errors and diverge from head position. A workaround could be to reinitialize the procedure every time it happens, checking a given error image threshold. Another factor to pay attention to is the use of filters when tracking, since jittering can occur. A simple mean filter for each of the translation and rotation coordinates can give reasonable results.

Summary

In this chapter, we discussed how Active Appearance Models can be combined with the POSIT algorithm in order to obtain a 3D head pose. An overview on how to create, train, and manipulate AAMs has been given, and you can use this background for any other field, such as medical, imaging, or industry. Besides dealing with AAMs, we got familiar with Delaunay subdivisions and learned how to use such an interesting structure as a triangulated mesh. We also showed you how to perform texture mapping in the triangles using OpenCV functions. Another interesting topic was approached in AAM fitting. Although only the inverse compositional project-out algorithm was described, we could easily obtain the results of years of research by simply using its output.

After enough theory and practice of AAMs, we dived into the details of POSIT in order to couple 2D measurements to 3D ones, explaining how to fit a 3D model using matchings between model points. We concluded the chapter by showing how to use all the tools in an online face tracker by detection, which yields 6 degrees of freedom head pose-3 degrees for rotation, and 3 for translation. The complete code for this chapter can be downloaded from http://www.packtpub.com/.

References

- *Active Appearance Models, T.F. Cootes, G. J. Edwards, and C. J. Taylor, ECCV, 2:484-498, 1998* (http://www.cs.cmu.edu/~efros/courses/AP06/Papers/cootes-eccv-98.pdf)

- *Active Shape Models-Their Training and Application, T.F. Cootes, C.J. Taylor, D.H. Cooper, and J. Graham, Computer Vision and Image Understanding, (61): 38-59, 1995* (http://www.wiau.man.ac.uk/~bim/Papers/cviu95.pdf)

- *The MUCT Landmarked Face Database, S. Milborrow, J. Morkel, and F. Nicolls, Pattern Recognition Association of South Africa, 2010* (http://www.milbo.org/muct/)

- *The IMM Face Database - An Annotated Dataset of 240 Face Images, Michael M. Nordstrom, Mads Larsen, Janusz Sierakowski, and Mikkel B.Stegmann, Informatics and Mathematical Modeling, Technical University of Denmark, 2004,* (http://www2.imm.dtu.dk/~aam/datasets/datasets.html)

- *Sur la sphère vide, B. Delaunay, Izvestia Akademii Nauk SSSR, Otdelenie Matematicheskikh i Estestvennykh Nauk, 7:793-800, 1934*

- *Active Appearance Models for Facial Expression Recognition and Monocular Head Pose Estimation Master Thesis, P. Martins, 2008*

- *Active Appearance Models Revisited, International Journal of Computer Vision, Vol. 60, No. 2, pp. 135 - 164, I. Mathews and S. Baker, November, 2004* (http://www.ri.cmu.edu/pub_files/pub4/matthews_iain_2004_2/matthews_iain_2004_2.pdf)

- *POSIT Tutorial, Javier Barandiaran* (http://opencv.willowgarage.com/wiki/Posit)

- *Model-Based Object Pose in 25 Lines of Code, International Journal of Computer Vision, 15, pp. 123-141, Dementhon and L.S Davis, 1995* (http://www.cfar.umd.edu/~daniel/daniel_papersfordownload/Pose25Lines.pdf)

6
Face Recognition Using Eigenfaces or Fisherfaces

In this chapter, we cover the following:

- Face detection
- Face preprocessing
- Training a machine-learning algorithm from collected faces
- Face recognition
- Finishing touches

Introduction to face recognition and face detection

Face recognition is the process of putting a label to a known face. Just like humans learn to recognize their family, friends, and celebrities just by seeing their face, there are many techniques for a computer to learn to recognize a known face.

These generally involve four main steps:

1. **Face detection**: This is the process of locating a face region in an image (a large rectangle near the center of the following screenshot). This step does not care who the person is, just that it is a human face.

2. **Face preprocessing**: This is the process of adjusting the face image to look more clear and similar to other faces (a small grayscale face in the top-center of the following screenshot).

3. **Collecting and learning faces**: This is the process of saving many preprocessed faces (for each person that should be recognized), and then learning how to recognize them.

4. **Face recognition**: This is the process that checks which of the collected people are most similar to the face in the camera (a small rectangle on the top-right of the following screenshot).

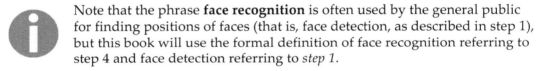

> Note that the phrase **face recognition** is often used by the general public for finding positions of faces (that is, face detection, as described in step 1), but this book will use the formal definition of face recognition referring to step 4 and face detection referring to *step 1*.

The following screenshot shows the final `WebcamFaceRec` project, including a small rectangle at the top-right corner highlighting the recognized person. Also notice the confidence bar that is next to the preprocessed face (a small face at the top-center of the rectangle marking the face), which in this case shows roughly 70 percent confidence that it has recognized the correct person:

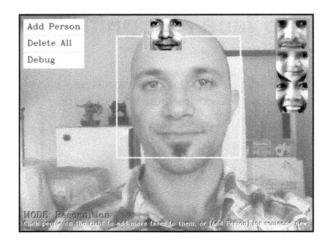

The current face detection techniques are quite reliable in real-world conditions, whereas current face recognition techniques are much less reliable when used in real-world conditions. For example, it is easy to find research papers showing face recognition accuracy rates above 95 percent, but when testing those same algorithms yourself, you may often find that accuracy is lower than 50 percent. This comes from the fact that current face recognition techniques are very sensitive to exact conditions in the images, such as the type of lighting, direction of lighting and shadows, exact orientation of the face, expression of the face, and the current mood of the person. If they are all kept constant when training (collecting images) as well as when testing (from the camera image), then face recognition should work well, but if the person was standing to the left-hand side of the lights in a room when training, and then stood to the right-hand side while testing with the camera, it may give quite bad results. So the dataset used for training is very important.

Face preprocessing (*step 2*) aims to reduce these problems, such as by making sure the face always appears to have similar brightness and contrast, and perhaps making sure the features of the face will always be in the same position (such as aligning the eyes and/or nose to certain positions). A good face preprocessing stage will help improve the reliability of the whole face recognition system, so this chapter will place some emphasis on face preprocessing methods.

Despite the big claims about face recognition for security in the media, it is unlikely that the current face recognition methods alone are reliable enough for any true security system, but they can be used for purposes that don't need high reliability, such as playing personalized music for different people entering a room or a robot that says your name when it sees you. There are also various practical extensions to face recognition, such as gender recognition, age recognition, and emotion recognition.

Step 1 - face detection

Until the year 2000, there were many different techniques used for finding faces, but all of them were either very slow, very unreliable, or both. A major change came in 2001 when Viola and Jones invented the Haar-based cascade classifier for object detection, and in 2002 when it was improved by Lienhart and Maydt. The result is an object detector that is both fast (it can detect faces in real time on a typical desktop with a VGA webcam) and reliable (it detects approximately 95 percent of frontal faces correctly). This object detector revolutionized the field of face recognition (as well as that of robotics and computer vision in general), as it finally allowed real-time face detection and face recognition, especially as Lienhart himself wrote the object detector that comes free with OpenCV! It works not only for frontal faces but also side-view faces (referred to as profile faces), eyes, mouths, noses, company logos, and many other objects.

This object detector was extended in OpenCV v2.0 to also use LBP features for detection based on work by Ahonen, Hadid, and Pietikäinen in 2006, as LBP-based detectors are potentially several times faster than Haar-based detectors, and don't have the licensing issues that many Haar detectors have.

The basic idea of the Haar-based face detector is that if you look at most frontal faces, the region with the eyes should be darker than the forehead and cheeks, and the region with the mouth should be darker than cheeks, and so on. It typically performs about 20 stages of comparisons like this to decide if it is a face or not, but it must do this at each possible position in the image and for each possible size of the face, so in fact it often does thousands of checks per image. The basic idea of the LBP-based face detector is similar to the Haar-based one, but it uses histograms of pixel intensity comparisons, such as edges, corners, and flat regions.

Rather than have a person decide which comparisons would best define a face, both Haar- and LBP-based face detectors can be automatically trained to find faces from a large set of images, with the information stored as XML files to be used later. These cascade classifier detectors are typically trained using at least 1,000 unique face images and 10,000 non-face images (for example, photos of trees, cars, and text), and the training process can take a long time even on a multi-core desktop (typically a few hours for LBP but 1week for Haar!). Luckily, OpenCV comes with some pretrained Haar and LBP detectors for you to use! In fact you can detect frontal faces, profile (side-view) faces, eyes, or noses just by loading different cascade classifier XML files to the object detector, and choose between the Haar or LBP detector, based on which XML file you choose.

Implementing face detection using OpenCV

As mentioned previously, OpenCV v2.4 comes with various, pretrained XML detectors that you can use for different purposes. The following table lists some of the most popular XML files:

Type of cascade classifier	XML filename
Face detector (default)	`haarcascade_frontalface_default.xml`
Face detector (fast Haar)	`haarcascade_frontalface_alt2.xml`
Face detector (fast LBP)	`lbpcascade_frontalface.xml`
Profile (side-looking) face detector	`haarcascade_profileface.xml`
Eye detector (separate for left and right)	`haarcascade_lefteye_2splits.xml`
Mouth detector	`haarcascade_mcs_mouth.xml`

Nose detector	`haarcascade_mcs_nose.xml`
Whole person detector	`haarcascade_fullbody.xml`

Haar-based detectors are stored in the `datahaarcascades` folder and LBP-based detectors are stored in the `datalbpcascades` folder of the OpenCV root folder, such as `C:opencvdatalbpcascades`.

For our face recognition project, we want to detect frontal faces, so let's use the LBP face detector because it is the fastest and doesn't have patent licensing issues. Note that this pretrained LBP face detector that comes with OpenCV v2.x is not tuned as well as the pretrained Haar face detectors, so if you want more reliable face detection then you may want to train your own LBP face detector or use a Haar face detector.

Loading a Haar or LBP detector for object or face detection

To perform object or face detection, first you must load the pretrained XML file using OpenCV's `CascadeClassifier` class as follows:

```
CascadeClassifier faceDetector;
faceDetector.load(faceCascadeFilename);
```

This can load Haar or LBP detectors just by giving a different filename. A very common mistake when using this is to provide the wrong folder or filename, but depending on your build environment, the `load()` method will either return `false` or generate a C++ exception (and exit your program with an assert error). So it is best to surround the `load()` method with a `try... catch` block and display a nice error message to the user if something went wrong. Many beginners skip checking for errors, but it is crucial to show a help message to the user when something did not load correctly, otherwise you may spend a very long time debugging other parts of your code before eventually realizing something did not load. A simple error message can be displayed as follows:

```
CascadeClassifier faceDetector;
try {
  faceDetector.load(faceCascadeFilename);
} catch (cv::Exception e) {}
if ( faceDetector.empty() ) {
  cerr << "ERROR: Couldn't load Face Detector (";
  cerr << faceCascadeFilename << ")!" << endl;
  exit(1);
}
```

Accessing the webcam

To grab frames from a computer's webcam or even from a video file, you can simply call the `VideoCapture::open()` function with the camera number or video filename, then grab the frames using the C++ stream operator, as mentioned in the section,*Accessing the webcam* in `Chapter 1`, *Cartoonifier and Skin Changer for Raspberry Pi.*

Detecting an object using the Haar or LBP Classifier

Now that we have loaded the classifier (just once during initialization), we can use it to detect faces in each new camera frame. But first, we should do some initial processing of the camera image just for face detection, by performing the following steps:

1. **Grayscale color conversion**: Face detection only works on grayscale images. So we should convert the color camera frame to grayscale.

2. **Shrinking the camera image**: The speed of face detection depends on the size of the input image (it is very slow for large images but fast for small images), and yet detection is still fairly reliable even at low resolutions. So we should shrink the camera image to a more reasonable size (or use a large value for `minFeatureSize` in the detector, as explained shortly).

3. **Histogram equalization**: Face detection is not as reliable in low-light conditions. So we should perform histogram equalization to improve the contrast and brightness.

Grayscale color conversion

We can easily convert an RGB color image to grayscale using the `cvtColor()` function. But we should do this only if we know we have a color image (that is, it is not a grayscale camera), and we must specify the format of our input image (usually 3-channel BGR on desktop or 4-channel BGRA on mobile). So we should allow three different input color formats, as shown in the following code:

```
Mat gray;
if (img.channels() == 3) {
  cvtColor(img, gray, CV_BGR2GRAY);
}
else if (img.channels() == 4) {
  cvtColor(img, gray, CV_BGRA2GRAY);
}
else {
  // Access the grayscale input image directly.
  gray = img;
```

```
    }
```

Shrinking the camera image

We can use the `resize()` function to shrink an image to a certain size or scale factor. Face detection usually works quite well for any image size greater than 240x240 pixels (unless you need to detect faces that are far away from the camera), because it will look for any faces larger than the `minFeatureSize` (typically 20x20 pixels). So let's shrink the camera image to be 320 pixels wide; it doesn't matter if the input is a VGA webcam or a five mega pixel HD camera. It is also important to remember and enlarge the detection results, because if you detect faces in a shrunk image then the results will also be shrunk. Note that instead of shrinking the input image, you could use a large value for the `minFeatureSize` variable in the detector instead. We must also ensure the image does not become fatter or thinner. For example, a widescreen 800x400 image when shrunk to 300x200 would make a person look thin. So we must keep the aspect ratio (the ratio of width to height) of the output the same as the input. Let's calculate how much to shrink the image width by, then apply the same scale factor to the height as well, as follows:

```
const int DETECTION_WIDTH = 320;
// Possibly shrink the image, to run much faster.
Mat smallImg;
float scale = img.cols / (float) DETECTION_WIDTH;
if (img.cols > DETECTION_WIDTH) {
  // Shrink the image while keeping the same aspect ratio.
  int scaledHeight = cvRound(img.rows / scale);
  resize(img, smallImg, Size(DETECTION_WIDTH, scaledHeight));
}
else {
  // Access the input directly since it is already small.
  smallImg = img;
}
```

Histogram equalization

We can easily perform histogram equalization to improve the contrast and brightness of an image, using the `equalizeHist()` function. Sometimes this will make the image look strange, but in general it should improve the brightness and contrast and help face detection. The `equalizeHist()` function is used as follows:

```
// Standardize the brightness & contrast, such as
// to improve dark images.
Mat equalizedImg;
equalizeHist(inputImg, equalizedImg);
```

Detecting the face

Now that we have converted the image to grayscale, shrunk the image, and equalized the histogram, we are ready to detect the faces using the `CascadeClassifier::detectMultiScale()` function! There are many parameters that we pass to this function:

- `minFeatureSize`: This parameter determines the minimum face size that we care about, typically 20x20 or 30x30 pixels but this depends on your use case and image size. If you are performing face detection on a webcam or smartphone where the face will always be very close to the camera, you could enlarge this to 80 x 80 to have much faster detections, or if you want to detect far away faces, such as on a beach with friends, then leave this as 20x20.

- `searchScaleFactor`: This parameter determines how many different sizes of faces to look for; typically it would be `1.1`, for good detection, or `1.2` for faster detection that does not find the face as often.

- `minNeighbors`: This parameter determines how sure the detector should be that it has detected a face, typically a value of `3` but you can set it higher if you want more reliable faces, even if many faces are not detected.

- `flags`: This parameter allows you to specify whether to look for all faces (default) or only look for the largest face (`CASCADE_FIND_BIGGEST_OBJECT`). If you only look for the largest face, it should run faster. There are several other parameters you can add to make the detection about 1% or 2% faster, such as `CASCADE_DO_ROUGH_SEARCH` or `CASCADE_SCALE_IMAGE`.

The output of the `detectMultiScale()` function will be a `std::vector` of the `cv::Rect` type object. For example, if it detects two faces then it will store an array of two rectangles in the output. The `detectMultiScale()` function is used as follows:

```
int flags = CASCADE_SCALE_IMAGE; // Search for many faces.
Size minFeatureSize(20, 20);      // Smallest face size.
float searchScaleFactor = 1.1f;   // How many sizes to search.
int minNeighbors = 4;             // Reliability vs many faces.

// Detect objects in the small grayscale image.
std::vector<Rect> faces;
faceDetector.detectMultiScale(img, faces, searchScaleFactor,
            minNeighbors, flags, minFeatureSize);
```

We can see if any faces were detected by looking at the number of elements stored in our vector of rectangles; that is, by using the `objects.size()` function.

As mentioned earlier, if we gave a shrunken image to the face detector, the results will also be shrunk, so we need to enlarge them if we want to know the face regions for the original image. We also need to make sure faces on the border of the image stay completely within the image, as OpenCV will now raise an exception if this happens, as shown by the following code:

```
// Enlarge the results if the image was temporarily shrunk.
if (img.cols > scaledWidth) {
  for (int i = 0; i < (int)objects.size(); i++ ) {
    objects[i].x = cvRound(objects[i].x * scale);
    objects[i].y = cvRound(objects[i].y * scale);
    objects[i].width = cvRound(objects[i].width * scale);
    objects[i].height = cvRound(objects[i].height * scale);
  }
}
// If the object is on a border, keep it in the image.
for (int i = 0; i < (int)objects.size(); i++ ) {
  if (objects[i].x < 0)
    objects[i].x = 0;
  if (objects[i].y < 0)
    objects[i].y = 0;
  if (objects[i].x + objects[i].width > img.cols)
    objects[i].x = img.cols - objects[i].width;
  if (objects[i].y + objects[i].height > img.rows)
    objects[i].y = img.rows - objects[i].height;
}
```

Note that the preceding code will look for all faces in the image, but if you only care about one face, then you could change the flag variable as follows:

```
int flags = CASCADE_FIND_BIGGEST_OBJECT |
            CASCADE_DO_ROUGH_SEARCH;
```

The WebcamFaceRec project includes a wrapper around OpenCV's Haar or LBP detector, to make it easier to find a face or eye within an image. For example:

```
Rect faceRect;    // Stores the result of the detection, or -1.
int scaledWidth = 320;    // Shrink the image before detection.
detectLargestObject(cameraImg, faceDetector, faceRect, scaledWidth);
if (faceRect.width > 0)
  cout << "We detected a face!" << endl;
```

Now that we have a face rectangle, we can use it in many ways, such as to extract or crop the face image from the original image. The following code allows us to access the face:

```
// Access just the face within the camera image.
Mat faceImg = cameraImg(faceRect);
```

The following image shows the typical rectangular region given by the face detector:

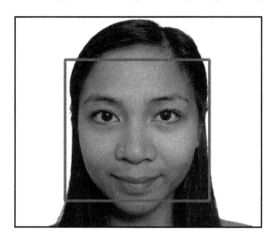

Step 2 - face preprocessing

As mentioned earlier, face recognition is extremely vulnerable to changes in lighting conditions, face orientation, face expression, and so on, so it is very important to reduce these differences as much as possible. Otherwise the face recognition algorithm will often think there is more similarity between faces of two different people in the same conditions than between two faces of the same person.

The easiest form of face preprocessing is just to apply histogram equalization using the `equalizeHist()` function, like we just did for face detection. This may be sufficient for some projects where the lighting and positional conditions won't change by much. But for reliability in real-world conditions, we need many sophisticated techniques, including facial feature detection (for example, detecting eyes, nose, mouth, and eyebrows). For simplicity, this chapter will just use eye detection and ignore other facial features such as the mouth and nose, which are less useful. The following image shows an enlarged view of a typical preprocessed face, using the techniques that will be covered in this section.

Eye detection

Eye detection can be very useful for face preprocessing, because for frontal faces you can always assume a person's eyes should be horizontal and on opposite locations of the face and should have a fairly standard position and size within a face, despite changes in facial expressions, lighting conditions, camera properties, distance to camera, and so on.

It is also useful to discard false positives when the face detector says it has detected a face and it is actually something else. It is rare that the face detector and two eye detectors will all be fooled at the same time, so if you only process images with a detected face and two detected eyes then it will not have many false positives (but will also give fewer faces for processing, as the eye detector will not work as often as the face detector).

Some of the pretrained eye detectors that come with OpenCV v2.4 can detect an eye whether it is open or closed, whereas some of them can only detect open eyes.

Eye detectors that detect open or closed eyes are as follows:

- `haarcascade_mcs_lefteye.xml` (and `haarcascade_mcs_righteye.xml`)
- `haarcascade_lefteye_2splits.xml` (and `haarcascade_righteye_2splits.xml`)

Eye detectors that detect open eyes only are as follows:

- `haarcascade_eye.xml`
- `haarcascade_eye_tree_eyeglasses.xml`

> As the open or closed eye detectors specify which eye they are trained on, you need to use a different detector for the left and the right eye, whereas the detectors for just open eyes can use the same detector for left or right eyes.
> The detector `haarcascade_eye_tree_eyeglasses.xml` can detect the eyes if the person is wearing glasses, but is not reliable if they don't wear glasses.
> If the XML filename says *left eye*, it means the actual left eye of the person, so in the camera image it would normally appear on the right-hand side of the face, not on the left-hand side!
> The list of four eye detectors mentioned is ranked in approximate order from most reliable to least reliable, so if you know you don't need to find people with glasses then the first detector is probably the best choice.

Eye search regions

For eye detection, it is important to crop the input image to just show the approximate eye region, just like doing face detection and then cropping to just a small rectangle where the left eye should be (if you are using the left eye detector) and the same for the right rectangle for the right eye detector.

If you just do eye detection on a whole face or whole photo then it will be much slower and less reliable. Different eye detectors are better suited to different regions of the face; for example, the `haarcascade_eye.xml` detector works best if it only searches in a very tight region around the actual eye, whereas the `haarcascade_mcs_lefteye.xml` and `haarcascade_lefteye_2splits.xml` detectors work best when there is a large region around the eye.

The following table lists some good search regions of the face for different eye detectors (when using the LBP face detector), using relative coordinates within the detected face rectangle:

Cascade classifier	EYE_SX	EYE_SY	EYE_SW	EYE_SH
`haarcascade_eye.xml`	0.16	0.26	0.30	0.28
`haarcascade_mcs_lefteye.xml`	0.10	0.19	0.40	0.36
`haarcascade_lefteye_2splits.xml`	0.12	0.17	0.37	0.36

Here is the source code to extract the left-eye and right-eye regions from a detected face:

```
int leftX = cvRound(face.cols * EYE_SX);
int topY = cvRound(face.rows * EYE_SY);
int widthX = cvRound(face.cols * EYE_SW);
int heightY = cvRound(face.rows * EYE_SH);
int rightX = cvRound(face.cols * (1.0-EYE_SX-EYE_SW));

Mat topLeftOfFace = faceImg(Rect(leftX, topY, widthX, heightY));
Mat topRightOfFace = faceImg(Rect(rightX, topY, widthX, heightY));
```

The following image shows the ideal search regions for the different eye detectors, where the `haarcascade_eye.xml` and `haarcascade_eye_tree_eyeglasses.xml` files are best with the small search region, while the `haarcascade_mcs_*eye.xml` and `haarcascade_*eye_2splits.xml` files are best with larger search regions. Note that the detected face rectangle is also shown, to give an idea of how large the eye search regions are compared to the detected face rectangle:

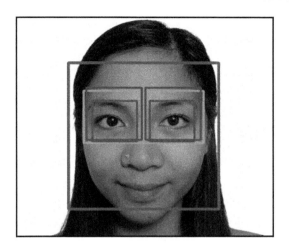

When using the eye search regions given in the preceding table, here are the approximate detection properties of the different eye detectors:

Cascade classifier	Reliability*	Speed**	Eyes found	Glasses
haarcascade_mcs_lefteye.xml	80%	18 msec	Open or closed	no
haarcascade_lefteye_2splits.xml	60%	7 msec	Open or closed	no
haarcascade_eye.xml	40%	5 msec	Open only	no
haarcascade_eye_tree_eyeglasses.xml	15%	10 msec	Open only	yes

* **Reliability** values show how often both eyes will be detected after LBP frontal face detection when no eyeglasses are worn and both eyes are open. If eyes are closed then the reliability may drop, or if eyeglasses are worn then both reliability and speed will drop.

** **Speed** values are in milliseconds for images scaled to the size of 320x240 pixels on an Intel Core i7 2.2 GHz (averaged across 1,000 photos). Speed is typically much faster when eyes are found than when eyes are not found, as it must scan the entire image, but the haarcascade_mcs_lefteye.xml is still much slower than the other eye detectors.

For example, if you shrink a photo to 320x240 pixels, perform a histogram equalization on it, use the LBP frontal face detector to get a face, then extract the *left-eye-region* and *right-eye-region* from the face using the `haarcascade_mcs_lefteye.xml` values, then perform a histogram equalization on each eye region. Then if you the `haarcascade_mcs_lefteye.xml` detector on the left eye (which is actually on the top-right side of your image) and use the `haarcascade_mcs_righteye.xml` detector on the right eye (the top-left part of your image), each eye detector should work in roughly 90 percent of photos with LBP-detected frontal faces. So if you want both eyes detected then it should work in roughly 80 percent of photos with LBP-detected frontal faces.

Note that while it is recommended to shrink the camera image before detecting faces, you should detect eyes at the full camera resolution because eyes will obviously be much smaller than faces, so you need as much resolution as you can get.

Based on the table, it seems that when choosing an eye detector to use, you should decide whether you want to detect closed eyes or only open eyes. And remember that you can even use a one eye detector, and if it does not detect an eye then you can try with another one.

For many tasks, it is useful to detect eyes whether they are opened or closed, so if speed is not crucial, it is best to search with the `mcs_*eye` detector first, and if it fails then search with the `eye_2splits` detector. But for face recognition, a person will appear quite different if their eyes are closed, so it is best to search with the plain `haarcascade_eye` detector first, and if it fails then search with the `haarcascade_eye_tree_eyeglasses` detector.

We can use the same `detectLargestObject()` function we used for face detection to search for eyes, but instead of asking to shrink the images before eye detection, we specify the full eye region width to get a better eye detection. It is easy to search for the left eye using one detector, and if it fails then try another detector (same for right eye). The eye detection is done as follows:

```
CascadeClassifier eyeDetector1("haarcascade_eye.xml");
CascadeClassifier eyeDetector2("haarcascade_eye_tree_eyeglasses.xml");
...
Rect leftEyeRect;    // Stores the detected eye.
// Search the left region using the 1st eye detector.
detectLargestObject(topLeftOfFace, eyeDetector1, leftEyeRect,
topLeftOfFace.cols);
// If it failed, search the left region using the 2nd eye
// detector.
if (leftEyeRect.width <= 0)
```

```
        detectLargestObject(topLeftOfFace, eyeDetector2,
                     leftEyeRect, topLeftOfFace.cols);
        // Get the left eye center if one of the eye detectors worked.
        Point leftEye = Point(-1,-1);
        if (leftEyeRect.width <= 0) {
          leftEye.x = leftEyeRect.x + leftEyeRect.width/2 + leftX;
          leftEye.y = leftEyeRect.y + leftEyeRect.height/2 + topY;
        }

        // Do the same for the right-eye
        ...

        // Check if both eyes were detected.
        if (leftEye.x >= 0 && rightEye.x >= 0) {
          ...
        }
```

With the face and both eyes detected, we'll perform face preprocessing by combining:

- **Geometrical transformation and cropping**: This process would include scaling, rotating, and translating the images so that the eyes are aligned, followed by the removal of the forehead, chin, ears, and background from the face image.
- **Separate histogram equalization for left and right sides**: This process standardizes the brightness and contrast on both the left- and right-hand sides of the face independently.
- **Smoothing**: This process reduces the image noise using a bilateral filter.
- **Elliptical mask**: The elliptical mask removes some remaining hair and background from the face image.

The following image shows the face preprocessing steps 1 to 4 applied to a detected face. Notice how the final image has good brightness and contrast on both sides of the face, whereas the original does not:

Geometrical transformation

It is important that the faces are all aligned together, otherwise the face-recognition algorithm might be comparing part of a nose with part of an eye, and so on. The output of face detection just seen will give aligned faces to some extent, but it is not very accurate (that is, the face rectangle will not always be starting from the same point on the forehead).

To have better alignment, we will use eye detection to align the face so the positions of the two detected eyes line up perfectly in the desired positions. We will do the geometrical transformation using the `warpAffine()` function, which is a single operation that will do four things:

- Rotate the face so that the two eyes are horizontal
- Scale the face so that the distance between the two eyes is always the same
- Translate the face so that the eyes are always centered horizontally and at a desired height
- Crop the outer parts of the face, since we want to crop away the image background, hair, forehead, ears, and chin

Affine Warping takes an affine matrix that transforms the two detected eye locations to the two desired eye locations, and then crops to a desired size and position. To generate this affine matrix, we will get the center between the eyes, calculate the angle at which the two detected eyes appear, and look at their distance apart as follows:

```cpp
// Get the center between the 2 eyes.
Point2f eyesCenter;
eyesCenter.x = (leftEye.x + rightEye.x) * 0.5f;
eyesCenter.y = (leftEye.y + rightEye.y) * 0.5f;

// Get the angle between the 2 eyes.
double dy = (rightEye.y - leftEye.y);
double dx = (rightEye.x - leftEye.x);
double len = sqrt(dx*dx + dy*dy);

// Convert Radians to Degrees.
double angle = atan2(dy, dx) * 180.0/CV_PI;

// Hand measurements shown that the left eye center should
// ideally be roughly at (0.16, 0.14) of a scaled face image.
const double DESIRED_LEFT_EYE_X = 0.16;
const double DESIRED_RIGHT_EYE_X = (1.0f - 0.16);

// Get the amount we need to scale the image to be the desired
// fixed size we want.
const int DESIRED_FACE_WIDTH = 70;
const int DESIRED_FACE_HEIGHT = 70;
double desiredLen = (DESIRED_RIGHT_EYE_X - 0.16);
double scale = desiredLen * DESIRED_FACE_WIDTH / len;
```

Now we can transform the face (rotate, scale, and translate) to get the two detected eyes to be in the desired eye positions in an ideal face as follows:

```
// Get the transformation matrix for the desired angle & size.
Mat rot_mat = getRotationMatrix2D(eyesCenter, angle, scale);
// Shift the center of the eyes to be the desired center.
double ex = DESIRED_FACE_WIDTH * 0.5f - eyesCenter.x;
double ey = DESIRED_FACE_HEIGHT * DESIRED_LEFT_EYE_Y -
  eyesCenter.y;
rot_mat.at<double>(0, 2) += ex;
rot_mat.at<double>(1, 2) += ey;
// Transform the face image to the desired angle & size &
// position! Also clear the transformed image background to a
// default grey.
Mat warped = Mat(DESIRED_FACE_HEIGHT, DESIRED_FACE_WIDTH,
  CV_8U, Scalar(128));
warpAffine(gray, warped, rot_mat, warped.size());
```

Separate histogram equalization for left and right sides

In real-world conditions, it is common to have strong lighting on one half of the face and weak lighting on the other. This has an enormous effect on the face-recognition algorithm, as the left- and right-hand sides of the same face will seem like very different people. So we will perform histogram equalization separately on the left and right halves of the face, to have standardized brightness and contrast on each side of the face.

If we simply applied histogram equalization on the left half and then again on the right half, we would see a very distinct edge in the middle because the average brightness is likely to be different on the left and the right side, so to remove this edge, we will apply the two histogram equalizations gradually from the left-or right-hand side towards the center and mix it with a whole-face histogram equalization, so that the far left-hand side will use the left histogram equalization, the far right-hand side will use the right histogram equalization, and the center will use a smooth mix of the left or right value and the whole-face equalized value.

The following image shows how the left-equalized, whole-equalized, and right-equalized images are blended together:

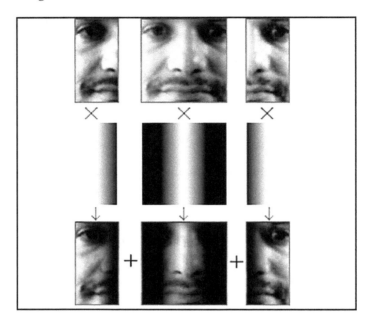

To perform this, we need copies of the whole face equalized as well as the left half equalized and the right half equalized, which is done as follows:

```
int w = faceImg.cols;
int h = faceImg.rows;
Mat wholeFace;
equalizeHist(faceImg, wholeFace);
int midX = w/2;
Mat leftSide = faceImg(Rect(0,0, midX,h));
Mat rightSide = faceImg(Rect(midX,0, w-midX,h));
equalizeHist(leftSide, leftSide);
equalizeHist(rightSide, rightSide);
```

Now we combine the three images together. As the images are small, we can easily access pixels directly using the `image.at<uchar>(y,x)` function even if it is slow; so let's merge the three images by directly accessing pixels in the three input images and output images, as follows:

```
for (int y=0; y<h; y++) {
    for (int x=0; x<w; x++) {
        int v;
        if (x < w/4) {
```

```
        // Left 25%: just use the left face.
        v = leftSide.at<uchar>(y,x);
    }
    else if (x < w*2/4) {
        // Mid-left 25%: blend the left face & whole face.
        int lv = leftSide.at<uchar>(y,x);
        int wv = wholeFace.at<uchar>(y,x);
        // Blend more of the whole face as it moves
        // further right along the face.
        float f = (x - w*1/4) / (float)(w/4);
        v = cvRound((1.0f - f) * lv + (f) * wv);
    }
    else if (x < w*3/4) {
        // Mid-right 25%: blend right face & whole face.
        int rv = rightSide.at<uchar>(y,x-midX);
        int wv = wholeFace.at<uchar>(y,x);
        // Blend more of the right-side face as it moves
        // further right along the face.
        float f = (x - w*2/4) / (float)(w/4);
        v = cvRound((1.0f - f) * wv + (f) * rv);
    }
    else {
        // Right 25%: just use the right face.
        v = rightSide.at<uchar>(y,x-midX);
    }
    faceImg.at<uchar>(y,x) = v;
  } // end x loop
} //end y loop
```

This separated histogram equalization should significantly help reduce the effect of different lighting on the left- and right-hand sides of the face, but we must understand that it won't completely remove the effect of one-sided lighting, since the face is a complex 3D shape with many shadows.

Smoothing

To reduce the effect of pixel noise, we will use a bilateral filter on the face, as a bilateral filter is very good at smoothing, most of an image while keeping edges sharp. Histogram equalization can significantly increase the pixel noise, so we will make the filter strength 20 to cover heavy pixel noise, but use a neighborhood of just two pixels as we want to heavily smooth the tiny pixel noise but not the large image regions, as follows:

```
Mat filtered = Mat(warped.size(), CV_8U);
bilateralFilter(warped, filtered, 0, 20.0, 2.0);
```

Elliptical mask

Although we have already removed most of the image background and forehead and hair when we did the geometrical transformation, we can apply an elliptical mask to remove some of the corner region such as the neck, which might be in shadow from the face, particularly if the face is not looking perfectly straight towards the camera. To create the mask, we will draw a black-filled ellipse onto a white image. One ellipse to perform this has a horizontal radius of 0.5 (that is, it covers the face width perfectly), a vertical radius of 0.8 (as faces are usually taller than they are wide), and centered at the coordinates 0.5, 0.4, as shown in the following image, where the elliptical mask has removed some unwanted corners from the face:

We can apply the mask when calling the `cv::setTo()` function, which would normally set a whole image to a certain pixel value, but as we will give a mask image, it will only set some parts to the given pixel value. We will fill the image in gray so that it should have less contrast to the rest of the face:

```
// Draw a black-filled ellipse in the middle of the image.
// First we initialize the mask image to white (255).
Mat mask = Mat(warped.size(), CV_8UC1, Scalar(255));
double dw = DESIRED_FACE_WIDTH;
double dh = DESIRED_FACE_HEIGHT;
Point faceCenter = Point( cvRound(dw * 0.5),
  cvRound(dh * 0.4) );
Size size = Size( cvRound(dw * 0.5), cvRound(dh * 0.8) );
ellipse(mask, faceCenter, size, 0, 0, 360, Scalar(0),
  CV_FILLED);

// Apply the elliptical mask on the face, to remove corners.
// Sets corners to gray, without touching the inner face.
filtered.setTo(Scalar(128), mask);
```

The following enlarged image shows a sample result from all the face preprocessing stages. Notice it is much more consistent for face recognition at a different brightness, face rotations, angle from camera, backgrounds, positions of lights, and so on. This preprocessed face will be used as input to the face-recognition stages, both when collecting faces for training, and when trying to recognize input faces:

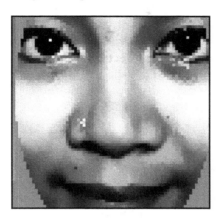

Step 3 - Collecting faces and learning from them

Collecting faces can be just as simple as putting each newly preprocessed face into an array of preprocessed faces from the camera, as well as putting a label into an array (to specify which person the face was taken from). For example, you could use 10 preprocessed faces of the first person and 10 preprocessed faces of a second person, so the input to the face-recognition algorithm will be an array of 20 preprocessed faces and an array of 20 integers (where the first 10 numbers are 0 and the next 10 numbers are 1).

The face-recognition algorithm will then learn how to distinguish between the faces of the different people. This is referred to as the training phase and the collected faces are referred to as the training set. After the face-recognition algorithm has finished training, you could then save the generated knowledge to a file or memory and later use it to recognize which person is seen in front of the camera. This is referred to as the testing phase. If you used it directly from a camera input then the preprocessed face would be referred to as the test image, and if you tested with many images (such as from a folder of image files), it would be referred to as the testing set.

It is important that you provide a good training set that covers the types of variations you expect to occur in your testing set. For example, if you will only test with faces that are looking perfectly straight ahead (such as ID photos), then you only need to provide training images with faces that are looking perfectly straight ahead. But if the person might be looking to the left or up, then you should make sure the training set will also include faces of that person doing this, otherwise the face-recognition algorithm will have trouble recognizing them, as their face will appear quite different. This also applies to other factors such as facial expression (for example, if the person is always smiling in the training set but not smiling in the testing set) or lighting direction (for example, a strong light is to the left-hand side in the training set but to the right-hand side in the testing set), then the face recognition algorithm will have difficulty recognizing them. The face preprocessing steps that we just saw will help reduce these issues, but it certainly won't remove these factors, particularly the direction in which the face is looking, as it has a large effect on the position of all elements in the face.

One way to obtain a good training set that will cover many different real-world conditions is for each person to rotate their head from looking left, to up, to right, to down, then looking directly straight. Then the person tilts their head sideways and then up and down, while also changing their facial expression, such as alternating between smiling, looking angry, and having a neutral face. If each person follows a routine such as this while collecting faces, then there is a much better chance of recognizing everyone in the real-world conditions.

For even better results, it should be performed again with one or two more locations or directions, such as by turning the camera around by 180 degrees and walking in the opposite direction of the camera and then repeating the whole routine, so that the training set would include many different lighting conditions.

So in general, having 100 training faces for each person is likely to give better results than having just 10 training faces for each person, but if all 100 faces look almost identical then it will still perform badly because it is more important that the training set has enough variety to cover the testing set, rather than to just have a large number of faces. So to make sure the faces in the training set are not all too similar, we should add a noticeable delay between each collected face. For example, if the camera is running at 30 frames per second, then it might collect 100 faces in just several seconds when the person has not had time to move around, so it is better to collect just one face per second, while the person moves their face around. Another simple method to improve the variation in the training set is to only collect a face if it is noticeably different from the previously collected face.

Collecting preprocessed faces for training

To make sure there is at least a 1 second gap between collecting new faces, we need to measure how much time has passed. This is done as follows:

```
// Check how long since the previous face was added.
double current_time = (double)getTickCount();
double timeDiff_seconds = (current_time -
  old_time) / getTickFrequency();
```

To compare the similarity of two images, pixel by pixel, you can find the relative L2 error, which just involves subtracting one image from the other, summing the squared value of it, and then getting the square root of it. So if the person had not moved at all, subtracting the current face with the previous face should give a very low number at each pixel, but if they had just moved slightly in any direction, subtracting the pixels would give a large number and so the L2 error will be high. As the result is summed over all pixels, the value will depend on the image resolution. So to get the mean error, we should divide this value by the total number of pixels in the image. Let's put this in a handy function, getSimilarity(), as follows:

```
double getSimilarity(const Mat A, const Mat B) {
  // Calculate the L2 relative error between the 2 images.
  double errorL2 = norm(A, B, CV_L2);
  // Scale the value since L2 is summed across all pixels.
  double similarity = errorL2 / (double)(A.rows * A.cols);
  return similarity;
}

...

// Check if this face looks different from the previous face.
double imageDiff = MAX_DBL;
if (old_prepreprocessedFaceprepreprocessedFace.data) {
  imageDiff = getSimilarity(preprocessedFace,
    old_prepreprocessedFace);
}
```

This similarity will often be less than 0.2 if the image did not move much, and higher than 0.4 if the image did move, so let's use 0.3 as our threshold for collecting a new face.

There are many tricks we can play to obtain more training data, such as using mirrored faces, adding random noise, shifting the face by a few pixels, scaling the face by a percentage, or rotating the face by a few degrees (even though we specifically tried to remove these effects when preprocessing the face!). Let's add mirrored faces to the training set, so that we have both a larger training set as well as a reduction in the problems of asymmetrical faces or if a user is always oriented slightly to the left or right during training but not testing. This is done as follows:

```
// Only process the face if it's noticeably different from the
// previous frame and there has been a noticeable time gap.
if ((imageDiff > 0.3) && (timeDiff_seconds > 1.0)) {
  // Also add the mirror image to the training set.
  Mat mirroredFace;
  flip(preprocessedFace, mirroredFace, 1);

  // Add the face & mirrored face to the detected face lists.
  preprocessedFaces.push_back(preprocessedFace);
  preprocessedFaces.push_back(mirroredFace);
  faceLabels.push_back(m_selectedPerson);
  faceLabels.push_back(m_selectedPerson);

  // Keep a copy of the processed face,
  // to compare on next iteration.
  old_prepreprocessedFace = preprocessedFace;
  old_time = current_time;
}
```

This will collect the `std::vector` arrays `preprocessedFaces` and `faceLabels` for a preprocessed face as well as the label or ID number of that person (assuming it is in the integer `m_selectedPerson` variable).

To make it more obvious to the user that we have added their current face to the collection, you could provide a visual notification by either displaying a large white rectangle over the whole image or just displaying their face for just a fraction of a second so they realize a photo was taken. With OpenCV's C++ interface, you can use the + overloaded `cv::Mat` operator to add a value to every pixel in the image and have it clipped to 255 (using `saturate_cast`, so it doesn't overflow from white back to black!) Assuming `displayedFrame` will be a copy of the color camera frame that should be shown, insert this after the preceding code for face collection:

```
// Get access to the face region-of-interest.
Mat displayedFaceRegion = displayedFrame(faceRect);
// Add some brightness to each pixel of the face region.
displayedFaceRegion += CV_RGB(90,90,90);
```

Training the face recognition system from collected faces

After you have collected enough faces for each person to recognize, you must train the system to learn the data using a machine-learning algorithm suited for face recognition. There are many different face-recognition algorithms in the literature, the simplest of which are Eigenfaces and Artificial Neural Networks. Eigenfaces tends to work better than ANNs, and despite its simplicity, it tends to work almost as well as many more complex face-recognition algorithms, so it has become very popular as the basic face-recognition algorithm for beginners as well as for new algorithms to be compared to.

Any reader who wishes to work further on face recognition is recommended to read the theory behind:

- Eigenfaces (also referred to as **Principal Component Analysis** (PCA)
- Fisherfaces (also referred to as **Linear Discriminant Analysis** (LDA)
- Other classic face recognition algorithms (many are available at http://www.face
  -rec.org/algorithms/)
- Newer face recognition algorithms in recent Computer Vision research papers (such as CVPR and ICCV at http://www.cvpapers.com/), as there are hundreds of face recognition papers published each year

However, you don't need to understand the theory of these algorithms in order to use them as shown in this book. Thanks to the OpenCV team and Philipp Wagner's libfacerec contribution, OpenCV v2.4.1 provided cv::Algorithm as a simple and generic method to perform face recognition using one of several different algorithms (even selectable at runtime) without necessarily understanding how they are implemented. You can find the available algorithms in your version of OpenCV by using the Algorithm::getList() function, such as with this code:

```
vector<string> algorithms;
Algorithm::getList(algorithms);
cout << "Algorithms: " << algorithms.size() << endl;
for (int i=0; i<algorithms.size(); i++) {
  cout << algorithms[i] << endl;
}
```

Here are the three face-recognition algorithms available in OpenCV v2.4.1:

- FaceRecognizer.Eigenfaces: Eigenfaces, also referred to as PCA, first used by Turk and Pentland in 1991.

- `FaceRecognizer.Fisherfaces`: Fisherfaces, also referred to as LDA, invented by Belhumeur, Hespanha, and Kriegman in 1997.
- `FaceRecognizer.LBPH`: Local Binary Pattern Histograms, invented by Ahonen, Hadid, and Pietikäinen in 2004.

 More information on these face-recognition algorithm implementations can be found with documentation, samples, and Python equivalents for each of them on Philipp Wagner's websites (http://bytefish.de/blog and http://bytefish.de/dev/libfacerec/).

These face recognition-algorithms are available through the `FaceRecognizer` class in OpenCV's `contrib` module. Due to dynamic linking, it is possible that your program is linked to the `contrib` module but it is not actually loaded at runtime (if it was deemed as not required). So it is recommended to call the `cv::initModule_contrib()` function before trying to access the `FaceRecognizer` algorithms. This function is only available from OpenCV v2.4.1, so it also ensures that the face-recognition algorithms are at least available to you at compile time:

```
// Load the "contrib" module is dynamically at runtime.
bool haveContribModule = initModule_contrib();
if (!haveContribModule) {
    cerr << "ERROR: The 'contrib' module is needed for ";
    cerr << "FaceRecognizer but hasn't been loaded to OpenCV!";
    cerr << endl;
    exit(1);
}
```

To use one of the face-recognition algorithms, we must create a `FaceRecognizer` object using the `cv::Algorithm::create<FaceRecognizer>()` function. We pass the name of the face-recognition algorithm we want to use, as a string to this create function. This will give us access to that algorithm, if it is available in the OpenCV version. So it may be used as a runtime error check to ensure the user has OpenCV v2.4.1 or newer. For example:

```
string facerecAlgorithm = "FaceRecognizer.Fisherfaces";
Ptr<FaceRecognizer> model;
// Use OpenCV's new FaceRecognizer in the "contrib" module:
model = Algorithm::create<FaceRecognizer>(facerecAlgorithm);
if (model.empty()) {
    cerr << "ERROR: The FaceRecognizer [" << facerecAlgorithm;
    cerr << "] is not available in your version of OpenCV. ";
    cerr << "Please update to OpenCV v2.4.1 or newer." << endl;
    exit(1);
}
```

Once we have loaded the `FaceRecognizer` algorithm, we simply call the `FaceRecognizer::train()` function with our collected face data as follows:

```
// Do the actual training from the collected faces.
model->train(preprocessedFaces, faceLabels);
```

This one line of code will run the whole face recognition training algorithm that you selected (for example, Eigenfaces, Fisherfaces, or potentially other algorithms). If you have just a few people with less than 20 faces, then this training should return very quickly, but if you have many people with many faces, it is possible that `train()` function will take several seconds or even minutes to process all the data.

Viewing the learned knowledge

While it is not necessary, it is quite useful to view the internal data structures that the face-recognition algorithm generated when learning your training data, particularly if you understand the theory behind the algorithm you selected and want to verify if it worked or find out why it is not working as you hoped. The internal data structures can be different for different algorithms, but luckily they are the same for eigenfaces and fisherfaces, so let's just look at those two. They are both based on 1D eigenvector matrices that appear somewhat like faces when viewed as 2D images, therefore it is common to refer as eigenvectors as eigenfaces when using the **Eigenface** algorithm or as fisherfaces when using the **Fisherface** algorithm.

In simple terms, the basic principle of Eigenfaces is that it will calculate a set of special images (eigenfaces) and blending ratios (eigenvalues), which when combined in different ways can generate each of the images in the training set but can also be used to differentiate the many face images in the training set from each other. For example, if some of the faces in the training set had a moustache and some did not, then there would be at least one eigenface that shows a moustache, and so the training faces with a moustache would have a high blending ratio for that eigenface to show that it has a moustache, and the faces without a moustache would have a low blending ratio for that eigenvector. If the training set had five people with 20 faces for each person, then there would be 100 eigenfaces and eigenvalues to differentiate the 100 total faces in the training set, and in fact these would be sorted so the first few eigenfaces and eigenvalues would be the most critical differentiators, and the last few eigenfaces and eigenvalues would just be random pixel noises that don't actually help to differentiate the data. So it is common practice to discard some of the last eigenfaces and just keep the first 50 or so eigenfaces.

In comparison, the basic principle of Fisherfaces is that instead of calculating a special eigenvector and eigenvalue for each image in the training set, it only calculates one special eigenvector and eigenvalue for each person. So in the preceding example that has fivepeople with 20 faces for each person, the Eigenfaces algorithm would use 100 eigenfaces and eigenvalues whereas the Fisherfaces algorithm would use just five fisherfaces and eigenvalues.

To access the internal data structures of the Eigenfaces and Fisherfaces algorithms, we must use the `cv::Algorithm::get()` function to obtain them at runtime, as there is no access to them at compile time. The data structures are used internally as part of mathematical calculations rather than for image processing, so they are usually stored as floating-point numbers typically ranging between 0.0 and 1.0, rather than 8-bit `uchar` pixels ranging from 0 to 255, similar to pixels in regular images. Also, they are often either a 1D row or column matrix or they make up one of the many 1D rows or columns of a larger matrix. So before you can display many of these internal data structures, you must reshape them to be the correct rectangular shape, and convert them to 8-bit `uchar` pixels between 0 and 255. As the matrix data might range from 0.0 to 1.0 or -1.0 to 1.0 or anything else, you can use the `cv::normalize()` function with the `cv::NORM_MINMAX` option to make sure it outputs data ranging between 0 and 255 no matter what the input range may be. Let's create a function to perform this reshaping to a rectangle and conversion to 8-bit pixels for us as follows:

```
// Convert the matrix row or column (float matrix) to a
// rectangular 8-bit image that can be displayed or saved.
// Scales the values to be between 0 to 255.
Mat getImageFrom1DFloatMat(const Mat matrixRow, int height)
{
  // Make a rectangular shaped image instead of a single row.
  Mat rectangularMat = matrixRow.reshape(1, height);
  // Scale the values to be between 0 to 255 and store them
  // as a regular 8-bit uchar image.
  Mat dst;
  normalize(rectangularMat, dst, 0, 255, NORM_MINMAX,
    CV_8UC1);
  return dst;
}
```

To make it easier to debug OpenCV code and even more so, when internally debugging the `cv::Algorithm` data structure, we can use the `ImageUtils.cpp` and `ImageUtils.h` files to display information about a `cv::Mat` structure easily as follows:

```
Mat img = ...;
printMatInfo(img, "My Image");
```

You will see something similar to the following printed to your console:

```
My Image: 640w480h 3ch 8bpp, range[79,253][20,58][18,87]
```

This tells you that it is 640 elements wide and 480 high (that is, a 640 x 480 image or a 480 x 640 matrix, depending on how you view it), with three channels per pixel that are 8-bits each (that is, a regular BGR image), and it shows the min and max value in the image for each of the color channels.

> It is also possible to print the actual contents of an image or matrix by using the `printMat()` function instead of the `printMatInfo()` function. This is quite handy for viewing matrices and multichannel-float matrices as these can be quite tricky to view for beginners.
> The `ImageUtils` code is mostly for OpenCV's C interface, but is gradually including more of the C++ interface over time. The most recent version can be found at http://shervinemami.info/openCV.html.

Average face

Both the Eigenfaces and Fisherfaces algorithms first calculate the average face that is the mathematical average of all the training images, so they can subtract the average image from each facial image to have better face recognition results. So let's view the average face from our training set. The average face is named `mean` in the Eigenfaces and Fisherfaces implementations, shown as follows:

```
Mat averageFace = model->get<Mat>("mean");
printMatInfo(averageFace, "averageFace (row)");
// Convert a 1D float row matrix to a regular 8-bit image.
averageFace = getImageFrom1DFloatMat(averageFace, faceHeight);
printMatInfo(averageFace, "averageFace");
imshow("averageFace", averageFace);
```

You should now see an average face image on your screen similar to the following (enlarged) image that is a combination of a man, a woman, and a baby. You should also see similar text to this shown on your console:

```
averageFace (row): 4900w1h 1ch 64bpp, range[5.21,251.47]
averageFace: 70w70h 1ch 8bpp, range[0,255]
```

The image would appear as shown in the following screenshot:

Notice that averageFace (row) was a single row matrix of 64-bit floats, whereas averageFace is a rectangular image with 8-bit pixels covering the full range from 0 to 255.

Eigenvalues, Eigenfaces, and Fisherfaces

Let's view the actual component values in the eigenvalues (as text):

```
Mat eigenvalues = model->get<Mat>("eigenvalues");
printMat(eigenvalues, "eigenvalues");
```

For Eigenfaces, there is one eigenvalue for each face, so if we have three people with four faces each, we get a column vector with 12 eigenvalues sorted from best to worst as follows:

```
eigenvalues: 1w18h 1ch 64bpp, range[4.52e+04,2.02836e+06]
2.03e+06
1.09e+06
5.23e+05
4.04e+05
2.66e+05
2.31e+05
1.85e+05
1.23e+05
9.18e+04
7.61e+04
6.91e+04
4.52e+04
```

For Fisherfaces, there is just one eigenvalue for each extra person, so if there are three people with four faces each, we just get a row vector with two eigenvalues as follows:

```
eigenvalues: 2w1h 1ch 64bpp, range[152.4,316.6]
317, 152
```

To view the eigenvectors (as Eigenface or Fisherface images), we must extract them as columns from the big eigenvectors matrix. As data in OpenCV and C/C++ is normally stored in matrices using row-major order, it means that to extract a column, we should use the Mat::clone() function to ensure the data will be continuous, otherwise we can't reshape the data to a rectangle. Once we have a continuous column Mat, we can display the eigenvectors using the getImageFrom1DFloatMat() function just like we did for the average face:

```
// Get the eigenvectors
Mat eigenvectors = model->get<Mat>("eigenvectors");
printMatInfo(eigenvectors, "eigenvectors");

// Show the best 20 eigenfaces
for (int i = 0; i < min(20, eigenvectors.cols); i++) {
  // Create a continuous column vector from eigenvector #i.
  Mat eigenvector = eigenvectors.col(i).clone();

  Mat eigenface = getImageFrom1DFloatMat(eigenvector,
    faceHeight);
  imshow(format("Eigenface%d", i), eigenface);
}
```

The following figure displays eigenvectors as images. You can see that for three people with four faces, there are 12 Eigenfaces (left-hand side of the figure) or two Fisherfaces (right-hand side):

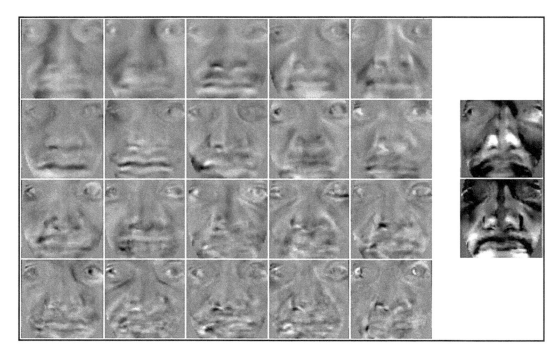

Notice that both Eigenfaces and Fisherfaces seem to have the resemblance of some facial features but they don't really look like faces. This is simply because the average face was subtracted from them, so they just show the differences for each Eigenface from the average face. The numbering shows which Eigenface it is, because they are always ordered from the most significant Eigenface to the least significant Eigenface, and if you have 50 or more Eigenfaces then the later Eigenfaces will often just show random image noise and therefore should be discarded.

Step 4 - face recognition

Now that we have trained the Eigenfaces or Fisherfaces machine-learning algorithm with our set of training images and face labels, we are finally ready to figure out who a person is, just from a facial image! This last step is referred to as face recognition or face identification.

Face identification - recognizing people from their face

Thanks to OpenCV's `FaceRecognizer` class, we can identify the person in a photo simply by calling the `FaceRecognizer::predict()` function on a facial image as follows:

```
int identity = model->predict(preprocessedFace);
```

This `identity` value will be the label number that we originally used when collecting faces for training. For example, 0 for the first person, 1 for the second person, and so on.

The problem with this identification is that it will always predict one of the given people, even if the input photo is of an unknown person or of a car. It would still tell you which person is the most likely person in that photo, so it can be difficult to trust the result! The solution is to obtain a confidence metric so we can judge how reliable the result is, and if it seems that the confidence is too low then we assume it is an unknown person.

Face verification - validating that it is the claimed person

To confirm if the result of the prediction is reliable or whether it should be taken as an unknown person, we perform **face verification** (also referred to as **face authentication**), to obtain a confidence metric showing whether the single face image is similar to the claimed person (as opposed to face identification, which we just performed, comparing the single face image with many people).

OpenCV's `FaceRecognizer` class can return a confidence metric when you call the `predict()` function but unfortunately the confidence metric is simply based on the distance in eigen-subspace, so it is not very reliable. The method we will use is to reconstruct the facial image using the *eigenvectors* and *eigenvalues*, and compare this reconstructed image with the input image. If the person had many of their faces included in the training set, then the reconstruction should work quite well from the learned eigenvectors and eigenvalues, but if the person did not have any faces in the training set (or did not have any that have similar lighting and facial expressions as the test image), then the reconstructed face will look very different from the input face, signaling that it is probably an unknown face.

Remember we said earlier that the Eigenfaces and Fisherfaces algorithms are based on the notion that an image can be roughly represented as a set of eigenvectors (special face images) and eigenvalues (blending ratios). So if we combine all the eigenvectors with the eigenvalues from one of the faces in the training set then we should obtain a fairly close replica of that original training image. The same applies with other images that are similar to the training set--if we combine the trained eigenvectors with the eigenvalues from a similar test image, we should be able to reconstruct an image that is somewhat a replica to the test image.

Once again, OpenCV's `FaceRecognizer` class makes it quite easy to generate a reconstructed face from any input image, by using the `subspaceProject()` function to project onto the eigenspace and the `subspaceReconstruct()` function to go back from eigenspace to image space. The trick is that we need to convert it from a floating-point row matrix to a rectangular 8-bit image (like we did when displaying the average face and eigenfaces), but we don't want to normalize the data, as it is already in the ideal scale to compare with the original image. If we normalized the data, it would have a different brightness and contrast from the input image, and it would become difficult to compare the image similarity just by using the L2 relative error. This is done as follows:

```
// Get some required data from the FaceRecognizer model.
Mat eigenvectors = model->get<Mat>("eigenvectors");
Mat averageFaceRow = model->get<Mat>("mean");

// Project the input image onto the eigenspace.
Mat projection = subspaceProject(eigenvectors, averageFaceRow,
  preprocessedFace.reshape(1,1));

// Generate the reconstructed face back from the eigenspace.
Mat reconstructionRow = subspaceReconstruct(eigenvectors,
  averageFaceRow, projection);

// Make it a rectangular shaped image instead of a single row.
Mat reconstructionMat = reconstructionRow.reshape(1,
  faceHeight);

// Convert the floating-point pixels to regular 8-bit uchar.
Mat reconstructedFace = Mat(reconstructionMat.size(), CV_8U);
reconstructionMat.convertTo(reconstructedFace, CV_8U, 1, 0);
```

The following image shows two typical reconstructed faces. The face on the left-hand side was reconstructed well because it was from a known person, whereas the face on the right-hand side was reconstructed badly because it was from an unknown person or a known person but with unknown lighting conditions/facial expression/face direction:

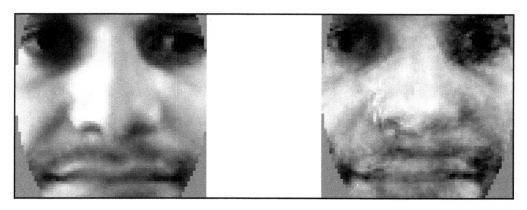

We can now calculate how similar this reconstructed face is to the input face by using the same getSimilarity() function we created previously for comparing two images, where a value less than 0.3 implies that the two images are very similar. For Eigenfaces, there is one eigenvector for each face, so reconstruction tends to work well and therefore we can typically use a threshold of 0.5, but Fisherfaces has just one eigenvector for each person, so reconstruction will not work as well and therefore it needs a higher threshold, say 0.7. This is done as follows:

```
similarity = getSimilarity(preprocessedFace, reconstructedFace);
if (similarity > UNKNOWN_PERSON_THRESHOLD) {
  identity = -1;    // Unknown person.
}
```

Now you can just print the identity to the console, or use it for wherever your imagination takes you! Remember that this face-recognition method and this face-verification method are only reliable in the certain conditions that you train them for. So to obtain good recognition accuracy, you will need to ensure that the training set of each person covers the full range of lighting conditions, facial expressions, and angles that you expect to test with. The face preprocessing stage helped reduce some differences with lighting conditions and in-plane rotation (if the person tilts their head towards their left or right shoulder), but for other differences, such as out-of-plane rotation (if the person turns their head towards the left-hand side or right-hand side), it will only work if it is covered well in your training set.

Finishing touches - saving and loading files

You could potentially add a command-line based method that processes input files and saves them to the disk, or even perform face detection, face preprocessing and/or face recognition as a web service, and so on. For these types of projects, it is quite easy to add the desired functionality by using the `save` and `load` functions of the `FaceRecognizer` class. You may also want to save the trained data and then load it on the program's start up.

Saving the trained model to an XML or YML file is very easy:

```
model->save("trainedModel.yml");
```

You may also want to save the array of preprocessed faces and labels, if you want to add more data to the training set later.

For example, here is some sample code for loading the trained model from a file. Note that you must specify the face-recognition algorithm (for example, `FaceRecognizer.Eigenfaces` or `FaceRecognizer.Fisherfaces`) that was originally used to create the trained model:

```
string facerecAlgorithm = "FaceRecognizer.Fisherfaces";
model = Algorithm::create<FaceRecognizer>(facerecAlgorithm);
Mat labels;
try {
  model->load("trainedModel.yml");
  labels = model->get<Mat>("labels");
} catch (cv::Exception &e) {}
if (labels.rows <= 0) {
  cerr << "ERROR: Couldn't load trained data from "
          "[trainedModel.yml]!" << endl;
  exit(1);
}
```

Finishing touches - making a nice and interactive GUI

While the code given so far in this chapter is sufficient for a whole face recognition system, there still needs to be a way to put the data into the system and a way to use it. Many face recognition systems for research will choose the ideal input to be text files listing where the static image files are stored on the computer, as well as other important data such as the true name or identity of the person and perhaps true pixel coordinates of regions of the face (such as ground truth of where the face and eye centers actually are). This would either be collected manually or by another face recognition system.

The ideal output would then be a text file comparing the recognition results with the ground truth, so that statistics may be obtained for comparing the face recognition system with other face recognition systems.

However, as the face recognition system in this chapter is designed for learning as well as practical fun purposes, rather than competing with the latest research methods, it is useful to have an easy-to-use GUI that allows face collection, training, and testing, interactively from the webcam in real time. So this section will provide an interactive GUI providing these features. The reader is expected to either use this provided GUI that comes with this book, or to modify the GUI for their own purposes, or to ignore this GUI and design their own GUI to perform the face recognition techniques discussed so far.

As we need the GUI to perform multiple tasks, let's create a set of modes or states that the GUI will have, with buttons or mouse clicks for the user to change modes:

- **Startup**: This state loads and initializes the data and webcam.
- **Detection**: This state detects faces and shows them with preprocessing, until the user clicks on the **Add Person** button.
- **Collection**: This state collects faces for the current person, until the user clicks anywhere in the window. This also shows the most recent face of each person. The user clicks either one of the existing people or the **Add Person** button, to collect faces for different people.
- **Training**: In this state, the system is trained with the help of all the collected faces of all the collected people.
- **Recognition**: This consists of highlighting the recognized person and showing a confidence meter. The user clicks either one of the people or the **Add Person** button, to return to mode 2 (*Collection*).

To quit, the user can hit the *Esc* key in the window at any time. Let's also add a **Delete All** mode that restarts a new face recognition system, and a **Debug** button that toggles the display of extra debug info. We can create an enumerated mode variable to show the current mode.

Drawing the GUI elements

To display the current mode on the screen, let's create a function to draw text easily. OpenCV comes with a cv::putText() function with several fonts and anti-aliasing, but it can be tricky to place the text in the correct location that you want. Luckily, there is also a cv::getTextSize() function to calculate the bounding box around the text, so we can create a wrapper function to make it easier to place text.

We want to be able to place text along any edge of the window and make sure it is completely visible and also to allow placing multiple lines or words of text next to each other without overwriting each other. So here is a wrapper function to allow you to specify either left-justified or right-justified, as well as to specify top-justified or bottom-justified, and return the bounding box, so we can easily draw multiple lines of text on any corner or edge of the window:

```
// Draw text into an image. Defaults to top-left-justified
// text, so give negative x coords for right-justified text,
// and/or negative y coords for bottom-justified text.
// Returns the bounding rect around the drawn text.
Rect drawString(Mat img, string text, Point coord, Scalar
    color, float fontScale = 0.6f, int thickness = 1,
    int fontFace = FONT_HERSHEY_COMPLEX);
```

Now to display the current mode on the GUI, as the background of the window will be the camera feed, it is quite possible that if we simply draw text over the camera feed; it might be the same color as the camera background! So let's just draw a black shadow of text that is just 1 pixel apart from the foreground text we want to draw. Let's also draw a line of helpful text below it, so the user knows the steps to follow. Here is an example of how to draw some text using the drawString() function:

```
string msg = "Click [Add Person] when ready to collect faces.";
// Draw it as black shadow & again as white text.
float txtSize = 0.4;
int BORDER = 10;
drawString (displayedFrame, msg, Point(BORDER, -BORDER-2),
    CV_RGB(0,0,0), txtSize);
Rect rcHelp = drawString(displayedFrame, msg, Point(BORDER+1,
    -BORDER-1), CV_RGB(255,255,255), txtSize);
```

The following partial screenshot shows the mode and info at the bottom of the GUI window, overlaid on top of the camera image:

We mentioned that we want a few GUI buttons, so let's create a function to draw a GUI button easily as follows:

```
// Draw a GUI button into the image, using drawString().
// Can give a minWidth to have several buttons of same width.
// Returns the bounding rect around the drawn button.
Rect drawButton(Mat img, string text, Point coord,
```

```
    int minWidth = 0)
{
    const int B = 10;
    Point textCoord = Point(coord.x + B, coord.y + B);
    // Get the bounding box around the text.
    Rect rcText = drawString(img, text, textCoord,
        CV_RGB(0,0,0));
    // Draw a filled rectangle around the text.
    Rect rcButton = Rect(rcText.x - B, rcText.y - B,
        rcText.width + 2*B, rcText.height + 2*B);
    // Set a minimum button width.
    if (rcButton.width < minWidth)
        rcButton.width = minWidth;
    // Make a semi-transparent white rectangle.
    Mat matButton = img(rcButton);
    matButton += CV_RGB(90, 90, 90);
    // Draw a non-transparent white border.
    rectangle(img, rcButton, CV_RGB(200,200,200), 1, CV_AA);

    // Draw the actual text that will be displayed.
    drawString(img, text, textCoord, CV_RGB(10,55,20));

    return rcButton;
}
```

Now we create several clickable GUI buttons using the `drawButton()` function, which will always be shown at the top-left of the GUI, as shown in the following partial screenshot:

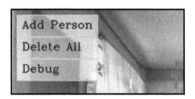

As we mentioned, the GUI program has some modes that it switches between (as a finite state machine), beginning with the Startup mode. We will store the current mode as the `m_mode` variable.

Startup mode

In the Startup mode, we just need to load the XML detector files to detect the face and eyes and initialize the webcam, which we've already covered. Let's also create a main GUI window with a mouse callback function that OpenCV will call whenever the user moves or clicks their mouse in our window. It may also be desirable to set the camera resolution to something reasonable; for example, 640x480, if the camera supports it. This is done as follows:

```
// Create a GUI window for display on the screen.
namedWindow(windowName);

// Call "onMouse()" when the user clicks in the window.
setMouseCallback(windowName, onMouse, 0);

// Set the camera resolution. Only works for some systems.
videoCapture.set(CV_CAP_PROP_FRAME_WIDTH, 640);
videoCapture.set(CV_CAP_PROP_FRAME_HEIGHT, 480);

// We're already initialized, so let's start in Detection mode.
m_mode = MODE_DETECTION;
```

Detection mode

In the Detection mode, we want to continuously detect faces and eyes, draw rectangles or circles around them to show the detection result, and show the current preprocessed face. In fact, we will want these to be displayed no matter which mode we are in. The only thing special about the Detection mode is that it will change to the next mode (*Collection*) when the user clicks the **Add Person** button.

If you remember from the detection step previously in this chapter, the output of our detection stage will be:

- `Mat preprocessedFace`: The preprocessed face (if face and eyes were detected).
- `Rect faceRect`: The detected face region coordinates.
- `Point leftEye, rightEye`: The detected left and right eye center coordinates.

So we should check if a preprocessed face was returned and draw a rectangle and circles around the face and eyes if they were detected as follows:

```
bool gotFaceAndEyes = false;
if (preprocessedFace.data)
  gotFaceAndEyes = true;
```

```
if (faceRect.width > 0) {
  // Draw an anti-aliased rectangle around the detected face.
  rectangle(displayedFrame, faceRect, CV_RGB(255, 255, 0), 2,
    CV_AA);

  // Draw light-blue anti-aliased circles for the 2 eyes.
  Scalar eyeColor = CV_RGB(0,255,255);
  if (leftEye.x >= 0) {   // Check if the eye was detected
    circle(displayedFrame, Point(faceRect.x + leftEye.x,
      faceRect.y + leftEye.y), 6, eyeColor, 1, CV_AA);
  }
  if (rightEye.x >= 0) {    // Check if the eye was detected
    circle(displayedFrame, Point(faceRect.x + rightEye.x,
      faceRect.y + rightEye.y), 6, eyeColor, 1, CV_AA);
  }
}
```

We will overlay the current preprocessed face at the top-center of the window as follows:

```
int cx = (displayedFrame.cols - faceWidth) / 2;
if (preprocessedFace.data) {
  // Get a BGR version of the face, since the output is BGR.
  Mat srcBGR = Mat(preprocessedFace.size(), CV_8UC3);
  cvtColor(preprocessedFace, srcBGR, CV_GRAY2BGR);

  // Get the destination ROI.
  Rect dstRC = Rect(cx, BORDER, faceWidth, faceHeight);
  Mat dstROI = displayedFrame(dstRC);

  // Copy the pixels from src to dst.
  srcBGR.copyTo(dstROI);
}
// Draw an anti-aliased border around the face.
rectangle(displayedFrame, Rect(cx-1, BORDER-1, faceWidth+2,
  faceHeight+2), CV_RGB(200,200,200), 1, CV_AA);
```

The following screenshot shows the displayed GUI when in the Detection mode. The preprocessed face is shown at the top-center, and the detected face and eyes are marked:

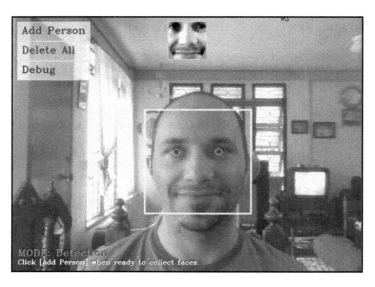

Collection mode

We enter the Collection mode when the user clicks on the **Add Person** button to signal that they want to begin collecting faces for a new person. As mentioned previously, we have limited the face collection to one face per second and then only if it has changed noticeably from the previously collected face. And remember, we decided to collect not only the preprocessed face but also the mirror image of the preprocessed face.

In the Collection mode, we want to show the most recent face of each known person and let the user click on one of those people to add more faces to them or click the **Add Person** button to add a new person to the collection. The user must click somewhere in the middle of the window to continue to the next (*Training mode*) mode.

So first we need to keep a reference to the latest face that was collected for each person. We'll do this by updating the m_latestFaces array of integers, which just stores the array index of each person, from the big preprocessedFaces array (that is, the collection of all faces of all the people). As we also store the mirrored face in that array, we want to reference the second last face, not the last face. This code should be appended to the code that adds a new face (and mirrored face) to the preprocessedFaces array as follows:

```
    // Keep a reference to the latest face of each person.
```

```
m_latestFaces[m_selectedPerson] = preprocessedFaces.size() - 2;
```

We just have to remember to always grow or shrink the `m_latestFaces` array whenever a new person is added or deleted (for example, due to the user clicking on the **Add Person** button). Now let's display the most recent face for each of the collected people, on the right-hand side of the window (both in the Collection mode and Recognition mode later) as follows:

```
m_gui_faces_left = displayedFrame.cols - BORDER - faceWidth;
m_gui_faces_top = BORDER;
for (int i=0; i<m_numPersons; i++) {
  int index = m_latestFaces[i];
  if (index >= 0 && index < (int)preprocessedFaces.size()) {
    Mat srcGray = preprocessedFaces[index];
    if (srcGray.data) {
      // Get a BGR face, since the output is BGR.
      Mat srcBGR = Mat(srcGray.size(), CV_8UC3);
      cvtColor(srcGray, srcBGR, CV_GRAY2BGR);

      // Get the destination ROI
      int y = min(m_gui_faces_top + i * faceHeight,
      displayedFrame.rows - faceHeight);
      Rect dstRC = Rect(m_gui_faces_left, y, faceWidth,
      faceHeight);
      Mat dstROI = displayedFrame(dstRC);

      // Copy the pixels from src to dst.
      srcBGR.copyTo(dstROI);
    }
  }
}
```

We also want to highlight the current person being collected, using a thick red border around their face. This is done as follows:

```
if (m_mode == MODE_COLLECT_FACES) {
  if (m_selectedPerson >= 0 &&
    m_selectedPerson < m_numPersons) {
    int y = min(m_gui_faces_top + m_selectedPerson *
    faceHeight, displayedFrame.rows - faceHeight);
    Rect rc = Rect(m_gui_faces_left, y, faceWidth, faceHeight);
    rectangle(displayedFrame, rc, CV_RGB(255,0,0), 3, CV_AA);
  }
}
```

The following partial screenshot shows the typical display when faces for several people have been collected. The user can click any of the people at the top-right to collect more faces for that person.

Training mode

When the user finally clicks in the middle of the window, the face-recognition algorithm will begin training on all the collected faces. But it is important to make sure there have been enough faces or people collected, otherwise the program may crash. In general, this just requires making sure there is at least one face in the training set (which implies there is at least one person). But the Fisherfaces algorithm looks for comparisons between people, so if there are less than two people in the training set, it will also crash. So we must check whether the selected face-recognition algorithm is Fisherfaces. If it is, then we require at least two people with faces, otherwise we require at least one person with a face. If there isn't enough data, then the program goes back to the Collection mode so the user can add more faces before training.

To check if there are at least two people with collected faces, we can make sure that when a user clicks on the **Add Person** button, a new person is only added if there isn't any empty person (that is, a person that was added but does not have any collected faces yet). If there are just two people and we are using the Fisherfaces algorithm, then we must make sure an `m_latestFaces` reference was set for the last person during the Collection mode. `m_latestFaces[i]` is initialized to -1 when there still haven't been any faces added to that person, and then it becomes `0` or higher once faces for that person have been added. This is done as follows:

```
// Check if there is enough data to train from.
bool haveEnoughData = true;
if (!strcmp(facerecAlgorithm, "FaceRecognizer.Fisherfaces")) {
  if ((m_numPersons < 2) ||
  (m_numPersons == 2 && m_latestFaces[1] < 0) ) {
```

```
          cout << "Fisherfaces needs >= 2 people!" << endl;
          haveEnoughData = false;
      }
  }
  if (m_numPersons < 1 || preprocessedFaces.size() <= 0 ||
      preprocessedFaces.size() != faceLabels.size()) {
      cout << "Need data before it can be learnt!" << endl;
      haveEnoughData = false;
  }

  if (haveEnoughData) {
      // Train collected faces using Eigenfaces or Fisherfaces.
      model = learnCollectedFaces(preprocessedFaces, faceLabels,
              facerecAlgorithm);

      // Now that training is over, we can start recognizing!
      m_mode = MODE_RECOGNITION;
  }
  else {
      // Not enough training data, go back to Collection mode!
      m_mode = MODE_COLLECT_FACES;
  }
```

The training may take a fraction of a second or it may take several seconds or even minutes, depending on how much data is collected. Once the training of collected faces is complete, the face recognition system will automatically enter the *Recognition mode*.

Recognition mode

In the Recognition mode, a confidence meter is shown next to the preprocessed face, so the user knows how reliable the recognition is. If the confidence level is higher than the unknown threshold, it will draw a green rectangle around the recognized person to show the result easily. The user can add more faces for further training if they click on the **Add Person** button or one of the existing people, which causes the program to return to the Collection mode.

Now we have obtained the recognized identity and the similarity with the reconstructed face as mentioned earlier. To display the confidence meter, we know that the L2 similarity value is generally between 0 to 0.5 for high confidence and between 0.5 to 1.0 for low confidence, so we can just subtract it from 1.0 to get the confidence level between 0.0 to 1.0.

Then we just draw a filled rectangle using the confidence level as the ratio shown as follows:

```
int cx = (displayedFrame.cols - faceWidth) / 2;
Point ptBottomRight = Point(cx - 5, BORDER + faceHeight);
Point ptTopLeft = Point(cx - 15, BORDER);

// Draw a gray line showing the threshold for "unknown" people.
Point ptThreshold = Point(ptTopLeft.x, ptBottomRight.y -
  (1.0 - UNKNOWN_PERSON_THRESHOLD) * faceHeight);
rectangle(displayedFrame, ptThreshold, Point(ptBottomRight.x,
ptThreshold.y), CV_RGB(200,200,200), 1, CV_AA);

// Crop the confidence rating between 0 to 1 to fit in the bar.
double confidenceRatio = 1.0 - min(max(similarity, 0.0), 1.0);
Point ptConfidence = Point(ptTopLeft.x, ptBottomRight.y -
  confidenceRatio * faceHeight);

// Show the light-blue confidence bar.
rectangle(displayedFrame, ptConfidence, ptBottomRight,
  CV_RGB(0,255,255), CV_FILLED, CV_AA);

// Show the gray border of the bar.
rectangle(displayedFrame, ptTopLeft, ptBottomRight,
  CV_RGB(200,200,200), 1, CV_AA);
```

To highlight the recognized person, we draw a green rectangle around their face as follows:

```
if (identity >= 0 && identity < 1000) {
  int y = min(m_gui_faces_top + identity * faceHeight,
    displayedFrame.rows - faceHeight);
  Rect rc = Rect(m_gui_faces_left, y, faceWidth, faceHeight);
  rectangle(displayedFrame, rc, CV_RGB(0,255,0), 3, CV_AA);
}
```

The following partial screenshot shows a typical display when running in Recognition mode, showing the confidence meter next to the preprocessed face at the top-center, and highlighting the recognized person in the top-right corner.

Checking and handling mouse clicks

Now that we have all our GUI elements drawn, we just need to process mouse events. When we initialized the display window, we told OpenCV that we want a mouse event callback to our onMouse function.

We don't care about mouse movement, only the mouse clicks, so first we skip the mouse events that aren't for the left-mouse-button click as follows:

```
void onMouse(int event, int x, int y, int, void*)
{
  if (event != CV_EVENT_LBUTTONDOWN)
    return;

  Point pt = Point(x,y);

  ... (handle mouse clicks)
  ...
}
```

As we obtained the drawn rectangle bounds of the buttons when drawing them, we just check if the mouse click location is in any of our button regions by calling OpenCV's inside() function. Now we can check for each button we have created.

When the user clicks on the **Add Person** button, we just add 1 to the m_numPersons variable, allocate more space in the m_latestFaces variable, select the new person for collection, and begin the Collection mode (no matter which mode we were previously in).

But there is one complication; to ensure that we have at least one face for each person when training, we will only allocate space for a new person if there isn't already a person with zero faces. This will ensure that we can always check the value of m_latestFaces[m_numPersons-1] to see if a face has been collected for every person. This is done as follows:

```
if (pt.inside(m_btnAddPerson)) {
  // Ensure there isn't a person without collected faces.
  if ((m_numPersons==0) ||
     (m_latestFaces[m_numPersons-1] >= 0)) {
     // Add a new person.
     m_numPersons++;
     m_latestFaces.push_back(-1);
  }
  m_selectedPerson = m_numPersons - 1;
  m_mode = MODE_COLLECT_FACES;
}
```

This method can be used to test for other button clicks, such as toggling the debug flag as follows:

```
else if (pt.inside(m_btnDebug)) {
  m_debug = !m_debug;
}
```

To handle the **Delete All** button, we need to empty various data structures that are local to our main loop (that is, not accessible from the mouse event callback function), so we change to the **Delete All** mode and then we can delete everything from inside the main loop. We also must deal with the user clicking the main window (that is, not a button). If they clicked on one of the people on the right-hand side, then we want to select that person and change to the Collection mode. Or if they clicked in the main window while in the Collection mode, then we want to change to the Training mode. This is done as follows:

```
else {
    // Check if the user clicked on a face from the list.
    int clickedPerson = -1;
    for (int i=0; i<m_numPersons; i++) {
        if (m_gui_faces_top >= 0) {
            Rect rcFace = Rect(m_gui_faces_left,
            m_gui_faces_top + i * faceHeight, faceWidth, faceHeight);
            if (pt.inside(rcFace)) {
                clickedPerson = i;
                break;
            }
        }
    }
    // Change the selected person, if the user clicked a face.
    if (clickedPerson >= 0) {
        // Change the current person & collect more photos.
        m_selectedPerson = clickedPerson;
        m_mode = MODE_COLLECT_FACES;
    }
    // Otherwise they clicked in the center.
    else {
        // Change to training mode if it was collecting faces.
        if (m_mode == MODE_COLLECT_FACES) {
            m_mode = MODE_TRAINING;
        }
    }
}
```

Summary

This chapter has shown you all the steps required to create a real-time face recognition app, with enough preprocessing to allow some differences between the training set conditions and the testing set conditions, just using basic algorithms. We used face detection to find the location of a face within the camera image, followed by several forms of face preprocessing to reduce the effects of different lighting conditions, camera and face orientations, and facial expressions. We then trained an Eigenfaces or Fisherfaces machine-learning system with the preprocessed faces we collected, and finally we performed face recognition to see who the person is with face verification providing a confidence metric in case it is an unknown person.

Rather than providing a command-line tool that processes image files in an offline manner, we combined all the preceding steps into a self-contained real-time GUI program to allow immediate use of the face recognition system. You should be able to modify the behavior of the system for your own purposes, such as to allow an automatic login of your computer, or if you are interested in improving the recognition reliability then you can read conference papers about recent advances in face recognition to potentially improve each step of the program until it is reliable enough for your specific needs. For example, you could improve the face preprocessing stages, or use a more advanced machine-learning algorithm, or an even better face verification algorithm, based on methods at http://www.face-rec.org/al gorithms/ and http://www.cvpapers.com.

References

- *Rapid Object Detection using a Boosted Cascade of Simple Features, P. Viola and M.J. Jones, Proceedings of the IEEE Transactions on CVPR 2001, Vol. 1, pp. 511-518*
- *An Extended Set of Haar-like Features for Rapid Object Detection, R. Lienhart and J. Maydt, Proceedings of the IEEE Transactions on ICIP 2002, Vol. 1, pp. 900-903*
- *Face Description with Local Binary Patterns: Application to Face Recognition, T. Ahonen, A. Hadid and M. Pietikäinen, Proceedings of the IEEE Transactions on PAMI 2006, Vol. 28, Issue 12, pp. 2037-2041*

- *Learning OpenCV: Computer Vision with the OpenCV Library, G. Bradski and A. Kaehler, pp. 186-190, O'Reilly Media.*

- *Eigenfaces for recognition, M. Turk and A. Pentland, Journal of Cognitive Neuroscience 3, pp. 71-86*

- *Eigenfaces vs. Fisherfaces: Recognition using class specific linear projection, P.N. Belhumeur, J. Hespanha and D. Kriegman, Proceedings of the IEEE Transactions on PAMI 1997, Vol. 19, Issue 7, pp. 711-720*

- *Face Recognition with Local Binary Patterns, T. Ahonen, A. Hadid and M. Pietikäinen, Computer Vision - ECCV 2004, pp. 469-48*

Index